Cl

Close to Home
A materialist analysis of women's oppression

Christine Delphy
Translated and edited by Diana Leonard

The University of Massachusetts Press   Amherst, 1984

Printed in Great Britain
First published in the United States by
The University of Massachusetts Press, 1984

LC 84-40285

ISBN 0-87023-453-6 cloth;

0-87023-454-4 paper

Contents

Preface

This collection contains papers published between 1970 and 1981 by Christine Delphy, a leading activist in the French women's liberation movement, who has been described by Simone de Beauvoir as France's most exciting feminist theorist.

Christine Delphy's work has only slowly become available in English. An article of hers, 'The main enemy', formed part of the first major publication from the women's movement in France in 1970[1]*, and it was translated and sold in mimeoed form at the 1974 Women's Liberation Conference in Edinburgh. It was then reissued, together with two other articles, in a pamphlet from the Women's Research and Resources Centre in London in 1977. A few other translations of her work have been scattered through a variety of academic collections and journals in subsequent years, including the American journal *Feminist Issues*.[2] When the WRRC Publications group went into collaboration with Hutchinson Education, we decided, rather than reissuing *The Main Enemy*, to produce a new and larger collection of Delphy's papers so as to give English and non-academic readers a better appreciation of the development and importance of her work.

'The main enemy' contains the core of one strand of Christine Delphy's work: a theoretical analysis of the feminist 'discovery' of housework as unpaid work within the family, central to an understanding of women's oppression today. Delphy's conceptions of the domestic mode of production, of marriage as a labour contract, and of the economic importance of marriage to women have been developed with increasing sophistication in her work on the ways in which divorce constitutes a continuation of marriage in a different form, on the class

---

* Superior figures refer to the Notes and references at the end of each chapter.

position of women, and on the definition of housework. She was among the first in the recent wave of feminism to stress the structural import- ance of the family in understanding women's situation, and she has continued to stress the significance of divisions *within* the family – unlike those socialist feminists who have taken up the economics of the family as a topic, but whose writings have in fact deflected attention from women's oppression within it (for example, by continuing to focus on the functions 'the family' performs in relation to 'the reproduction of capitalism').

Delphy's economic analysis of the family does not, of course, com- prise any and everything there is to be said about women and the family. In particular, as she notes in her Introduction to this collection, it deals only tangentially with the issues of sexuality and violence. But it does explain much about the pressures towards heterosexuality and marriage which exist for all women, about women's position within the labour market as less than freely contracting agents, about employers prefer- ence for employing married men,[3] and about women and inheritance (including the low investment made in women's education).

A second important element in Delphy's work, which runs through all the articles included here, is a dissection of patriarchal ideologies: an untangling of the deeply entrenched ways of interpreting the world which support and continue male dominance. In a number of papers she looks at the recourse made in a variety of explanations of the divisions between men and women to 'natural facts', 'universal values', differences of 'need' and 'skills', or to women's childbearing capacities. She also exposes the various inventions of the Origins of Humanity which have thrust back into pre-history a set of sexual divisions parallel to those of the west today, which are then used to 'explain' the evolution of our present system. She strongly criticizes the presumption that 'men' and 'women' exist as biologically based categories prior to and independently of the power relationship which currently exists between them. Delphy also lays bare the presumptions about women's intrinsic worthlessness which are built into theories of the functions of the family – which assume the domestic work women do must somehow be about something else, something important, like helping to maintain class divisions, since it is clearly so trivial as not to be worth exploiting in its own right. And she also shows how the idea that the public and private spheres are eternal categories 'givers' of nature (and that the latter, the public sphere or the economy, is the determining influence), is built into the heart of marxist and sociological theories. Such theories therefore cannot allow for the fact that this division, and the opposition of public and private, is itself a social construct.

A final strand in many of the papers is a discussion of the politics and strategy of the women's liberation movement. Delphy looks at the reasons why an autonomous women's movement is needed if women's oppression is to be not only struggled against, but recognized at all; at why excluding men does not constitute 'inverse sexism'; at divisions within the movement and how different groups' use of terms (for example, patriarchy/patriarchal) reflects deep differences of analysis; at the problem in demanding Wages for Housework; at the importance of remaining angry and of struggling against self-hatred; and the problems of (and for) intellectuals within political movements.

Christine Delphy's style, the content of her arguments, and the specific targets for criticism which she selects, are, naturally enough, within a French tradition – although she is well apprised of debates and events in the English-speaking world. It is worth noting particularly in her work (as elsewhere in the French women's movement)[4] the influence of the French tradition of philosophic and logical analysis, the importance of psychoanalysis in intellectual life, her training as a sociologist and her related concern with the situation of rural women, and her sense of a need for constant vigilance against the left and the traditions of intellectual marxism.

Delphy's work is firmly social constructionist and in line with the brand of radical feminism which has for some years dissociated itself from the biologism of Shulamith Firestone (1971). Delphy has a particularly forceful and analytic style, which she justifies by stressing the importance in the development of feminism of the freedom to criticize ideas put forward by feminists as well as by non- or antifeminists. She argues that moving forwards necessarily involves critiques of existing work, but in so doing we must be careful to attack the ideas, not the individual who advanced them (unless, of course, the writer is clearly acting in bad faith). Much of Delphy's own work – including several articles included here – takes this form: routing out idealist (including biologistic, individualistic and psychologistic) thinking in the works of Frederick Engels, Claude Alzon, Annie Leclerc, and Michèle Barrett and Mary McIntosh. Delphy argues that *all* knowledge is political and that it is not sufficient to counter one set of ideas with another view of the world: we must also show the first set of ideas to be *ideological*. That is to say, we must demonstrate the material relationships which exist within a society, and show how particular ideas support the continuation of the objective interests of oppressor groups.

The salience of Lacanian psychoanlysis in French academic life and for feminism can be seen from the existence of an entire group, Psychoanalysis and Politics (familiarly referred to as 'Psych et Po'), within the French women's movement, and from the attention given by intellectuals to the work of Luce Irigaray, Julia Kristeva and Hélène Cixous, whose writings dominate a recent collection purporting to represent *The New French Feminism* (Marks 1982). Christine Delphy has been a vigorous opponent of the ideas of Psych et Po (and their commercial and related practices,[5] for many years – as has the journal she helped to found, *Questions Féministes* (now *Nouvelles Questions Féministes*). She argues that men and women are made not born, that there are no differences of essence between the sexes, and that our bodies do not 'speak': do not require or restrict the possible meanings we give to anatomical features. Rather, how we understand and experience our organs and actions is socially determined and could be wholly different (and is in other cultures). She also stresses throughout her work that the relationships which exist between men and women are *power* relationships, and that no understanding of gender, sexuality or sexual orientation can be divorced from this for an instant. To 'revalue' feminity within our existing society is therefore to celebrate masochism.

In such arguments Delphy is in full accord with her sociological colleagues (or at least with those who carry the principles they hold dear in other realms into the arena of the analysis of gender). Her sociological background is also evident in her concern with the situation of the wives and daughters of small farmers in France, since, as in many European countries, France still has a substantial peasant-agriculturalist population and a flourishing school of rural sociology. The lives of country men and women have been relatively well documented, and with an attention to the economics of family life quite unlike that of sociological studies of town dwellers.

Those who argue that all aspects of society were totally transformed by the transition to industrial capitalism have criticized Delphy for too frequently using examples drawn from rural families to make points about all families. Her response would be that it is possible that many aspects of families were not changed all that much by the Industrial Revolution. At the very least we need more empirical historical investigation to show what *has* changed; at present much is asserted or presumed and little proved. She would also argue that *contemporary* farm families are sufficiently distant from many of us to enable us to see features of *their* families' lives clearly, which then in return show us things we had taken for granted in our own situations. It is in any case amazingly ethnocentric for English or American urban intellectuals to suggest the wives and daughters of small farmers can be ignored because they are just a 'backward minority'.

Difficulties in the relationship between the women's movement and socialist groups in France have a long history. Feminists and socialists have felt ambivalent about each other for at least two hundred years, and the entryist tactics exercised by those within the 'class struggle tendency' within the WLM in France during the 1970s created new suspicions. Chistine Delphy has consistently argued for a completely autonomous women's movement, but her work on the oppression of women is clearly marxist in origin. However, she *uses and develops* marxism, meeting marxist orthodoxy head on. She argues that while historical materialism as developed by Marx is an important tool for analysing any form of oppression, what has become 'marxism' holds back rather than facilitates the struggle for women's liberation. Orthodox marxism and marxist feminist analysis seek all the time to tie the oppression of women to the oppression of the working class. They try to show what use women's oppression has for capitalism or how women should relate to the class struggle . . . and thus exonerate men, and divert women's energies from feminism. Delphy argues for a return to Marx's own methods and practice, and against a digging around for what Marx himself (or subsequent marxists) have had to say on a topic which did not particularly concern him (or them), in analysing women's oppression.

Those who criticize Delphy for not using 'marxist' concepts 'as they should be used' or who think that by adding 'patriarchy' to 'capitalism' they have integrated feminism with marxism, are therefore talking at cross purposes with her.[6] She has said clearly that feminism cannot use concepts developed to explain capitalist class relationships because they precisely occlude the oppression which is specific to women. Nor, she argues, can we move immediately to looking at how the oppression of women relates to or 'articulates with' capitalist oppression[7] – because we are still far from understanding women's oppression. First, we must look much more deeply, and within an autonomous and women-only movement, at women's oppression. We must start by taking ourselves and our oppression as seriously as we take men and men's oppression – even if as women we find it excruciatingly difficult to devote such time and care to ourselves!

The papers included here were written over a ten year period, and while they have been edited slightly to cut out repetitions and a few specialized discussions, and in some cases retranslated, no attempt has been made to update the arguments or the examples. All the debates Christine Delphy raises here still continue: whether men can be feminists; whether individuals can make their marriages egalitarian; whether 'bourgeois' women and heterosexual women are retrogressive members of the women's movement; how to counter naturalistic thinking in commonsense and scholarly accounts of the world. . . . In short, how best to understand and struggle against the multiple oppressions women endure. This collection demonstrates the sophistication of Delphy's argument that structurally men are the agents and beneficiaries of the subordination of women. We hope it will contribute towards open discussion of the oppression of women and means to change, since her work, while intellectually radical and rigorous, gives ways of confronting and explaining men's oppression of women without alienating any groups of women, without attaching individual responsibility to men, without closing off avenues by prescribing currently correct behaviour, and leaving open the question of the relationship between feminism and socialist, anti-racist and other movements for liberation.

Diana Leonard
November 1983

Notes and references

1   A double issue of the journal *Partisans* (nos. 50 and 51) from Maspero, entitled *Libération des femmes – année zero.*

2   *Feminist Issues* began in 1980 as the English-language edition of the French radical feminist journal *Questions Féministes*, which Christine Delphy had helped to establish in 1977. In 1981, following a split in the editorial collective in France over radical lesbianism (see Duchen 1984), *Feminist Issues* has in practice sided with those

Delphy opposed. It has therefore not published any of her more recent work.

3   Delphy's ideas on this have been used recently by Janet Finch in a review of the extent to which wives are *Married to* (their husband's) *Job* (1983).

4   I draw here on the analysis of the *Mouvement de Libération des Femmes* in Duchen (1983).

5   For further details on Psychanalyse et Politique, see Lewis (1981), Douglas (1980), and Kandel (1980).

6   cf. Molineux (1979), Barrett and McIntosh (1979), and Eisenstein (1979).

7   Here she differs from Hartmann (1974), although in many respects they agree.

1. Introduction to the collection

The analysis of patriarchy in our society which I have been developing for the last fourteen years has a history. I arrived at my conceptualization starting from two apparently unrelated theoretical concerns: one was to study the transmission of family property (patrimony), and the other was to reply to the criticisms of the women's liberation movement which come from the left.

But these concerns were only apparently unrelated because in fact, when I started to do research, I wanted to work 'on women', which is to say, for me, on women's oppression. Since my director of studies at the time told me that this was impossible, I chose to study the inheritance of property instead, hoping to get back to my initial interest eventually, by an indirect route.

In my research I discovered first what a huge quantity of goods change hands without passing through the market. These goods change hands through the family – as gifts or inheritance. I also discovered that the science of economics, which purports to concern itself with everything related to the exchange of goods in society, is in fact concerned only with *one* of the systems of production, circulation and consumption of goods: that of the market.

At this time (between 1968 and 1970) I was also taking part in one of the two groups which initially helped create the new feminist movement in France. I was very annoyed – and I was not alone, though like the hero of *Catch 22* I thought I was being personally got at! – by one of the men in this mixed group. He claimed that the oppression of women could not be equal in importance to that of the proletariat since, he said, although women were oppressed, they were not 'exploited'.

I was well aware that there was something wrong with this formulation. In that group at least we recognized that women earn half as much as men and work twice as hard: but apparently their oppression nevertheless had, in theory, no economic dimension!

While by the early 1970s we knew that housework existed – it was no longer invisible or non-work – we saw the problem of housework as principally a question of an unfair division of boring tasks; and since we didn't ask the relevant questions about it, we not surprisingly didn't get any relevant answers. My work on patrimony (i.e. on the economic aspects of the non-market sphere, or, to put it another way, on the non-market sphere of the economy) served to help me find and pose these questions.

Around this same time others were also discovering the theoretical, as well as the practical, importance of housework. But because they came at it via a different route from mine, they arrived at rather different conclusions. Analysis of gifts and the inheritance of property within the family helped me to demystify the market. This prevented my getting caught in the classic trap of opposing exchange-value and use-value: an opposition which led the pioneers (Benston and Larguia), and also others who came later, into a number of impasses – or rather, round in circles from which they could find no escape. By showing that this opposition only makes sense if one takes the viewpoint of the market, I was able to propose a theory from another viewpoint; a theory in which non-market-value, instead of being a *problem* in understanding house-work, is one of the clues to elucidating its specific nature. By taking this non-value as a constitutive element of housework, I was able:

1   to show that housework's exclusion from the market was the cause, and not the consequence, of its not being paid for;
2   that this exclusion involves not only housework, or particular types of work, but rather social *actors*; or, to be more precise, work done within certain social relations; and
3   that in seeking to understand housework it is a mistake to see it as a particular set of tasks, whether one is seeking to describe them or to explain them in terms of their 'intrinsic usefulness'.

I have taken up all these points again in my recent work, but they were present, at least in bud, in 'The Main Enemy' (1970). From this time onwards I have been able to propose a theoretical rather than an empirical analysis of housework, which I see as a particular part of the much larger category of 'domestic work', thanks to my initial creation of the concept of the 'domestic mode of production'.

Patriarchy

Since 1970 I have used the term 'patriarchy', and in all my work I have tried to specify and delimit this word and to state precisely the relationship between patriarchy and the domestic mode of production. I am still working on this. If I have used a fairly vague term, it has been so as to show from the start that I consider the oppression of women *to be a system*. But the question is, what constitutes the system and how does it function? The concept has to be filled in, and this can only be done bit by bit.

I have, however, since entering the field, restricted the meaning I attach to the term patriarchy. For many it is synonymous with 'the subordination of women'. It carries this meaning for me too, but with this qualification: I add the words 'here and now'. This makes a big difference. When I hear it said, as I often do, that 'patriarchy has changed since the origins of agriculture', or 'from the eighteenth century to the present', I know that people are not talking about 'my' patriarchy. What I study is not an ahistoric entity which has wandered down through the centuries, but something peculiar to contemporary industrial societies. I do not believe in the theory of 'survivals' – and here I am in agreement with other sociologists and anthropologists. An institution which exists today cannot be explained by the simple fact that it existed in the past, even if this past is recent. I do not deny that certain elements of patriarchy today resemble elements of the 'patriarchy' of six thousand years ago or that of two hundred years ago; what I deny is that this continuation – in so far as it is a *continuation* (i.e. in so far as it really concerns the same thing) – does not in itself constitute an explanation.

Many people think that when they have found the birth of an institution in the past, they hold the key to its present existence. But they have in fact explained neither its present existence, nor even its birth (its past appearance), for they must explain its existence at each and every moment in the context prevailing at that time; and its persistence today (if it really is persistence) must be explained by the present context. Some so-called 'historical' explanations are in fact ahistorical, precisely because they do not take account of the given conditions of each period. This is not history, but mere dating. History is precious if it is well conducted: if each period is examined in the same way as the present period. A science of the past, worthy of the name, cannot be anything other than a series of synchronic analyses.

The search for 'origins' is a caricature of even this falsely historical procedure, and this is one of the reasons I have denounced it, and why I shall continue to denounce it each and every time it surfaces – which is, alas, all too frequently. (The other reason I denounce the search for origins is because of its hidden naturalistic presuppositions.) But from the scientific point of view, it is as illegitimate to seek keys to the present situation in the nineteenth century as in primitive societies.

Since 1970, then, I have been saying that patriarchy is the system of subordination of women to men in contemporary industrial societies, that this system has an economic base, and that this base is the domestic mode of production. Needless to say, these three ideas have been, and remain, highly controversial.

The domestic mode of production

Like all modes of production, the domestic mode of production is also a mode of consumption and circulation of goods.

While it is difficult in the capitalist mode of production to identify the form of consumption which distinguishes individuals of the dominant class from those of the dominated, at least at first sight, since consumption is mediated by the wage, things are very different in the domestic mode. Here consumption is of primary importance and has the power to discriminate, for one of the essential differences between the two modes of production lies in the fact that those exploited by the domestic mode of production are not *paid* but rather *maintained*. In this mode, therefore, consumption is not separate from production, and the unequal sharing of goods is not mediated by money.

Consumption in the family has to be studied if we want not only to be able to evaluate the quantitative exploitation of various members, but also to understand what maintenance consists of and how it differs from a wage. Too many people today still 'translate' maintenance into its monetary equivalent, as if a woman who receives a coat receives the value of the coat. In so doing they abolish the crucial distinction between a wage and retribution in kind, produced by the presence or absence of a monetary transaction. This distinction creates the difference between self-selected and non-free consumption, and is independent of the 'value' of the goods consumed.

Every mode of production is also a mode of circulation. The mode of circulation peculiar to the domestic mode of production is the transmission of patrimony, which is regulated in part by the rules of inheritance. But it is not limited to these. It is an area which has been fairly well studied in some sectors of our society (e.g. farming), but completely ignored in others. With the transmission of family property we can see, on the one hand, the difference between the abstract model and the concrete society, and on the other the consequences of the fact that our social system (or more precisely the representation which has been made of it, i.e. our model of our social system) is composed of several sub-systems, several modes of production.

Studying how possessions are passed from one generation to the next in the family is interesting because it shows the mechanisms which produce complementary and antagonistic classes at work. It shows how owners are divided from non-owners of the means of production.

The effect of the dispossession of one group is clear in the agricultural world for instance. Those who do not inherit – women and younger siblings – work unpaid for their husbands and inheriting brothers. Domestic circulation (the rules of inheritance and succession) here *flows directly* into patriarchal relations of production.

Patrimonial transmission is equally interesting and important at another level, in reconstituting the capitalist mode of production generation after generation. It not only creates possessors and non-possessors inside each family, it also creates this division *between* families.

The latter is the only aspect of patrimonial transmission which has really been studied to date. The former system, the division into classes *within* a kin group, is passed over in silence by sociologists and anthropologists alike. Indeed they pretend – against all the evidence, and in particular against all the evidence on the division of society into genders – that *all* the children in a family in our society inherit the goods and status of the head of the family equally. But of course, the fact that the reconstitution of capitalist classes is the only effect of patrimonial transmission recognized by (traditional) sociology makes this effect no less real. This is indeed one of the times when the domestic mode of production *meets* the capitalist mode and where they *interpenetrate* each other.

Depriving women of the means of production by patrimonial transmission is not, however, the only way in which they are dispossessed of direct access to their means of subsistence, if only because many families simply do not have any family property to transmit or *not* to transmit to them. The same effect is produced by the systematic discrimination which women face in the *wage*-labour market. (Let us for the moment call it the dual labour market.) This also pushes women to enter domestic relations of production, mainly by getting married, though some may act as housekeepers for kin.

The situation of women in the labour market has been relatively well studied. The only originality in my approach in this field has been to invert the direction of links usually established. While ordinarily it is seen as 'the family situation' which influences the capacity of women to work 'outside', I have tried to show that the situation created for women in the labour market itself constitutes an objective incentive to marry, and hence that the labour market plays a role in the exploitation of their domestic work.

How should we conceptualize this fact? How should we interpret it with regard to the relations between capitalism, patriarchy and the domestic mode of production? Should we talk of capitalist mechanisms in the service of the domestic mode of production? Or should we speak of domestic mechanisms at work in the labour market? Whatever the reply – and the question will stay open for a long time – one thing is clear: whether it is a matter of patrimonial transmission (which assists if it does not create relations of production other than those which are strictly domestic), or the capitalist labour market (which assists if it does not create relations of production other than capitalist ones), the two systems are tightly linked and have a relationship of mutual aid and assistance.

What is more, the relations between patriarchy and the domestic mode of production are themselves not ones of simple superimposition. The domestic mode of production is in places more extensive than patriarchy, and in places less. The same is true also of the capitalist mode of production: one of its institutions, the labour market, is in part ruled, or used, by patriarchy.

The domestic mode of production, therefore, does not give a total account of even the economic dimensions of women's subordination. It certainly does not account for other dimensions of this subordination, in particular those oppressions which are just as material as economic exploitation, such as the general violence from men to women and the violence associated with sexual relations between them. Some of these forms of violence can be shown to be related to the appropriation of women's labour power – as C. Hennequin, E. de Lesseps and I demonstrated in the case of the prohibition on abortion and conception (1970). Since raising children requires work, and since this work is extorted from *women*, it can be argued that men are afraid women will try to escape motherhood, or excessive motherhood, by limiting the number of children they bear. Men therefore ensure they always have the means to withdraw control of childbearing from women. Making abortion illegal is one such means. Putting pressure on women to be heterosexual and, within this sexuality, to 'choose' practices which result in impregnation, is another. The same sort of reasoning has been applied to marital violence (Hanmer 1978) and rape (Féministes Revolutionnaires 1976).

However, to be fair, the links established so far between such oppressions and the domestic mode of production are too tenuous to be called full explanations. There remain therefore whole sections of women's oppression which are only very partially, if at all, explained by my theory. This may be a shortcoming; but it is certainly not an involuntary shortcoming. It is rather a consequence of certain refusals, and of methodological choices on my part.

On methodology

I distrust theories which seek from the outset to explain every aspect of the oppression of women. I distrust them for two reasons.

The first, general, reason is that theories which seek to explain everything about a particular situation, themselves remain particular. In being too glued to their object, to what is specific to it, they themselves become specific and are therefore unable to locate their object among other similar things (e.g. among other oppressions) because they do not possess the tools to make it comparable.

The explanatory power of a theory (or concept or hypothesis) is tied to its capacity to find what is common to several phenomena of the same order, and hence to its capacity to go beyond the phenomenal reality of (i.e. what is immediately present in) each case. The belief that the reason for the existence of things is to be found beyond their appearance, that it is 'hidden', is integral to scientific procedure (though it can, of course, be contested). This is why I do not accept the objection which has been made to my use of the concepts of 'mode of production' and 'class'. It has been suggested that these concepts were created to describe other situations, and that in using them I deny the specificity of women's oppression. This overlooks the fact that all analysis proceeds by 'butchery'. To understand a phenomenon, we begin by breaking it down into bits, which are later reassembled. Why? So that the bits shall be the same for all instances of the phenomenon being studied. (The phenomenon I study is the subordination of one group by another; the oppression of women being one instance of it.) The recompositions we later obtain are then comparable. To understand is first to compare. This is how all sciences proceed, and it is how we proceed in everyday life: how you and I describe a person, a place, a situation, to people who are not able to have direct experience of them. With a few concepts a geographer can describe any landscape.

Non-specific concepts are used in theories, however, not so much to describe things as to explain them (although all description requires a classification, hence at the start an explanation; and conversely all explanation is also a description in so far as it can itself be further explained). The aim of analysis is explanation.

The bits into which a phenomenon is broken down are not those of immediate perception. (The economic dimension, for instance, is not an 'obvious' category for thinking about the family today, but then it was also not an obvious one for thinking about any phenomenon what-soever a few centuries ago, even those which our current language now calls 'the economy'.) It follows, therefore, that when the bits are reassembled, the results are in no way restitutions of the objects initially treated, but rather models: images of the realities underlying and *causing* the objects.

The initial 'objects' are in any case not 'pure' facts, but rather the immediate perception of things, informed in a non-explicit fashion by a certain view of the world (what Feyerabend referred to as 'natural evidences').

Thus, on the one hand, the more a theory pretends to be 'general' (in regard to its object), the more it has descriptive power and the less it has explanatory power; and on the other, the more it is held in fief to immediate perception, precisely because to have a descriptive power it must stick to the 'facts', the more it is ideological.

The other reason for my distrust of theories which try to be 'total' is that, even when they do not aim to 'cover' everything, they still aim to explain everything by a single 'cause'; and when their concern is women's oppression, this thirst for a single cause generally leads straight into the arms of naturalism.

Naturalism

Naturalism is a major sin for which we are not responsible since it is the indigenous theory of (the rationalization for) women's oppression in our society. Today it is applied to the oppression of women and of people 'of colour', but scarcely a century ago it was also used to explain the oppression of the proletariat. People do not sufficiently recognize that in the nineteenth century the exploitation of the working class was justified by the 'natural' (today one would say the 'genetic') inferiority of its members. And naturalism continues to infect (and the word is not too strong) feminist thinking. Naturalism is, of course, even more obvious in anti-feminist thinking, but it is still present in large measure in feminism.

Feminists have been shouting for at least twelve years, and still shout, whenever they hear it said that the subordination of women is caused by the inferiority of our natural capacities. But, at the same time, the vast majority continue to think that 'we mustn't ignore biology'. But why not exactly? No one is denying the anatomical differences between male and female humans or their different parts in producing babies, any more than they deny that some humans have black and some white skins. But since science has thrown out all 'biological explanations' of the oppression of the working class and non-whites, one after another, we might have thought that this type of account of *hierarchies* would have been discredited. This century has seen the collapse of such racist theories – even though one quarter of primatologists keep trying to save them from annihilation – but the role that biology never merited historically it does not merit logically either. Why should we, in trying to explain the division of society into hierarchical groups, attach ourselves to the bodily type of the individuals who compose, or are thought to compose, these groups? The pertinence of the *question* (not to speak of the pertinence of the replies furnished) still remains to be demonstrated so far as I am concerned.

Naturalist 'explanations' choose the biology of the moment anyway. In the eighteenth century it was women's wandering uteruses which made us inferior, in the last century it was our (feeble) muscles, in the 1950s, the (deleterious) influence of our hormones on our moods, today it is the (bad) lateralization of our brains or our ability to breastfeed or our capacity for caring. Feminists are outraged by such 'theories', but none has yet explained to me how they differ fundamentally from the explanation in terms of women's ability to *gestate* which is so in favour today under the name of 'reproduction'.

One of the axioms, if not the fundamental axiom, of my approach is that women and men are *social* groups. I start from the incontestable fact that they are socially named, socially differentiated, and socially pertinent, and I seek to understand these social practices. How are they realized? What are they for? It may be (and again this remains to be proven) that women are (also) females, and that men are (also) males, but it is women and men that interest me, not females and males. Even if one gives minimal weight to this social aspect, if one contents oneself with stating the pertinence of sex for society, one is obliged to consider this pertinence as a social fact, which therefore requires an equally social explanation. (Just because it was a male sociologist, Emile Durkheim, who first forcefully stated this as an axiom does not make it any less true!) This is why an important part of my work is devoted to denouncing explicitly naturalistic approaches: to denouncing approaches which seek a natural explanation for a social fact, and why I want to dislodge all approaches which implicitly bear the stamp of this reductionism.

Gender

A considerable theoretical step forward was taken ten years ago with the creation of the concept of 'gender'. However, the term is unfortunately little used in French and not systematically used in English. As a result we continue to get entangled in the different meanings of the word 'sex' or are constrained to use paraphrases (e.g. 'sexual divisions in society'). The concept of gender carries in one word both a recognition of the social aspect of the 'sexual' dichotomy and the need to treat it as such. It consequently detaches the social from the anatomical-biological aspect of sex, but it has only done so partially. If gender was from the start a social construction, it was not built on just any thing. It was set on anatomical sex like the beret on the head of the legendary Frenchman. And since its creation, gender, far from taking wing, has on the contrary seemed to cling on to its daddy. It is almost never seen on its own, but almost always in composite expressions, such as 'sex and gender' or 'sex/gender' – the 'and' or the dash serving to buttress rather than to separate the two. When two words are always associated, they become redundant. When, in addition, the association is not reciprocal – when 'sex' can happily dispense with 'gender' – the optional addition of the second term seems but a way of paying lip-service to the social aspects.

The concept of 'gender' has thus not taken off as I would have hoped, nor has it given rise to the theoretical development which it carried in embryo. Rather, it now seems to be taken at its most minimal. It is accepted that the 'roles' of the sexes vary according to the society, but it is this *variability* which is taken to sum up the social aspect of sex. The content (gender) may vary from society to society, but the basis (sexual division) itself does not. Gayle Rubin, for example, maintains that in human society sex inevitably gives birth to gender (Rubin 1975). In other words, the fact that humans reproduce sexually and that males and females look different contains within itself not only the capacity but also the *necessity* of a *social* division, albeit the social form varies greatly. The very existence of genders – of different social positions for men and women (or more correctly for females and males) – is thus taken as given and as not requiring explanation. Only the content of these positions and their (eventual, according to Rubin) hierarchy are a matter for investigation. Those who, like me, took gender seriously find themselves today pretty isolated.

Sex classes

I gave above my reasons for mistrusting 'specific' explanations. They may perhaps not totally explain for readers why I use the term 'class' to refer to the division between men and women. I do this because the concept of class best meets the needs of analysis as described above. That is to say, it allows an object, the oppression of women, to be broken down into small sections, or, more precisely, into non-specific *dimensions* – though it perhaps does this no better than another concept might. The concept of class has a further advantage however: it is the only concept I know which at least partially responds to the strict requirements of a *social* explanation. It is perhaps not totally satisfactory, but it is the least unsatisfactory of all the terms used to analyse oppression.

Some talk of men and women as being 'groups', but the term 'groups' says nothing about their mode of constitution. It can be thought that two groups – the dominant and the dominated – each has an origin which is *sui generis*; that having already come into existence, they later enter into a relationship; and that this relationship, at a still later time, becomes characterized by domination. The concept of class, however, inverts this scheme. It implies that each group cannot be considered separately from the other, because they are bound together by a relationship of domination; nor can they even be considered together but independently of this relationship. Characterizing this relationship as one of economic exploitation, the concept of class additionally puts social domination at the heart of the explanation of hierarchy. The motives – material profit in the widest sense – attributed to this domination can be discussed, and even challenged or changed, without the fundamental scheme needing to be changed. Class is a dichotomous concept and it has, because of this, its limitations; but on the other hand, we can see how well it applies to the exhaustive, hierarchical, and precisely dichotomous classifications which are internal to a given society – like the classification into men *or* women (adult/child, white/ non-white, etc.). The concept of class starts from the idea of social construction and specifies the implications of it. Groups are no longer *sui generis*, constituted before coming into relation with one another. On the contrary, it is their relationship which constitutes them as such. It is therefore a question of discovering the social practices, the social relations, which, in constituting the division of gender, create the groups of gender (called 'of sex').

I have put forward the hypothesis that the domestic relations of production constitute one such class relationship. But family relationships do not account for the whole of the 'gender' system, and they also concern other categorizations (e.g. by age). I would put forward as a second hypothesis that other systems of relationship constitutive of gender division also exist – and these remain to be discovered. If we think of each of these systems as a circle, then the gender division is the zone illuminated by the projection of these circles on one another. Each system of relations, taken separately, is not specific, either to gender division or to another categorization. But these systems of relationships can combine in various different ways, each of which is unique. According to this hypothesis, it is the particular combination of several systems of relationships, of which none is specific, which gives its singularity to division by gender.

Needless to say, much still needs to be done before we reach a complete understanding of the domestic mode of production, and still more before we know about the nature of other systems which oppress women and which articulate with the domestic mode of production to form contemporary patriarchy. We are further still from understanding the systems of subordination to which women have been subject in past and in non-industrial societies. My work, and that of hundreds of other feminists, has barely begun.

2. Women in stratification studies*

Over the past ten years, increasing attention has been given to the place of women in society, and this has included concern with their position within the system of social stratification. Most studies of social inequalities have, however, continued to take the family to be 'a solidary unit of equivalent valuation' and to assume that the class position of the family is entirely determined by the socio-economic status of the head of the household.

Joan Acker in an important paper distinguished four further assumptions implicit in such studies, of which the two most important are: first, that the status of a wife is (assumed to be) equal to that of her husband, at least as regards her position in the class structure; and second, that the fact that women are *not* equal to men in many ways . . . is irrelevant to the structure of stratification systems (Acker 1973, p. 937).

This latter assumption itself implies, on the one hand, that wider inequalities have no influence on the (assumed) 'equality' of wives, and on the other that relationships within a couple (whose members are seen as equals) cannot be the cause of wider inequalities. Thus while some criticize the fact that a wife's occupation is not taken into account when grading the family, on the grounds that it contributes to the family income, they nevertheless themselves retain the family as the unit of stratification. (Archer and Giner 1971, p. 14).

Acker goes further, however, and criticizes, first, the inconsistency of the practice of classifying a woman by her own occupation so long as she is unmarried and then abandoning this criterion the day she marries; and second, the assumption that the family is a single unit of equivalent

---

* This article first appeared in Andrée Michel (ed.), *Femmes, sexisme et sociétés*, Presses Universitaires de France, Paris 1977. An English translation was included by H. Roberts in her edited collection, *Doing Feminist Research*, Routledge and Kegan Paul 1981.

status, i.e. that it is socially homogeneous, even when the woman is not in paid employment.

She suggests, first, that a woman's own occupation should be taken into account whatever her marital status; and, second, that the role of women without paid work (i.e. housewives) should be considered as an occupation and given a particular place on the occupational scale.

Studying the treatment of women in French analyses of stratification clearly reveals the same sorts of assumption as have been found in work on other western societies, and in many respects I am in full agreement with Acker and others. However, in my opinion it is not sufficient to treat these assumptions as methodological errors or ideological biases which need only to be deplored and corrected. I feel that they should be considered and analysed as unintentional indices (as opposed to analyses) of a hidden social structure.

What these writers have done is draw attention to inconsistencies in the criteria used in the classification of women, and, in particular, to the use of a double standard: that paid work is taken into account for single but not for married women. But they have not examined what this 'inconsistency' itself reveals: the use of a double standard in determining social class membership. Occupation, the universal measure of an individual's social class, is, in the case of women, and only of women, replaced by a completely different criterion – marriage.

It follows from this that women are not integrated into the description of the social structure by applying a rule governing the concept of social stratification, but rather by abandoning this rule. This in my opinion is the principal contradiction in such studies and I believe an analysis of this contradiction to be very fruitful.

Premises underlying social stratification studies

The concept of stratification is based on two major premises. First, every modern society consists of hierarchical groups, whether this hierarchy is seen as a dichotomy (marxist theory taken up by non-marxist writers (Bottomore 1965)), or as a continuous scale (as in American sociology). Second, the principle according to which these groups are ranked and individuals included in them is based on their place in the production process in its fullest sense, i.e. including not only their technical function, but also their relations of production in the marxist sense. These criteria are combined in occupation, or, rather, occupation can be analysed according to these dimensions. It therefore serves as an index to categorize individuals into hierarchically organized socio-economic groups. These are usually further grouped into broader categories, for which the term 'class' is used by marxist and non-marxist writers alike.

In this paper I shall use the term 'occupation' to indicate the criteria according to which individuals are placed within the hierarchy, and 'class' to indicate the hierarchically organized groups making up the social structures which together form the system of social stratification or the class system. I shall also be using the term 'relations of production' because it explicitly denotes a class system (i.e. a system where occupational groups are regrouped in two broad antagonistic classes in a particular economic formation), whereas the term 'category' denotes a point on a continuum of prestige and income, with no sense of antagonism and class struggle.

The universal index for classifying individuals and for determining their class position is occupation. It is the only index used to classify individual men, the basic assumption being that all men occupy some sort of place in production. In all modern western societies something like 50 per cent of women 'do not work', that is to say, they have no paid employment. This category is used in studies of economic activity, but not in studies of social stratification. In what ways, then, do stratification studies include women, and how are women represented?

Naville (1971), for example, takes the class structure to be synonymous with occupational divisions among the active population and he therefore excludes from the class structure any individuals without paid work – and thus all women occupied full-time in the home. Girard (1961) goes further and equates the class structure with occupational divisions among economically active males alone, thus excluding not only individuals without employment and women in the home, but *all women*. In Naville's work, the active population is described without being divided by sex, with the implication that 'economically active' women are on a par with their male counterparts, whether they are married or single. The most common practice, however, is to take account of a woman's marital status, and to grade married women by their husbands' occupations and single women by their jobs. A married woman's own position, that is to say, having a job – and one job rather than another, or not having a job at all, is thus usually not taken into account in determining her class membership.

I shall illustrate this by discussing two studies which exemplify these practices. One is particularly well known to me, as I took part in it, and the other is a classic in French social stratification literature.

Comparing the social class of brothers and sisters

The first study, the primary objective of which was to determine the inherited assets of a sample of self-employed workers, also sought to measure and compare the backgrounds and current positions of husbands and wives and their brothers and sisters (siblings). It looked particularly at the relative social mobility of brothers and sisters. The socio-professional categories used were the ten main categories of INSEE (the French National Institute for Statistics and Economic Studies), grouped for the purpose of analysis into three main 'classes': upper, middle and lower.

The population studied comprised married couples and included 10 per cent of women. Consequently 90 per cent of the spouses of those studied were women, and 10 per cent were men. The 10 per cent of women included in the study were classified, like the men, in terms of their own occupation. Their husbands, the 10 per cent of male spouses, were also classified in terms of their own occupations. But the class membership of female spouses was determined by two criteria, used not together but as alternatives: employed women were classified according to their own occupation; while women who were not employed were classified according to their husband's occupation.

Other individuals were also classified – the brothers and sisters of the respondents and the brothers and sisters of the spouses – with the aim of evaluating the comparative mobility of individuals within groups of siblings. Brothers of the respondent or of the spouse were classified according to their occupations; but for sisters, whether they were sisters of the respondent or of the spouse, the criterion of classification varied according to whether they were single or married. Their class position was determined by *their* occupation if they were single, but by their *husband's* occupation if they were married.

Two points should be noted from the above. First, all the women in the study were dealt with according to two criteria, whereas men were dealt with according to only one; and second, all the women in the study were not considered according to the *same* two criteria.

There are, therefore, three problems to be considered. First, the dual standard applied to one part of the female population; second, the dual standard applied to the other part of the female population; and third, the relationship between these two dual standards.

To begin with the last, and perhaps least important, of these problems: what broader view of stratification does this double use of a dual standard point to? That is to say, what is implied by comparing one population classified by two heterogeneous criteria with another population classified by two different heterogeneous critera? For the sake of clarity, I shall limit myself to the case of women and their siblings.

Siblings of women in the study

The position (in terms of their own occupation) of women studied was compared to:

1   the position of their brothers (in terms of their occupations);
2   the position of their single sisters (in terms of their own occupations); and
3   the position by marriage of their married sisters (in terms of the occupation of their husbands).

Siblings of female spouses

The differing social class positions of the brothers and sisters of the wives of respondents (classified according to (1), (2) and (3) above), were compared to the wives' own social class position if they were employed, or, if they were not, to their social class position through marriage, i.e. to their husband's social class position.

One might well ask what the social homogeneity rates of siblings and indices of social mobility mean when calculated in this way! A description is as good as its initial definitions, but only so long as one keeps to the *same* definitions. One can only compare like with like, and one must avoid combining incompatible categories.

But would the study have been valid if the women studied, their spouses, and the women who were sisters, had been dealt with consistently? It would not, because in that case we would have moved from a double dual standard to a single dual standard. The treatment of sisters would come within the scope of Acker's critique: only single women would be classified by their own occupation; married women, whether or not they had an occupation, would be classified according to their husbands' occupation. However, female spouses would be dealt with in a way which would satisfy Acker, since their occupation, if they had one, would be taken into account.

Acker's two main criticisms are in fact as follows:

1 since many women do not have a man (to give them a social class position), we must consider their own occupations; and
2 it is illogical, having taken occupation into consideration when women are single, not to take it into consideration when they are married.

The implication of this is that if no married woman had an occupation, it would be less problematic, if not perfectly legitimate, to assign a woman to her husband's social class.

But from the point of view of consistency, the problem is not solved by taking the occupation of married women into account. That certainly eliminates *one* of the differences in the way in which the female population is considered: both married women and single women are then classified according to their own occupations. But this does not deal with all the problems. For instance, in the study referred to, the population of female spouses (for whom occupation was taken into account when it was present) is nevertheless still not treated consistently, since some women (with a job) are classified according to their own occupation and others (without a job) are classified according to their husband's. Thus, not only are female spouses not all classified in the same way, but the whole female population is treated differently from the population of men, since the former have two criteria applied to them, and the latter only one (that of their own occupation).

Comparing the social class of husband and wife

Since in most research the unit of stratification is taken to be the family, comparisons between spouses are not usually made as this is seen as unnecessary. Even if they were deemed necessary, it would be impossible – precisely because, given the dogmatic assumption of homogeneity of status within the family, the social class of the husband is automatically attributed to the wife. There is no way to compare social class positions which by definition are identical.

Nevertheless, certain studies do try to make this comparison, at least in theory. The concept of homogamy (marriage within or across sectors of society), for example, is by definition a measure of distance – and in particular socio-economic distance – between spouses. In order to make such calculations it would seem necessary that the positions to be compared be evaluated; i.e. that we know the class of the wife and of the husband. But even this necessity can be bypassed.

In *Le Choix du conjoint* (*Choosing a Spouse*, 1964) Alain Girard looks at homogamy of origin by assessing the distance between the social class of the husband's father and that of the wife's father. But in order to measure homogamy at the time of marriage (that is to say, the gap between the spouses' own social class positions), he compares the class position of the husband with the class position of the wife's *father*. As he himself recognizes, 'since social status is defined by occupation, in order to be completely rigorous one would have to compare the occupations of the spouses'. But, he adds, 'a large number of women do not have a job, or only have one on a temporary basis until marriage. Thus it is *preferable* [my emphasis] to consider the occupation of their fathers.' One might well ask what 'preferable' means here. Are we to understand that if a characteristic (in this case occupation) is not a good indicator of what we are seeking to measure (in this case a woman's own social class position), we are justified in abandoning this dimension in order to keep the indicator, even if it means changing the population studied (i.e. studying the fathers instead of the women themselves)?

If we look more closely, however, we see it is not a case of a methodological error, but a theoretical choice: 'the milieu from which the woman comes being more *significant* than her occupation' (my emphasis). The theory underlying this choice and the criteria according to which the father's occupation is judged 'more significant' are, however, left unexplained. The father's occupation is not 'more significant' for husbands because it is their own occupation that counts.

As far as Girard is concerned, social background is for some reason more significant for women, whereas for husbands it is their own occupation which is crucial. This reasoning, whatever it may be, merits discussion, or at least comment. If what is a 'significant' indicator is not the same for women as for men, it is because *they are not part of the same system of reference*. But there is no justification offered for the choice of different indicators, and no explanation of the reference systems implicitly used.

Not only is the social class distance within the couple not measured, but the choice of indices used prevents any comparison between them. Operationally, the concept of a woman's own position does not exist.

The purported theoretical aim is to study women as members of social groups and as subjects of relationships. But these groups are *operationally* defined as being made up exclusively of men, and women are *operationally* defined as being mediators and not subjects in social relationships with men.

This problem is not specific to Girard's study. Just as in his study husbands are compared with their fathers-in-law, in the preceding study it was brothers being compared with their brothers-in-law and not their sisters; and in social mobility studies, fathers are compared not with their daughters but with their sons-in-law. These sorts of comparison lead us to an important problem: that of the principles according to which women are included in social groups and the theoretical implications of the criteria used to determine women's class membership. But before discussing the theoretical implications further, we must examine the consequences the criteria used have for measuring social distance between husbands and wives.

The critiques of the treatment of women in stratification studies suggest that it is *offensive* to women to be classified according to their husband's occupation, particularly when they have an occupation of their own, and that this leads to a distortion in possible comparisons between women, and between couples (e.g. between those with one or two incomes). But, as we have seen above, so far as women are concerned, taking their own occupations into account resolves nothing. Nor is anything resolved when comparisons are actually made between husband and wife, since in the first study, unlike Girard's, *some* women *were* classified according to their own occupations, which allowed us to evaluate their social distance from their husbands. But all women without employment were put into the same social class as their husbands. The net result was that if, *like her husband*, a woman had an occupation, this distanced her from him in terms of social ranking; while if, *unlike her husband*, she was not employed, this brought her closer to him in terms of ranking. Thus, even when a woman's own occupation is taken into account, putting women who are not employed into their husbands' social class distorts the comparison between the social class position of husband and wife.

Marriage and the class position of women

In systematically attributing to a woman without an occupation the occupation of her husband, an essential dichotomous variable – that of the presence or absence of economic independence – is obscured. A woman who has an occupation, generally of a lower status than that of her husband, is put in a lower social class than the woman with the same husband but without an occupation (who is put in the same social class as her husband). More particularly, a woman who works, generally in a job of lower status than that of her husband, is considered to be more distanced socially from her husband than a woman who does not work outside the home. The fact that a woman is comparable to her husband from the point of view of economic independence distances her from him in sociological terms. Putting a non-employed woman into her husband's social class does not just obscure this fact, it completely reverses its meaning.

What is fundamentally in question in the classification of married women without an occupation (and sometimes even with one) in the same class as their husbands is thus that a criterion is being used which is alien to social stratification theory, namely *the criterion of association through marriage*.

Critics have complained that the occupation of married women is not taken into account in studies of stratification. Implicit in this criticism is the assumption of an association between occupation and social class position. If we accept this assumption, we must conclude that individuals without an occupation have no social class position of their own, and are, therefore, neither a part of, nor capable of being a part of, the stratification system. But if we cannot bring ourselves to admit that one part of the population has no social existence, we must conclude that *not having an occupation in itself constitutes a specific position*, which is the position of individuals in this situation.

Consequently, the same criticism which is made of the allocation of married women who *do* have an occupation of their own to their husbands' social class (i.e. the fact that their own occupation is not taken into account), can also be applied to women who *do not* have a job. For women who do not have a job, *their* own social position is not taken into account, i.e. it is not treated as an economic situation. (Nor is it treated as the absence of a social position, which, strictly speaking, makes it impossible to classify them with *any* group.) Quite illogically, it is considered as both a necessary and sufficient reason for attributing to them, without further examination, *someone else's* social class.

We have seen that the class structure is frequently equated with the occupational distribution of the economically active male population; or at best, with the total economically active population. In the first case no woman, and in the second no full-time housewife, is included in this social structure. From an operational point of view then, classes include few or no women.

Nevertheless, it must be admitted by the layperson and the social scientist alike, that women, if not actually within the class system, can hardly be anywhere else. The concept of a class system as a stratification system is exhaustive, in the sense that it is supposed to cover all the possibilities in a given society. This aim is never challenged even by those who criticize specific features of the concept or the criteria used.

Jackson (1968), for example, mentions the problem of categorizing the 'dependent sections of the population such as the old, the young and married women'. For him, 'classifying those who are not part of the work force in a stratification system based on industrial occupations presents difficulties.' But apparently he sees these as being purely technical, because, although he recognizes them, this does not lead him to put forward a stratification system based on criteria which *would* be applicable to the whole population. Nor does it lead him to challenge the universal claims of a system which is manifestly partial, since, by his own admission, it is concerned with only one section of the population.

In the light of this we can draw out several assumptions implicit in the study of social stratification which can be added to those put forward at the beginning:

1   The absence of an occupation is seen as meaning the absence of a place of one's own in the class structure.
2   Marriage is considered a valid criterion for determining class membership only so far as women are concerned. (No man is classified according to his wife's occupation, even when he himself has no occupation.)
3   Marriage is used over and above occupation for women, even for those who live on their own, since women who *do* have an occupation are *usually* classified according to their husband's social class.
4   Marriage puts a woman into the same relations of production as her husband. Since determination of class membership through one's own occupation and its determination through marriage are judged to be equivalent, an indirect relationship to class is thus clearly judged to be equivalent to a direct one.

But in reality, not having an occupation does constitute a specific situation. Even having an indirect relationship to an occupation constitutes a specific situation. The latter situation characterizes women and only women. Thus, wives and daughters constitute a sociological class where membership is defined indirectly, as opposed to the sociological class of men where class membership is defined directly. A woman's own position in sociology is that of having a place in the stratification system which is mediated and conditioned by a personal relationship (to a father or husband).

Marriage as a class position for women

At the level of knowledge, sociology reflects and reproduces a social class, just as membership of a class reflects and reproduces an actual economic situation. The relationship of women without an occupation to the economic world is a mediated and not a direct one. Women without jobs are not part of the economic sphere (the labour market and the system of industrial wage-labour) whose operation determines the critieria for social stratification. Nevertheless, they do have a relationship to production, a means of earning their living. But what they participate in is a mode of production which is not part of classical economics, or rather of economics as classically defined. They are neither selling what they produce for money, nor their labour for a wage. Their labour power is being given in return for maintenance. Thus, not only are they not a concrete part of the labour force, but on a theoretical level too, they are not integrated into the classical mode of production (wage labour, capitalist or socialist). Their specific relationship to production cannot be reduced to the analytical categories derived from classical economics. Their labour relationship is part of a specific mode of production, different from and parallel to the wage-labour mode.

The existence of this particular mode of production, which I first described as patriarchal in 1970, had previously been unacknowledged and has only slowly begun to gain some recognition. The specific patriarchal relations of production of married women, whether or not they also have a classical relationship to production (i.e. paid work), are characterized by dependence. And it is this dependence which provides the basis for putting women in the same social class as their husbands. What is more, it is only *as* dependents that women are seen to belong to the social class of their husbands. Having made use of this dependent status to put women in the *same* social class as their husbands, sociologists are anxious to forget this necessary condition, and to forget that it is *the* crucial criterion for allocating women to a socio-economic class. Sociologists use it, and must use it in order to affirm class parity between husband and wife; but having done this, they obscure the premises used and consider only the result. They treat this class parity as a predominant factor in the couple relationship. Or rather, this so-called class parity is used to minimize the dependency relationship within the couple. The relations between the man and woman within the couple, and particularly her economic dependence on him, are always treated as secondary, since the shared social status – seen as more general and therefore carrying more weight in determining an individual's situation – is supposed to override internal disparities. Unfortunately, this 'parity of status' is based necessarily and exclusively on women's dependence.

The actual situation is, therefore, the reverse of the one put forward. Not only do the relations of production which put husband and wife into patriarchal and antagonistic classes override commonality of industrial class, since they precede it both chronologically and logically, but they contradict it, since women without an occupation are by definition outside the industrial class system. Certain women, however, in so far as they have an occupation, fall within the confines of the industrial class system. Nevertheless, the fact that their dependence on their husbands is chosen as an index of class membership more frequently than their own occupation, constitutes a sign, though not the only one, that the patriarchal class system overrides the industrial one.

Thus, the criteria used in determining the class membership of women, if they are analysed correctly, clearly reveal the true position of women. Sociology, however, by reproducing social reality at the level of knowledge, prevents us, *ipso facto*, from analysing and clarifying the situation. On the contrary, sociology uses this relationship of dependence in order to situate women within the classical system of stratification. It thus obscures the fact that women form part of *another* mode of production. Sociology roots its analyses in the specific antagonistic relations of production between husbands and wives, and then not only denies this relationship, but transforms it into its very opposite: a relationship between equals.

3. Sharing the same table: consumption and the family*

If there is one universally recognized function of the family it is 'consumption'. It would be tedious to list all the books and articles which mention this, because there is no sociologist, and more generally no author dealing with the family, who does not at least allude to it. It is presented as one of the principal functions of 'the modern family'.

If it is granted that the family is the institution (or one of the institutions) which fulfils this function, we might have expected that the next step would have been to study the ways in which the family satisfies what are undoubtedly seen as some basic biological needs of its individual members. But despite the social and theoretical importance of both the family and the 'function' of consumption, there is a strikingly poor literature on the topic. Not a single known study of the family takes consumption as its theme of research, or even sets out the ground for such research.

If consumption and the family were not the object of specific investigations, we might at least have expected to see it discussed in general theoretical introductions. But, after its obligatory and quasi-ritual mention, it is little developed. Indeed, the assertion of the existence of a consumption function is often put in the form of a negatively phrased sentence. That is to say, the function of consumption is presented as the *only remaining* function of the family within the economic order: what remains to it of a glorious past, of the global economic role it used to play. Its mention is an integral part of the – often advanced, never

* This paper first appeared in *Cahiers Internationaux de Sociologie* (1974), pp. 23–41. An English translation was included in C. C. Harris *et al.* (eds.), *The Sociology of the Family: New Directions for Britain*, Sociological Review Monograph, **28**, (1979).

substantiated – thesis that the family in general (and not certain forms of the family) has recently been excluded from any role in production whatsoever (and not only from production for the market). It is as if consumption was put forward to give credit to the thesis of the loss of the family's role in production, and at the same time to affirm that – despite this vicissitude – the family continues to be necessary within the economic order. Hence, even at a theoretical level, the function of consumption is not treated in and of itself by those who study the family. E. M. Duvall's sentence (1957, p. 58) 'Families have shifted from production to consumption' is exemplary of this kind of thinking. It is considered only in a general historical perspective: from the point of view of the evolution of the family and its gains and losses of 'functionality'.

When we look at past work on family consumption, it rapidly becomes clear that the term 'consumption' is used to designate market demand. The titles of articles and journals lead us to think that what is being studied is individual consumption, but the consumption they describe is not that of any actual person, but is rather the purchase of goods and services on the market by households (generally in the person of the housewife). Such studies let it be thought that the family, which is a collective agent on the market, is equally a collective agent in consumption.[1] An INSEE study (the French equivalent of the Government Social Survey's *Family Expenditure Survey*) says explicitly:

The field covered by this enquiry is that of expenditure on goods and services: purchase of products, consumption taking place outside the home, and payment for loans and services.

It is clear here that all consumption by members of the household (and this includes children at boarding school for instance), wherever it occurs, is taken into account in evaluating the standard of living of *households*.

Thus the use of the term consumption implies that individual consumption is being studied, while the way in which consumption is observed in practice – the relating of all consumption to the household – requires that distribution within the family should be studied. But not only do studies of individual consumption or sharing within the family not exist, the themes are not so much as broached, even theoretically, and it is precisely the choice of the household as the unit of observation which prevents such studies being possible using existing data. Taking

the family as a unit does not allow family consumption to be studied –
only the consumption of aggregates of families. What is studied is no
longer the families themselves, but the way in which they differ from
each other, or form groups. Moreover, the only difference between
families which these studies are explicitly interested in studying, is that
of 'the comparative standard of living of different socio-economic
groups' (Jousselin 1972, p. 141).

This comparison *itself* actually also suffers from the definition of the
household, e.g. servants (waged and apprenticed) lodging in a household are held to be part of it from the point of view of consumption. The
result is that studies of the standard of living of farm workers' households, for example, do not include those who lodge with – and who are
consequently trapped by – the household of their boss. And these are
those whose standard of living is lowest. Excluding them from farm
workers' households has the effect of raising the average standard of
living of the latter, while their being 'captive' has the effect of lowering
the average standard of living of the households to which they are
attached, i.e. those of the class of their masters. These two effects
together lead to a not inconsiderable diminution of the economic
distance between the two classes.

But distortions brought about in comparisons of social categories are
a minor defect compared to the major sin of considering the very place –
the household – where certain class relations are exercised (e.g. those of
servant and master) as the place where they are annulled.

The absence of studies of distribution has a positive meaning. It
means that the only pertinent perspective is how the family is a unit
within a larger whole, because this is the only perspective considered.
Above all, it lets it be thought that the family, a unity *vis-à-vis* the
outside, is also one within itself. One of the images which the term 'unit
of consumption' evokes is that of common – i.e. homogeneous – consumption. It connotes at one and the same time *common consumption*,
and *undifferentiated consumption*.

Differences of consumption within families

However, such connotations of common and undifferentiated consumption are contradicted by the facts of everyday experience. Here the
disparities of consumption between family members are not only

visible, but recognized as *constitutive* of family structure. Differences in consumption are seen as correlated with the existence of different family statuses. Differential consumption plays a major role both in the perception of these statuses by outsiders and in the appreciation of their particular statuses by those involved.

Existing studies of consumption are, however, based on the opposite assumption. And they do not rest content with ignoring individual consumption: they pretend to know about it without having studied it. Thus:

The average annual consumption *per head* . . . is obtained simply [sic] by dividing the values entered in the table . . . by the number of persons.
(INSEE 1973)

It should be remembered, however, that among the individuals whom we are thus invited to consider as benefiting in equal shares from all the goods consumed in the household to which they are attributed, are not only children in boarding schools, and soldiers on military service, but also servants, waged employees and apprentices. Thus, while pretending to ignore the whole topic, existing studies of consumption in fact assume (impose) a theory of distribution – an egalitarian theory.

It is likely that the processes described above are no chance effects and that their convergence is no coincidence. The use of the term 'unit of consumption' – which in denoting a simple unit of reckoning connotes a unitas (union and communion) – tends to make the study of distribution seem pointless; and statistical practice, for its part, by always taking the household as the only unit of observation, makes any empirical research impossible. All these processes converge to prevent any study of real distribution, for on the one hand such a study would risk undermining the whole basis of existing research by showing it to be founded on an implicit postulate – that of egalitarian distribution; while on the other hand it could not but confirm what is apprehended impressionistically by everyday experience – the existence of differential consumption.[2]

Study of the consumption function of the family should consist of studying the role of the family as the distribution centre for its members, and research should take as its object the effect of family status on individual consumption. But, as has been noted above, not one of the studies which refers to the family as a unit of consumption so much as outlines the limits of what does or does not enter into this unit, so the very framework of the research has still to be defined. Does individual consumption within the family involve consumption effected collectively, with all the members of the family present, regardless of place? Or is it consumption that occurs at home, whichever members may be present? Or is it consumption by members of the family, whatever the place and whichever individuals are present? Among the criteria which could be envisaged, besides the place (at home or outside) and the presence or absence of the family as a collective, must be the nature of the consumption. Would specific consumption (e.g. connected with a job) be opposed to common consumption, or consumption of the same sort of thing (e.g. consumption of food) – these latter alone being considered familial?

If the subject of research is the role of the family as a distribution point, it seems obvious that all individual consumption should be considered as familial since it is based on the status of the individual in the family whatever the place, the modalities, or the form it may take. But in the absence of even elementary reflections and investigation in this area we must proceed empirically and cautiously. In fact it is much more a matter of using examples to set out the directing hypothesis for a new approach to family consumption than of stating the methodological outlines for a systematic study.

I shall try to set out the outlines of such an approach in the remainder of this article, using examples chosen from the area of non-specific consumption, effected mainly at home, even if not in the presence of the whole family, since such consumption, and particularly the consumption of food, is the most evidently familial. It is the family seated around the table which most approximates the image of a really communist community, of a really equitable distribution, and which seems most sheltered from the effects of hierarchy.

I shall also deal with families on very low incomes, since there is a sentiment that inequality is less cruel when it is a case of individuals getting more or less of what is already a surplus, rather than when it is a question of individuals getting more or less than the minimum needed for a healthy life. It tends to be thought that families on the breadline must and do share what little they have.[3]

Both experts and the uninitiated like to situate the western version of 'subsistence' within rural, and above all within peasant, families. Here production for self-consumption is relatively important compared to that destined for the market, and this suggests a self-sufficiency, especially in food, which though far from existing in reality, is close to the golden age of the popular imagination (which is curiously situated in the nineteenth century).

It is in this type of family that some of the lowest incomes within industrial society are to be found and here that the standard of living is at its lowest. It is also here that it is most recognized that *all* family members do hard physical work. It is thus the last place where one would expect to find differential consumption of food. Therefore, if it can be shown that such differential consumption does exist, there seem good grounds for expecting it to exist in *all* families: that it is part and parcel of the *structure* of the family. That is to say, the stress given here to the rural family, and to the consumption of food, is not due to a particular interest in these areas as such, but rather to a belief that once the fact of differential consumption is established and established here (for the reasons evoked above), it will require further research into its principles and functioning, i.e. its existence as an institution. It will involve, in sum, the freeing of a problematic which will allow us to return to new concrete studies since future research will no longer be aimless: its problematic will have been constructed.

The distribution of food in peasant families

There is, needless to say, no scientifically collected information which can be used in considering whether there is or is not differential consumption in poor farm families. On the contrary, so-called scientific data have been collected in just such a way as to mask it. But, as was said earlier, the point of this essay is not to present new facts, but to look at facts, which are universally known to the social actors, from a new angle.[4] So I shall therefore draw on descriptive studies and personal knowledge.

In the traditional rural family (of the eighteenth and early nineteenth centuries in Britain, and still today in marginal family smallholdings of the type that predominate in south-west France and much of southern Europe), consumption of food varies greatly according to the individual's status in the family. This variation concerns the quantity of food and sets apart primarily children and adults, and women and men. But among the adults the old eat less than those who are mature, and the junior members eat less than the head of the family. It is he who takes the biggest pieces. He also takes the best: variation concerns quality as much as quantity.

Children are fed exclusively on milk, flour and sugar until two or three years old. The old, particularly the infirm elderly, return to a similar regime based on cereals and milk, bread-soups (*panade*) and broths.

Meat is rarely on the menu, and even more rarely on the menu for everyone. It often appears on the table to be consumed only by the head of the family, especially if it is butcher's meat. Less expensive meat – chickens reared on the farm, preserves made at home – are not subject to such exclusive privilege. However, women and children will never have the choice piece, which is reserved for the father (or, on social occasions, for distinguished guests). Thus according to Cazaurang (1968), the prime pieces of ham, a prime food in itself, fall to the future son-in-law. Infants and the elderly never touch it. Alcohol is another food whose consumption is strongly differentiated. It is for adult men, to the exclusion of women and children.

Respect for food prohibitions is obtained by both coercion and the internalization of these prohibitions. The physical infirmity of young children and the old makes coercion so easy that it becomes not useless but invisible. It is mainly necessary, and becomes visible, in relation to children during the period when they are 'thieves': i.e. when they have not yet internalized the prohibitions.

Hence many types of food which are kept in the kitchen are put in high-up places, on hanging shelves (*planches à pain*) or on the tops of cupboards, where only people of adult height can reach them. This coercion by height is so classic that many folk tales have as their hero a child who has decided to outmanoeuvre it. The tale generally tells of the confident solution of the problem by the hero using a stool, and of the unhappy outcome in a punishment, either mediated (inflicted by an adult hand) or immediate (coming from the sky in the shape of indigestion). A brand of jam has even chosen for its trademark the picture of a little girl dipping her fingers into a jar: she is perched on a chair.

But if certain foodstuffs are physically protected only from children, others are protected from the whole family:

Provisions which it is thought should not be allowed into the kitchen are put in the bedroom, especially in the master's bedroom. For pieces of pork meat, such as sausages, the stay in the upper storey enables them to finish drying out. Further, it shields them from the temptation of the young, who are always

hungry. The same line of thought leads to the week's supply of bread being put on a shelf from which it is only given out as needed
(Cazaurang 1968, p. 97, t II).

Some of the measures which back up prohibitions with physical obstacles apply to the whole household – except for the women, or rather except for the mistress of the house. These measures would in fact be inconvenient if applied to her because it is she who prepares all the food. She therefore has access to all the foodstuffs, even to those which she does not eat. But this access is clearly tied to her operations as preparer. Alcohol escapes her operations because its preparation is a masculine prerogative. The physical taboo to which it is subject may extend to the mistress of the house: often the 'master's' bottle is touched only by his hand.

Repression in all its aspects – punishments and threats, verbal injunctions, physical obstacles and taboos on contact – play only a security role, except with regard to children, or perhaps even (as in the case of the bottle of alcohol) only a symbolic role in founding and maintaining differential consumption. For this is essentially a customary act (i.e. the constraints are internalized and reproduced as spontaneous behaviour by those involved). A whole corpus of proverbs, sayings and beliefs are both tokens of the content of the roles and the justification for these roles.

Sometimes these precepts seem like observations from experience – 'women eat less than men'. Sometimes they are in the shape of advice on hygiene – 'such food is "bad" or "good" ' – with the prescriptive aspect on differential consumption only appearing in the second part of the phrase, where it is revealed that this 'goodness' or 'badness' strikes the organs in a selective manner according to the status of their possessors. Thus 'jam spoils (*only*) *children's* teeth', 'wine gives (*only*) *men* strength', etc. The waiter in the restaurant where the young David Copperfield was stranded when he was travelling alone explained to him in the same vein that the beer which had been served to the youth would be fatal for him, and he saved David from death by gulping it down for him. At other times the norm is prescribed under the guise of aesthetic considerations – 'There's nothing more ugly than a drunken woman' – or moral – 'a woman who drinks is worthless' (*femme de vin, femme de rien*) – which completely masks the repressive aspect, since it leaves those concerned free to be 'ugly' or 'worthless' and passes in silence over the anticipated benefit of such repression, i.e. the monopoly of a prized commodity. One could set against this the naïvity of an old farmer in the Lot region of France who exclaimed: 'Goodness me, a woman smoking . . . it's the first time I've ever seen that . . . but why not, after all, smoking's a pleasure.'

The total absence of proteins from the diet of infants and the elderly leads to food deficiencies which have serious repercussions on the development of the former and the ageing of the latter, and the life expectancy of everyone. Their relative absence in the diet of women leads to consequences for their general state of health, whose effects are doubled by the physiological burden of pregnancies, as was previously evidenced by the very high rates of maternal and infant mortality in rural areas. Nevertheless, it is held that babies and children do not need meat, and that women have 'less need' of it. Men, however, 'need' such noble food. Vegetables which do not 'hold to the body' and do not 'sustain a man', apparently nourish women and children.

Indigenous theory suggests a relationship between the stature of the individual and the quantity of food necessary for his or her constitution.[5] That this is a rationalization and not a principle of distribution is evident from the number of exceptions it suffers: a husband, a master, a father, or an eldest son, however puny he may be, does not give up his privileged share to a wife, a worker, a child, or a younger sibling, however heavily built or tall.

The theory of differential needs allows a third level of argument – that of differential expenditure of energy. This form of argument does not rest on the measure of energy really expended by the individual, but establishes an impersonal relationship between an activity and the expenditure of energy. This relationship is based on classifying activities into 'heavy' and 'light' work, but the classification is not based on the actual expenditure of energy required by the activity considered, but rather by the nature of the activities. It is not the technical operation itself which is the real criterion of the classification (carrying water is considered to be 'light work', carrying manure is 'heavy'), nor is it the labour of the task (cutting corn with a scythe is 'heavy work', gathering it into bundles and binding it is seen as 'light work'). Rather, throughout France, carrying water and gathering are, or were, exclusively work for women, while other sorts of carrying and harvesting were men's work. The criteria of classification of work into 'heavy' and 'light' rests, in fact, on the status of those who usually do it.

Certain work, reserved for men and hence supposedly 'heavy' in some regions, is reserved for women in others and there changes its qualifications. This applies, to give just a couple of examples from among many sex-related tasks, to earthing up potatoes and driving draught animals. When women do supposedly 'heavy' work in one particular region – either in an exceptional way, at certain times of year, or in an ordinary way, as in Brittany or in the Alps where they do all agricultural work – the evaluation of the energy they expend and need is not thereby modified. This is not surprising since this expenditure and their real needs are never measured nor compared. The simple counting of hours of physical activity per day (more than a third higher on average for women than for men) would lead one to think that, contrary to indigenous belief, women's expenditure and hence need for energy would be greater than men's. But the theory of 'needs', while invoking explicitly or referring itself implicitly to objective physiological imperatives, in fact ignores them totally.

Does it, then, take into account subjective needs and desires? Still less. It is clear that in determining the 'needs' of a given individual, the evaluation of those 'concerned' does not enter into it. The feeling of hunger experienced by children and adolescents does not lead to a conclusion that they need food. On the contrary, in reply to requests there is a set response: 'you don't need it', which suggests that need is different from, external to, and even antinomic to desire. The theory of needs thus calls on objectivity as against subjectivity, albeit (as we have seen) refusing any objective measurement.

This double contradiction is well expressed in the previously cited passage by Cazaurang:

It shields them (the pieces of meat) from the temptation of the young, *who are always hungry* . . . the week's supply of bread . . . is only given out *as needed*.

The needs to which he alludes are thus not those of the youngsters. Their present hunger will not be satisfied, and had their previous needs been covered, they would not be 'hungry'.

This quotation shows that a state of hunger is considered to be normal among the young, or rather that satiation does not form part of the needs which are recognized for them. 'To eat one's fill' is one of the pleasures of life and this objective always runs the risk of not being achieved. Nonetheless, a chronic feeling of hunger is not considered an attribute of adults as an age class, although it is attributed as a distinctive characteristic to adolescents in rural society. 'Hunger' as concerning, not specific cases, but a whole category of individuals, 'the young', is considered not a characteristic of their social condition but an irremediable physiological fact. In other societies, such as that of North America or even urban France, a state of perpetual non-satiation appears as just as subjectively undesirable and objectively injurious among the young as among adults.[6]

When peasant farmers say – and most do concede it – that 'we live better than before', it is often primarily to evoke those changes which have occurred in everyday experience. In this regard, today is compared advantageously to yesterday. This 'before' is repeatedly evoked with bitterness, as a period of deprivation of food, and in all cases this relates to childhood.

I remember, when I was a kid, I went out in the morning with the sheep. I went out with a 'drubbing' and that's all I had till evening (from an interview in the Lot Region).

The maintenance of differentials in consumption

If coercion is primarily used to make up for the lack of internalization of prohibitions among the young, and to create them, this is never so perfect that some slackening is not to be found. Between pure coercion and pure internalization, gossip plays a role, calling in the last resort on the presence of others and on shame, or its inverse, honour.

As Cazaurang again says:

A small gesture of an earlier mistress of the house is worth pointing out. She used to profit by the absence of other family members to yield to her gluttony. She would make herself some separate small dishes or simply coffee. If an intruder arrived unexpectedly, the *sinful* object was swiftly slid into the unlit oven near the hearth
(Cazaurang 1968, p. 124, my emphasis).

If for the young, food prohibitions – even when internalized – remain as constraints, especially since they are linked to a necessarily transitory status, for women they are integrated into a wider repressive system which allows a greater flexibility in its details. This system is the ideology of the role of wife and mother.

Women are in practice managers of the home and like all overseers they find themselves confronting situations for which no instructions exist. At such times a general principle takes over from the precise prohibitions which have become inappropriate. This general principle is simple: the wife and mother should always preserve the privileges of the husband and father, and 'sacrifice' herself.

Different modalities are used to this end in different societies. In Tunisia, for example, differential consumption is effected in a radically different way. Men have two or three meals a day while women have only one or two, and these meals never coincide. The women eat foodstuffs prepared once a year and obtained from second quality produce. The meals they make for men on the other hand use fresh and best quality ingredients. The rigorous separation of time, place and the basic substance of the meals makes any competition for the food between men and women impossible (Ferchiou 1968).

In France today, except for a few specific prohibitions – such as alcohol and tobacco – men and women eat 'from the same table' (*au même pain et pot*). Differential consumption derives essentially not from prohibition on this or that food, but from attributing women the smallest and most mediocre share of each food. It is difficult to say if it is the circumstances – sharing the same meal – which make necessary the creation and application of a general principle, or whether it is the existence of this principle which makes possible the preparation of but one meal. Perhaps it would be more appropriate to say that only such a principle could give an account of the variability of content of differential consumption.

In a particular social situation, in a given family and at a given standard of living, the content is not so flexible: the same dishes appear regularly on the table each week and it is not necessary to work out a new evaluation and a new distribution each time. The shares are fixed once and for all: in each family and in each chicken there is 'father's bit'.

Here again restrictions are experienced differently according to the degree of internalization and the transitory character or definitive status to which they are attached. For children, especially male children, they are persecutions on which they are revenged from the first occasion when they have access to the 'father's bit' which they have coveted for years. Women, however, think that they have chosen the piece to which they are entitled.

For instance, a young peasant farmer invited two city women to share his tea and opened a tin of paté. His aunt, an old woman who kept house for him because his mother was ill, was there. On her bread she put only the fat from around the paté, which had been scorned by the three other diners. The system not only requires women to restrain themselves, but also allows them a certain latitude by making them responsible for taking the decision as to the form of their restriction. Thus the meat of the paté had doubtless never been expressly forbidden to this old woman; but the obligation to leave the best part to others had been internalized as a moral imperative. She could have complied with it in a different way; she acted on her own initiative in giving herself the worst part; and above all the precise way of doing it was up to her. This attribution is experienced as a free choice and is often explained by the 'ordinary' motivation for choice: personal preference. When asked, the old woman replied that she liked fat.

But there is absolutely no need for sacrifice to be liked: it becomes second nature. The mistress of the house takes the smallest steak without thinking, and will not take one at all if by chance there are not enough for everyone. She will say 'I don't want any'; and nobody is surprised, she least of all, that it should always be the same person who 'doesn't want any'. There is also no need at all for her to refer to the ideology of sacrifice as an integral part of feminine nature, nor that she be aware of her generosity or abnegation. Recourse to a universal principle supposes an out of the ordinary situation where the purely mechanical conduct of everyday life no longer suffices to guide action.

When one moves from the country to the town, and from low income sectors to higher sectors, consumption of food increases and differential consumption becomes less marked in this area. Since the level of food consumption is higher, it might be expected that basic needs are better covered and that differences of consumption would more and more concern less visible qualities and modalities. Indeed, food being sufficiently abundant, it might be expected that differences in food consumption would tend to disappear completely and be replaced by, or only exist in, other areas.

However, the flexible character of differential consumption, the fact (discussed above) that it is not the specific content but the principles of attribution which are defined, allows other expressions of subordination when for one reason or another the household's scale of relative values is modified. One example can illustrate this move back to using food to express status differences, and this also illustrates the flexibility of the system.

In the last ten years France, and Paris in particular, experienced a shortage of potatoes which lasted for a fortnight. Since the demand for this basic commodity is relatively inelastic, prices rose and queues formed in front of the greengrocers. When questioned in one of these queues by a radio interviewer, a woman replied: 'I'll keep the potatoes for my husband. The children and I will eat pasta or rice.' In spite of the relative expense of potatoes it would not have been beyond the budget of the family to get enough for everyone, given the subjective importance they attach to them. On the other hand, if the value of the gratification did not compensate for the budgetary sacrifice, as the renunciation by the wife and children suggests, the husband should also logically have eaten pasta and rice. The solution adopted seems to be explained neither by the physiological impossibility for the husband to absorb products (replacements in this particular situation) which were in any case consumed in almost as regular a way as potatoes, nor by the economic situation of the family, but rather by the symbolic necessity of marking privileged and statutory access to goods which are rare (or become rare) – this access being both the sign and at the same time the reason for the hierarchy of consumption.

If differentiation were studied in all sectors of consumption it is likely that the following principle and its corollaries would be confirmed:

1   The rarest goods in each sector, and the most prestigious sectors of consumption, are subject to privileged access.
2   The relative difference between the standard of living of different family members stays more or less constant in all social situations (and increases in absolute value as the privileged access concerns more and more costly goods and/or the differentiation is exercised on an enlarged global volume).

Indeed, with growth in the part of the budget which is available for spending on things other than food, forms of consumption develop which were previously of little importance or non-existent. The raising of the general standard of living may thus allow the development of differentiation in certain existing areas. In addition, it allows the emergence of new areas of consumption which are fresh fields for the exercise of differentiation. For example, the acquisition of a car by a household in which previously everybody travelled by public transport, not only considerably increases the global difference in consumption – variance in the standard of living – between the user of the car and other family members, but above all it introduces differentiation into an area – transport – which up till then was undifferentiated.

The study of differential consumption cannot be reduced to the study of quantitative differences in access to particular goods, however, it is also qualitative. Does a child being taken for a Sunday outing consume the family car in the same way as the father who drives it? Above all, does it consume the same outing? The problems which are currently being put forcefully in rural areas when two generations live together, reveal – if one listens to those concerned – that the conflicts experienced divide not 'the generations', but rather concern the 'freely chosen' consumption which the 'invited' children want, and the 'compelled' consumption which is 'given' them (imposed) by their parent-hosts.

These examples seem to indicate that ways of consuming are perhaps more important than quantities consumed. But up to now the study of consumption has always been preoccupied with – has always meant exclusively – volumes, and the very existence of modes of consumption has not even been hinted at.

Yet consumption after all concerns not only goods but also services, and if the classical economic studies sometimes include under the rubric of 'self-consumption' goods which are made at home, they always ignore the services produced in the household. However, despite what the titles of research on household budgets may lead us to think, household consumption does not only involve what is bought on the market: we do not eat raw steaks or unpeeled potatoes at our family tables. We consume not only primary materials but also their preparation: the housework of the 'mistress of the house' (work of which the preparation of food constitutes only a part). The provider of these services does not consume them in equal manner with the non-providers, for diverse reasons (of which some are obvious: e.g. you cannot serve at table and be served at the same time). This point is considered further in Chapter 5, 'Housework or domestic work'.

Taking these services into consideration overturns not only the existing accounted evaluation of family consumption, it overturns at the same stroke the evaluation of family production, because these services are also 'self-produced'. Above all, it re-poses, at the level of production, the problems of the meaning of the very term 'unit' when applied to the family – i.e. the problem of the internal functioning of the family as an economic institution.

Notes and references

1 J. K. Galbraith in a recent book shares this critique of the idea of the 'household':

Though a household includes several individuals – husband, wife, off-spring, sometimes relatives or parents – with differing needs, tastes and preferences, all neoclassical theory holds it to be the same individual. (1973)

2 The history of the creation and construction from 1895 to the present of 'consumption scales' recounted by Perrot in *Le mode de vie des familles bourgeoises* (1961, pp. 21–40) is very instructive. In these studies, differential consumption is dissembled – as in the story of E. Allen Poe – by the act of bringing it to light. Three types of studies can be distinguished which, with apparently different methods, all lead to astonishingly similar scales.

In the first (Engels) 'the increase of weight and height represents the progression of expenditure of consumption'; it suggests lower coefficients of consumption of food for women and children.

Others ('budgetists') cling to the actual behaviour of households and 'discover' that consumption is indeed differentiated according to age and sex (thus 'confirming' the initial assumptions of the first school).

Lastly, the nutritionists try to evaluate the calorific needs of family members, but by 'considering that the expenditure on food of a family is proportional to the needs in calories of the people of whom it is composed' (i.e. by taking the actual consumption as the indicator of 'needs').

In corroborating the coefficients of the 'budgetists', those of the 'nutritionists' carry the guarantee that the actual expenditure well covers the 'calorific needs', and that differential expenditures are justified by different needs. In addition they give the impression that no consideration whatsoever, other than the provision of calories, enters into the consumption of food. It is implicit that differentiation of food intake cannot relate to quality but exclusively to calorific values. Quantities being adapted to needs, distribution is hence – in the full sense of the word – *just*.

3 This tendency to find what is morally unacceptable and also theoretically unthinkable – or at least not to think about it – overflows the

restricted area of consumption. Thus Engels (followed by Simone de Beauvoir) could see nothing in the hierarchy of the proletarian family other than a dulling 'remnant of brutality' which did not profoundly debase the essential 'equality in misfortune'. The latter attenuates the former and allows it alone to be conceived as empirical reality. This sentiment even overflows the limits of the family since (marxist) authors refuse to interpret hierarchies in terms of classes – i.e. in terms of exploitation – when they come across them in so-called 'subsistence' societies, modestly covering them over with the functionalist concept of 'power of redistribution'. The coincidence of the existence of surplus and the existence of social inequalities is thus not an empirical discovery but an element of dogma, according to which the creation of surplus explains the appearance of inequalities. See particularly Terray (1972).

4   I feel authorized by an illustrious mentor to choose 'homely facts' 'drawn from everyday life' when handling 'phenomena whose intimate place in men's life has sometimes shielded them from the impact of economic discussion' (Veblen 1953, p. xx).

5   The similarity between this indigenous theory and the basic postulates of consumption scales is striking. The latter 'scientifically' confirm the former. Thus the 'nutritional' scales (the most 'scientific') of 1918 are closer to the 'budgetary' scales of 1918 than to the 'nutritional' scales of 1970. The evaluation of the calorific needs of an individual thus vary with the allocation of food considered as 'normal' for that individual by the society (and the sociology) of his or her time.

6   Consumption scales give many indications on this subject, but since they cannot be analysed in detail here, let us simply stress the coincidence of the relative share of adolescents in food consumption – a coefficient of *84* in the USA in *1917* and *60* in France (CREDOC) in *1965* – and the existence or absence of a theory of adolescent hunger.

4. The main enemy*

Since the birth of the women's liberation movement in France, the United States and elsewhere, the marxist point of view has been represented by a line formulated outside the movement. This has been put forward by both traditional communist parties and more recently developed left groups, and it has been brought into the movement by militant women from these groups.

Most women in the movement consider this line unsatisfactory, in both theory and strategy, for two basic reasons:

1 it doesn't account for the oppression common to all women, and
2 it concentrates, not on the oppression of women, but on the consequences this oppression has for the proletariat (cf. the analysis in McAffee and Wood, 1969).

This is only possible because there is a flagrant contradiction between the principles which adherents of marxism claim to uphold and the way in which they have applied these principles to the situation of women. Historical materialism is based on the analysis of social antagonisms in terms of classes; classes being themselves defined by their place in the system of production. While these principles have supposedly been used to analyse the situation of women as women, the specific relations of women to production have in fact simply been ignored. That is to say there has been no class analysis of women. This theoretical failure has had immediate consequences.

---

* First published in *Partisans*, no. 54–5 (July–October 1970). An English translation by Lucy ap Roberts was sold in mimeoed form at the 1974 National Women's Liberation Conference in Edinburgh, and later included in a Women's Research and Resources Centre pamphlet with the same title in 1977.

1   The oppression of women is held to be a secondary consequence of (and derived from) the class struggle, which is currently defined exclusively as the oppression of the proletariat by Capital.

2   The continuing oppression of women in countries where capitalism as such has been destroyed is attributed to purely ideological factors. This implies an idealist and non-marxist definition of ideology. It treats it as a factor which can survive in the absence of any material oppression that it serves to rationalize.

These assumptions go against the dynamic of the women's movement, and hold back the development of women's awareness of a twofold need. First, a theoretical need: to find the structural reasons why the abolition of capitalist relations of production as such is not sufficient to free women; and second, a political need: to establish the women's movement as an autonomous force.

Hardly born, the movement has had to confront the following contradiction. At the very moment when it is becoming a revolutionary force, the only analysis which places the struggle of women in a global revolutionary perspective denies the first of these necessities (the need to seek the causes of the specific oppression of women), and offers no theoretical basis for the second (it allows, but does not establish the necessity, for an autonomous movement). The results of this contradiction are directly manifested within the movement in a general uneasiness, the appearance of opposing factions, and a difficulty in functioning. These are all due to the impossibility of defining a coherent practice so long as a gap exists between the theory to which we refer and the actual oppression of women against which we fight. This will continue so long as the very reason for the existence of the movement lacks a solid theoretical foundation.

The existence of this marxist line in practice holds back the movement – an effect which is obviously not accidental. My aim here is not to analyse the mechanisms by which this line came to be adopted by women themselves,[1] nor to show how this constitutes further proof of the existence of objective interests in the oppression of women – interests not confined to the capitalist class. Suffice to say that, because of this objective role in retarding the liberation of women, the existing marxist line must be regarded as the creation of groups interested in the subjection of women; and because of its non-scientific nature it can only be a marxist camouflage for theories which justify this subjection: that is, it is itself an ideology. But to repeat, my aim is not to question this line point by point (which I do elsewhere in other chapters in this book, cf. pp. 106 and 154), but to try to provide what the movement crucially needs at this moment: the basis for a materialist analysis of the oppression of women.

My concern certainly reflects an objective need in the movement, as is clear from the fact that in 1969–70, various attempts to provide such an account were made by a number of different women, separated by thousands of miles and having no contact one with another. In the United States, Margaret Benston wrote 'The political economy of women's liberation' (1969) and Suzie Olah 'The economic function of the oppression of women' (n.d.), in Cuba there was an article 'Against invisible work' (Larguia 1970) and in France the group FMA (Féminisme, Marxisme, Action)[2] produced an unpublished manifesto.

The relations of production entered into by women

In order to survive, each society must create material goods (production) and human beings (reproduction). The attempts at analysis just referred to all concentrate on the oppression of women in terms of their participation in family production (and not on those commonly stressed – i.e. reproduction). That is to say, they analyse domestic work and child-rearing as productive activities. They thus constitute the embryo of a radical feminist analysis based on marxist principles, and they reject the 'marxist' pseudo-theories of the family which ignore its economic function and see it as above all the site for the ideological indoctrination of 'future workers' (i.e. which see the family as existing in order to sustain indirectly the only form of exploitation recognized under capitalism: that of the workers). The new analyses show the family as itself the site of economic exploitation: that of women. Having shown that domestic work and child-rearing are, first, exclusively the responsibility of women, and, second, unpaid, these essays conclude that women have a specific relationship to production which is comparable to serfdom. But they do not go far enough. We need also:

1   to analyse the relationship between the *nature* of domestic goods and services and their *mode* of production;
2   to proceed to develop a class analysis of women; and
3   on the basis of this analysis, to trace the broad outlines of the

women's movement's political perspective in terms of our *goals, constituency* and *political alliances*.

All contemporary 'developed' societies, including 'socialist' ones, depend on the unpaid labour of women for domestic services and child-rearing. These services are furnished within the framework of a particular relationship to an individual (the husband). They are excluded from the realm of exchange and consequently have no *value*. They are unpaid. Whatever women receive in return is independent of the work which they perform because it is not handed out in exchange for that work (i.e. as a wage to which their work entitles them), but rather as a gift. The husband's only obligation, which is obviously in his own interest, is to provide for his wife's basic needs, in other words he maintains her labour power.

In the American and Cuban texts mentioned above there is an ambiguity, or rather a remnant of the dominant ideology. Although they recognize that domestic work is productive, they suggest – or say explicitly – that its non-value, its non-remuneration, and its exclusion from the domain of economic exchange, are due to the very nature of domestic services themselves. This idea is based on and expressed in two assumptions:

1   that women 'have no structural responsibility for the production of commodities' and are 'excluded from the realm of surplus value' (Benston 1969);
2   that women are restricted to activities which produce goods and services that have only 'use-value' and no 'exchange-value', and which do not create any 'surplus value' (Larguia 1970).

I contend, on the contrary, that far from it being the nature of the work performed by women which explains their relationship to production, it is their relations of production which explain why their work is excluded from the realm of value. It is women as economic agents who are excluded from the (exchange) market, not what they produce.

1   *The relations of production of domestic work described above, i.e. the non-remuneration of the wife's work by the household head, are not limited to products consumed within the family (child-rearing, domestic services) but apply also to products destined for the market when they are produced within the family, and to work done by other family members*

Women's participation in the creation of commodities and vital necessities is attested by the whole anthropological literature, and this constitutes an obstacle in the path of those ideologists who claim that they
can explain the inferior status of women by our secondary role in the
survival of the species – if not now, at least 'in the beginning'. In a later
chapter (p. 182) I shall look further at the phenomenon of 'naturalist'
ideologies which explain the present system by a myth of its origins. It is
enough to say here that anthropological evidence as a whole shows that
the economic importance of the work performed by women or by men is
unrelated to the social pre-eminence of one sex or the other. On the
contrary, all the anthropological and sociological evidence reveals an
inverse relationship: it reveals that the dominant classes make the
classes in their power do the productive work – that the pre-eminent sex
does less work.

In France today women's labour may be unpaid not only when it is
applied to products for use in the home, but also when it is applied to
goods and services for the market. This occurs in all those sectors where
the unit of production is the family (rather than the workshop or the
factory); i.e. on most farms, in small retail businesses, and in small craft
workshops. Thus work by women in family production is by no means
marginal.

In 1968, wives of small farmers, for example, devoted an average of
four hours a day to agricultural work (Bastide 1969). The 'rural crisis'
which France is experiencing is largely due to the fact that girls no
longer want to marry farmers, and by general consensus 'a farm can't be
run without a woman'. Michelet said that when a farmer couldn't afford
to hire a domestic worker he took a wife. This is still true. As the mother
of an unmarried farmer said to me: 'Michel needs someone to help him
and he can't find a servant. If only he could get married. . . .' In France
the tasks assigned to farmers' wives vary from region to region, but they
always raise young animals, and keep poultry and pigs. Otherwise they
are good for anything. They are the assistants, the subordinates, to
whom all the dirty, unpleasant, non-mechanized tasks are assigned. (In
particular they are given the milking if this is done by hand. This work
is so arduous and demands such a tiring schedule that some women now
demand exemption from it in their marriage contracts. Men take over
the work when it is mechanized.) Often the only source of cash which
enables the household to buy things which are not produced on the farm
is the sale of goods which are exclusively produced by the wife: i.e.

milk, eggs and poultry. But whatever her tasks on the farm may be, a wife's work is absolutely indispensable. A man alone cannot keep a farm without doubling his workload, and in the last resort he cannot manage it at all – and I speak here only of the actual farm work, since a man on his own with no children does not need a great many domestic services.

A wife's unpaid labour is therefore taken for granted in the economy of a farm, as is also the unpaid labour of younger brothers and sisters of the owner (who are literally disinherited), and that of children in some cases. Even though today in most cases younger siblings and children may threaten to leave a family enterprise unless they are paid (and some actually do leave), it is important to remember that their exploitation was *the rule* in every sector of the economy until industrialization (the end of the eighteenth century) and in agriculture until the Second World War.

Historically and etymologically the family is a unit of production. *Familia* in Latin means all the land, the slaves, the women and the children who were under the control of (the synonym for the property of) the father of the family. The father of the family dominated this unit as he still does today. The labour of the people who are under his authority belongs to him. In other words, a family is a group of individuals who owe their labour to a particular 'boss'.

Since the family is based on one individual's exploitation of those who are related to him by blood or by marriage, wherever the unit of production is still the family, this exploitation still exists. In Morocco for example:

In rural communities the women gather fruit and take care of the animals. These women receive no payment for their work; they are entitled to receive upkeep from the head of the family
(Nouase 1969).

It also continues in the West. In France today 7 million women are actually designated as 'working', i.e. as participating in production. Out of these 7 million, 1 million, are 'family helps', which is an official category meaning they work unpaid within a family business. Of those women who are working but not paid, almost eight out of ten are employed in agriculture.

The status of 'family help' is the consecration of family exploitation in official statistics, because it institutionalizes the fact that some producers are not paid, i.e. that the profits acquired from their production belong to their brother, husband or father. This status was invented after the war in order to allow these particular workers to receive social welfare benefits. (Most wives of small farmers, shopkeepers and craftsmen, however, continue to declare themselves to be 'unemployed'.) But even so, the number of women other than wives who participate in the production of commodities within the framework of family businesses is far larger than the number of women who are counted in the census as 'family helps'. Assuming that the number is underestimated by 40 per cent, there are 1,400,000 women out of 14 million adult women (between 17 and 64 years old) who are subject to this relationship of production, i.e. one woman in ten.

Thus the unpaid nature of married and unmarried women's labour in the family is still taken for granted. The unpaid labour of male children is however being called into question. More and more frequently, when a farming household is made up of different generations, the son demands that he be paid for his work and no longer 'recompensed' by the mere maintenance of his labour power. The suggestion that his wife might demand the same thing, however, that the young couple should receive two wages for two jobs, is greeted with total incomprehension. Thus, while the unpaid labour of men is strongly under attack (currently only one in forty-three 'working' men is a family help, as opposed to one in seven 'working' women), the unpaid labour of women is still institutionalized. It is institutionalized in practice in the bookkeeping of the state (through the status of family help), and also in the demands of opposition political parties. The MODEF,[3] for example, is demanding that each *family* farm be assured of an income equivalent to *one* wage, the implication being that the wife's labour, which is incorporated into household production, does not merit a wage – or perhaps rather, since the production of the wife is exchanged by the husband as his own, that her work belongs to him.

2 *The domestic services supplied by wives are no different from other so-called productive goods and services produced and consumed by the family*

In the traditional peasant farm economy, the family produces a large part of the goods which it consumes; it directly absorbs much of what it produces. But what it produces is at the same time saleable. There is no distinction here between use-value and exchange-value. The product which is consumed by the family, and thereby has a use-value, also has an exchange-value, since it could have been sold on the market. Conversely, if it had not been self-produced, it would have had to be replaced by its equivalent bought on the market.

Because of this, produce from the farm which is self-consumed is considered income by those concerned, and as part of production in the national economy (i.e. it is included in estimates of the gross national product). The only question raised is whether a pig eaten by the family should be valued at its selling price, i.e. the price for which it could have been sold (the profit missed by the enterprise), or at its purchase price, i.e. the price which would have had to have been paid had it not been produced (the cost avoided by the unit of consumption) (see p. 82).

When the producer and the consumer are one, as in the farming family, it is obvious that there is a continuum between production and consumption: you sow wheat in order to consume it, you mill it because you cannot consume it in the form of grains, you bake it because you cannot consume it in the form of flour. None of these operations is useful without the others because the goal is the final consumption. It is therefore absurd to introduce a break into the process. This, however, is what happens when only a part of the process is considered productive – up to and including the production of flour – and when the rest of the process, the baking of the bread for example, is considered nonproductive. Either all of the labour involved in making a product which is self-consumed is productive, or none of it is. The latter hypothesis is absurd because wheat which is eaten could have been sold on the market, in which case it would have had to have been replaced by its equivalent in food purchased on the market. When farmers produce only one crop or animal, and especially when they produce goods which they cannot consume, they must exchange products twice before they can consume something. (They sell the goods they produce, and purchase the goods they consume.) This masks the fact that the ultimate goal of all production is consumption. What breaks the continuum between production and consumption, however, is not the fact that some activities necessary for the final goal, consumption, are not productive, but that when production is *specialized*, consumption (the final object of all production) is mediated by exchange.

The example of self-consumption on small farms shows clearly that there is no essential difference between activities which are said to be 'productive' (like growing wheat and milling it) and domestic activities which are called 'non-productive' (like cooking the selfsame flour).

To sum up, on small farms men and women together create use-values which are:

a potentially exchange-values. Women and men produce milk, eggs and agricultural produce for their own consumption and for exchange. The desired level of consumption and the desired quantity of cash determine what they put on the market and what they consume themselves;

b some of the use-values are officially included in the calculation of production (the gross national product);

c 'productive' use-values are no different from 'non-productive' use-values created by the purely domestic labour of the housewife. They are both part of the same process of creation and transformation of raw materials (they are carried out on the same raw materials for the production of food) and have the same goal: self-consumption.[4]

3 *Just as there is a continuity and not a division between activities for self-consumption which are called productive and activities for self-consumption which are called non-productive (household activities), so there is continuity between the services furnished without pay by wives and commercialized services*

Many of the operations necessary to turn raw materials into consumable goods are now industrialized. Operations such as the manufacture of bread, clothes and preserved foods, which were once part of household activities, are now performed outside the home. Bakeries, clothing manufacturers and canning and freezing companies today *sell* goods incorporating paid labour which were, in the past, produced with unpaid labour by women. This manufacturing is considered production and is officially included in the national product. The labour involved in it is considered productive labour and the individuals who perform the work are producers. This was not the case when these goods were created with the unpaid labour of women.

When women in families cannot provide certain goods and services, these are *bought*. And in fact *all* the usual domestic services exist on the market. Delicatessens and restaurants offer prepared dishes, nurseries and babysitters offer child care, cleaning agencies and domestic servants offer housework, etc. Food, for example, which is the major item on household budgets in France (50 to 80 per cent of weekly outgoings) can either be bought ready to eat, thus paying for the value which has been added to the raw materials by the paid labour of the caterer, the restaurateur, etc., or it can be bought in raw form and labour applied to make it edible. Most households spend the bulk of their food budget on raw materials.

One might say that the household itself manufactures final products for consumption, just as a business firm manufactures final products. To do this the household uses labour (domestic), durable goods (domestic appliances) and raw materials (the intermediary products bought from the manufacturers), which are transformed by the household itself with the aid of a certain quantity of labour and capital. Looked at in this way, the only distinction between the household and the firm is that the household adds to production (which is the sole function of the firm) the activity of consumption (which is the goal of the production performed by the household itself with the aid of goods produced by a firm)

(Wolfelsperger 1970, p. 20).[5]

The final goal of production for the producer is consumption, either of his own products in a subsistence economy, or of the products of others in a specialized economy. The money he obtains from the exchange of specialized products, or the sale of his labour power on the market, is not sufficient to accomplish this goal. It has to be reached in two stages: first, by the purchase of raw materials for consumption using money earned by the sale of products or by paid labour; and second, the transformation of these primary materials by domestic labour into products which can be directly consumed.

We have then, on the one hand work inside the house which supplies a certain quantity of directly consumable goods, and on the other hand work outside the home which brings in a certain monetary income. But how is this income used? We can readily see that it is not used to purchase goods which can be directly consumed, as the traditional theory asserts, but, according to our hypotheses, it is used to contribute to the production of consumable final products; that is to say, the capital goods purchased with this income (raw materials and machines) contribute to this production

(Wolfelsperger 1970, p. 22).

What this bourgeois economist does not mention is that if most 'households' prefer to buy food in a raw form, it is because domestic labour is unpaid and because this labour is provided almost entirely by women. These facts give the lie to the ideology which says that the husband's wage buys everything the entire household consumes, while the housewife does not 'earn her own living', despite the hours of work she does each week (see Girard 1958 for figures on hours of housework).

The fact that women's labour is excluded from the zone of exchange therefore results not from the nature of what they produce, since their unpaid labour goes towards producing goods and services which:

a reach and are exchanged on the market (in agriculture, crafts and small retail businesses); and
b are paid for when done outside the family.

Their work is only *not* paid when it is done within the family; and all the work they do within the family is not paid, whatever its nature.

4 *The appropriation of women's labour power is nowadays largely limited to their unpaid provision (the exploitation) of domestic work and child-rearing*

With industrialization, the family was stripped of much of its function as a unit of production, except in certain sectors, because one of the main effects of industrialization was to make production for the market impracticable within the family. As a result, market production less and less incorporated the unpaid labour of wives and children. Or, to put it another way, wives' work could no longer be used for family production intended for exchange, since production for exchange was performed outside the family. As the industrial capitalist mode of production spread, the number of independent workers who could use the labour of their wives for exchange diminished, while the number of wage-earners who could not exchange this labour increased, and is still increasing.

In sectors where all production intended for exchange is performed by paid labour, the unpaid labour of a wife can now only be applied to production which is not intended for exchange. Or, to be more precise, the family mode of production – the exploitation of wives' (and other family members') unpaid labour – can no longer be applied to production intended for exchange. It must be pointed out, however, that this concerns exchange *by the husband*. A woman's agricultural labour, for instance, is only not paid for if it is performed within the family. She cannot exchange her *family* production on the market. In family production, she does not make use of her labour power; her husband makes use of it. He alone exchanges his wife's production on the market. In the same way, a woman does not make use of her housework as long as it is performed within the family; she can only exchange it outside the family. Thus women's production always has an exchange-value – i.e. it can always be exchanged by them – except when they work within the framework of the family. With industrialization, family production became limited to housework; or, more precisely, we call housework that to which the unpaid labour of the housewife has been limited.

Women's entry into industry as paid workers was the direct consequence of it becoming impossible to exploit their labour power completely within the family. However, the appropriation of their labour power by their husbands has been so absolute that even when women work outside the family, their wage still belongs to their husbands. A wife has legally had the use of her own wage in France since 1907, but in fact the custom in most marriages has been such as to annul this concession. All her earnings go into a common budget which the husband alone controls. Similarly a wife's entire labour power has been appropriated. Until 1965 a husband could prevent his wife working outside the home, and though since then women have legally had control of part of their own labour power (i.e. they have been legally free to work outside the home), they are in fact not free. Part of a woman's labour power is still appropriated since 'she must fulfil her family responsibilities' – that is, she must do the housework and raise children without pay. Not only has going out to work not freed women from domestic work, it has not been allowed to interfere with it either. Thus what women have been free to do has been to have a double workload in return for a certain amount of economic independence.

The situation of the married woman who has a job clearly reveals the legal appropriation of her labour power. Her provision of domestic work can in fact no longer be justified by the economic exchange to which the servitude of the housewife is often attributed, i.e. it can no longer be claimed that she performs domestic labour in return for her keep, that this upkeep is the equivalent of a wage, and that therefore her work is paid, since women who go out to work keep themselves. It is therefore clear that they perform domestic work *for nothing*.

Moreover, when a woman works 'outside', the cost of childcare and any extra taxes, etc., are paid for from *her* income. They are not taken from the couple's income as a whole. This shows that:

a it is believed that these services should be provided free, unlike other items such as housing and transport, which are considered as normal expenses; and
b the wife alone is exclusively responsible for providing these services, since it is deemed that the part of her wage which goes towards paying for them when she works outside the home is cancelled out, as though she had never earned the money in the first place. In terms of these calculations it is generally discovered that the wife earns 'almost nothing'.

5 *On this basis we can now outline the main elements of an analysis of the class position of women*

There are two modes of production in our society. Most goods are produced in the industrial mode. Domestic services, child-rearing and certain other goods are produced in the family mode. The first mode of production gives rise to capitalist exploitation. The second gives rise to familial, or more precisely, patriarchal exploitation.

307,000 men (who are family helps) out of about 15 million adult men are subject to patriarchal exploitation. They are mainly in agriculture and provide skilled services unpaid within the family. All married women (i.e. 80 per cent of adult women at any given moment) are subject to patriarchal exploitation. They provide minimally or unpaid domestic services and child-rearing within the family. The status of son or younger brother, on which the familial exploitation of men is based, is temporary, whereas the status of women is lifelong. Moreover, male family helps are not exploited because they are men, whereas women are exploited because they are women (wives).[6] While unpaid work in the farm, workshop or shop can be performed just as easily by men as by women members of the family, unpaid housework is performed exclusively by women, generally as wives of the heads of households.

The labour of women is appropriated for family production when the family is the unit producing for the market (wives of farmers, independent craftsmen and shopkeepers – approximately one million out of 14 million *adult* women in France) and is used exclusively for household production when the family no longer produces directly for the market (e.g. wives of wage-earners). In the first case the labour power of the woman is entirely appropriated; in the second her labour power is totally appropriated if she doesn't work outside the home, or partially appropriated if she does. (37.8 per cent of married women in France are economically 'active', but we must subtract from this figure the number of family helps – approximately 8,000,000 wives of farmers, independent craftsmen and shopkeepers.) The majority of married women thus had no independent income and work for their keep.

The difference between the family mode of production and the wage mode of capitalist production lies neither in the quantity of benefits given for work nor in the difference between the value of a wage and upkeep, but in the relations of production themselves. The wage-labourer sells his labour power for a fixed wage which depends on the service he provides. These services are also fixed: defined in quantity (hours of work) and kind (qualifications). The equivalents are determined according to a fixed scale (that is, by a price determined by the overall supply and demand on the labour market in the capitalist system) – a scale which is not subject to the will of either party. The employer and the employee have no personal influence on the terms of their contract and the individuals are interchangeable. The labour which is performed has a universal value and it is this value which the employer buys and over which the worker can bargain because it is possible for him to take his labour power elsewhere. The fact that it is precise services which are bought may enable the worker to increase his earnings by improving his performance, either in quantity or in kind.

The services which a married woman provides, on the contrary, are not fixed. They depend on the will of the employer, her husband. And these services are not paid according to a fixed scale. Her keep does not depend on her work, but on the wealth and goodwill of her husband. For the same work (for example, the rearing of three children) the wife of a business executive receives as much as ten times the benefits received by the wife of a manual worker. On the other hand, for the same benefits, a wife may furnish very different quantities and kinds of services, depending on the needs of her husband. For example, the housework of the wife of one bourgeois man may consist of running single-handedly a large house, while another may be given several servants to free her for the work of social display.

Since the benefits which wives receive have no relationship to the services which they provide, it is impossible for married women to improve their own standard of living by improving their services. The only solution for them is to provide the same services for a richer man. Thus the logical consequence of the non-value of women's family labour is the hunt for a good marriage. But even though a marriage with a man from the capitalist class can raise a woman's standard of living, it does not make her a member of that class. She herself does not own the means of production. Therefore her standard of living does not depend on her class relationship to the proletariat; but on her serf relations of production with her husband. In the vast majority of cases, wives of bourgeois men whose marriage ends must earn their own living as wage-workers. They therefore become in practice (with the additional handicaps of age and/or lack of professional training) the proletarians that they essentially were.

The non-value of a woman's work is shown by the independence of the services she renders from the upkeep she receives. This stems from the impossibility of *exchanging* her labour, which stems in turn from the impossibility of changing employers. (We need only compare the number of divorced women who remarry with the number of workers who change jobs within a given year.) In addition, the contract can be broken unilaterally by the husband even when a woman continues to provide adequate services. (Women are given care of the children on separation and only their upkeep is covered by alimony – when the payments are actually made. See Chapter 6, p. 93.)

In sum, while the wage-labourer depends on the market (on a theoretically unlimited number of employers), the married woman depends on one individual. While the wage-labourer sells his labour power, the married woman gives hers away. Exclusivity and non-payment are intimately connected.

6 *Providing unpaid labour within the framework of a universal and personal relationship (marriage) constitutes a relationship of slavery*

Since less than 10 per cent of all women over 25 have never been married in developed societies, chances are high that women will be married at some point in their lives. Thus effectively all women are destined to participate in these relations of production. As a group which is subjected to this relation of production, they constitute a class; as a category of human beings who are destined by birth to become members of this class, they constitute a caste.[7] The appropriation of their labour within marriage constitutes the oppression common to all women. Destined as women to become 'the wife of' someone, and thus destined for the same relations of production, women constitute but one class.

When they participate in capitalist production, women enter additionally into a second relation of production. Nearly 6 million women in France are integrated into capitalist production: 5,160,000 wage-workers and 675,000 self-employed. In the whole of France only 11,000 women are 'industrialists'. This small minority of women belongs to the capitalist class, while the majority of women who work belong to the proletariat. Within the latter class, they constitute a super-exploited caste, as is well known. This super-exploitation is clearly connected to their specific, familial exploitation as women.

In view of what has been said, we can see that it is about as accurate to say that the wife of a bourgeois man is herself bourgeois as it is to say that the slave of a plantation owner is himself a plantation owner. However, this *is* very commonly asserted. There is, equally, currently a confusion between women workers and the wives of workers. That is to say, women's class membership is sometimes based on a marxist definition of class – on their relationship to production – and sometimes on a conception of women as the property and extension of their husbands.

Society is divided into classes and women are not outside these classes; consequently the lot of every woman is linked to that of other women and men who belong to the same class and social category
(PCF 1970, p. 129).

But if only the capitalist mode of production is considered – as is usually the case – and if the same criteria are applied to women as men, then it can be seen that all women who do not work outside the home are outside the (proletariat/capitalist) class system. What is more, such women can only be reintegrated into the class system by determining their class membership according to non-marxist criteria (that is, by attributing them the class of their husbands). By pretending that women belong to their husband's class, the fact that wives belong, by definition, to a class *other* than that of their husbands is hidden. By pretending that marriage can take the place of relations of production in the capitalist system as the criterion for class membership in this system, the existence of another system of production is masked, and the fact that the relations of production within that system place husbands and wives into two antagonistic classes (the former benefiting materially from the exploitation of the latter) is hidden. The 'reintegration' of women into classes by defining them as the property of their husbands has as its objective precisely hiding the fact that they really *are* the property of their husbands.

If one merely wanted to rally women to the anti-capitalist struggle, it would be enough to show that, in so far as they are integrated into this mode of production (as wage-workers), the vast majority of women (nine out of ten women who work) have an objective interest in this struggle. But because women are assigned their husbands' class, the wives of the bourgeoisie (who are not integrated into capitalist production) are considered as enemies of the anti-capitalist struggle. It is thus clear that what is at issue is not so much a question of rallying *all* women to the anti-capitalist struggle, as of denying the existence of a *non-capitalist system of production*. In denying the existence of this system of production, the existence of relations of production specific to this system are also denied, and those who participate in this system are prevented from having the possibility of rebelling against it. The priority of the left, therefore, appears to be to preserve the patriarchal mode of production of domestic services (i.e. the unpaid performance of these services by women). In this regard it is revealing to compare the current ideas of the French Communist Party with Lenin's recommendations.[8] Lenin said:

The true liberation of women and true communism will only begin when the struggle of the masses against this petty domestic economy begins (led by the proletariat in power), or to be more precise, when this economy is totally transformed into large scale socialist economy

(Lenin, p. 462).

The Communist Party solution however is to: 'make domestic appliances available for all households which can lead to the mechanisation of domestic labour' (PCF 1970). According to the Communist Party, employers and the public administration should 'enable the working woman to fulfil her role as mother of a family' (PCF 1970). Lenin himself commented:

Among our comrades, there are many of whom one can unfortunately say, 'scratch the communist and you will find a Philistine'. There is no more convincing proof of this than the fact that men calmly watch their wives exhaust themselves at the petty monotonous work which absorbs their time and energy: housework. . . . There are few husbands, even within the proletariat, who would think of substantially lightening the labour and cares of their

wives, or even of doing away with these altogether by helping them with 'women's work'
    (quoted by Zetkin).

None the less, the Communist Party asserts that, 'an equal distribution of difficulties and fatigue in a household is a limited concept of equality' (PCF 1970).

The consequences of this analysis for the WLM

Patriarchal exploitation is the common, specific and main oppression of women.

1 *Common:* because it affects all married women (80 per cent of women at any given moment);
2 *Specific:* because only women are under an obligation to perform free domestic services;
3 *Main:* because even when women go out to work, the class membership they derive from that work is conditioned by their exploitation as women in the following ways. First, because access to the ownership of the means of production was forbidden them by marriage laws (until 1968 in France) and by the practice of inheritance (the majority of women who own property and employ other people are only children or widows). Second, because their earnings are cancelled out by the deduction of the value of the services which they are obliged to buy to replace their own unpaid services. And third, because the material conditions for the exercise of their outside occupation are dictated by their patriarchal oppression. On the one hand, the very possibility of women being employed is conditional on their fulfilling their primary 'family duties', which results in the work they do outside the home being either impossible or else added to their domestic work; while on the other, family duties are erected as a handicap by capitalism and used as a pretext to exploit women in their outside work.

It has not been possible in this chapter to study the relationship between the exploitation of women's productive capacity and the exploitation of their reproductive capacity. The control of reproduction is both the cause and the means for the second great material oppression of women – sexual exploitation. Control of reproduction is the second facet of the oppression of women. Establishing why and how these two forms of exploitation are affected and reinforced by each other, and why and how both have the same framework and institution, the family, should be one of the primary theoretical goals of the movement.

Such an analysis is basic to a study of the relationship between patriarchy and capitalism. It means that we must know what patriarchy is in order to understand to what extent it is theoretically independent of capitalism. Only such an understanding can enable us to account for the historical independence of these two systems. Only then will it be possible to establish the material basis for the connection between the struggle against patriarchy and the struggle against capitalism. So long as this connection remains based on unproven assumptions about the relative priority of the two struggles, which derive not from analysis but from a fear of upsetting the political practice and priorities established before the women's movement, we are condemned to theoretical confusion and to political ineffectiveness in the short term, and to historical failure in the long term.

This analysis should be followed by a class analysis which integrates individuals into both systems of exploitation (patriarchal and capitalist) according to their objective interests. This is necessary in the short term to enable us to mobilize for the immediate struggle, and in the long term to enable us to see how the dynamic of the struggle against patriarchy and the struggle against capitalism can be oriented to combine them in revolutionary struggle. (Needless to say, this must be the object of a continuing study whose bases will constantly be modified as the struggle evolves.)

For now, we can say that women will not be liberated unless the patriarchal system of production and reproduction is totally destroyed. Since this system is central to all known societies (however it originated), this liberation necessitates the total overthrow of the bases for all known societies. This overthrow cannot take place without a revolution, that is, the seizure of political power over ourselves presently held by others. This seizure of power should constitute the ultimate objective of the women's liberation movement, and the movement should prepare for a revolutionary struggle.

Our strategy should be centred on patriarchal oppression and should therefore include all individuals who are oppressed by patriarchy and who are hence interested in its destruction, that is all women. The work of mobilization must emphasize the solidarity of all people oppressed by the same system. To do this we must:

1 attack the problems of false consciousness, that is class consciousness determined according to membership in capitalist classes rather
than in patriarchal classes, and the identification of women under this
pretext with enemy patriarchal classes;
2 show how this false consciousness serves the interests of patriarchy
and detracts from our struggle.

Finally, in the immediate future, the political alliances and strategy of
the movement in relation to other groups, movements or revolutionary
parties should be based only on an unambiguous dedication on the part
of the latter to the goals of the women's movement. That is, on the basis
of their clearly and officially expressed desire to destroy patriarchy and
their actual participation in the revolutionary struggle for its destruction.

Notes and references

1 These are mechanisms of alienation and false consciousness which
    perpetuate oppression. The women are victims of oppression and
    not responsible for it.
2 *Féminisme, Marxisme, Action* was one of the first two neo-feminist
    groups in France. It started in 1968 as a mixed group (men and
    women) but gradually became a women's group. In 1970 it com-
    bined with another women's group and women who had previously
    been isolated from any group to become the *Mouvement de Liberation
    des Femmes* (MLF). (For further information on the history of the
    women's liberation movement in France, see Pisan and Tristan,
    1977.)
3 *Mouvement de Defense des Exploitations Familiales:* a French
    Communist Party organization concerned with agriculture.
4 Ernest Mandel in his *Marxist Economic Theory* confirms that the
    terms 'use-value' and 'exchange-value' refer to neither the nature
    nor the intrinsic value nor the productivity of the labour involved in
    different types of production, but simply to the use to which the
    production is put – immediate consumption or consumption
    mediated by exchange.
5 This piece by an economist is about domestic appliances and was
    written for a business conference on their production and sale.
6 In French the word 'femme' means both 'woman' and 'wife'. There
    are two words in the case of males: 'mari' meaning 'husband' and

'homme' meaning 'man'. Thus even on the level of vocabulary the biological fact of being a woman and the social role of wife are synonymous.

7 The point made in the previous footnote can be expanded. The term 'slav' has the same root as the French 'esclave' (slave). Here an entire ethnic group is bound to service from birth. In the same way the entire female population is bound to become women/wives.

8 Such attitudes are not restricted to the Communist Party alone within the left. The *Programme Commun*, the platform of the recently formed coalition of the Socialist Party and the Communist Party, recommends that women be allowed to leave their outside jobs five minutes early in order to do the shopping for their families before the stores close. A peculiar privilege indeed!

5. Housework or domestic work*

In the last few years a new object of knowledge has appeared for sociology and economics: housework. Of course, it had not really been ignored up until then, but it was only tackled in a descriptive and quantitative way. Theoretically limited as they may be, we in France owe to the first time-budget studies (Stoetzel 1948, Girard 1958 and 1959) a recognition of the number of daily hours of housework performed by married women. We owe to the new feminists, however, the posing, for the first time in history, of the question of housework as a *theoretical* problem.[1] Subsequently 'scientists' (and among them some of the most brilliant, such as J. K. Galbraith), although they did not produce a theory of housework, have at least not hesitated to recognize the importance of the problem. After a decent lapse of time, they have built into their accounts concepts forged for the most part outside the academic world.

The literature on housework grows each year – to the point where 'schools' are beginning to form. However, a consensus does still exist among the authors, mostly women, as to the major economic characteristics of housework. It is agreed, on the one hand, that housework is work (and that this is indeed the reason why it is being considered) and on the other that it is free/unpaid (which is why recognizing it *as* work was not automatic, but rather constituted a great step forward and a scientific discovery). But beyond these two points of agreement, the divergences begin. There is a debate, for example, about the 'productivity' of housework. Some put the stress on the aspect of 'work', in the sense of 'tasks' involved in housework; others on the 'unpaid' aspect, on the mode of production. Studies are sometimes focused on

* This article appeared first in A. Michel (ed.), *Les femmes dans la société marchande*, PUF, Paris 1978.

the use made of housework by – or the use for – capitalism, and sometimes on the meaning of this work for the direct producers: for women-wives.[2] All these points are obviously connected, but in spite of the interest generated by the question, and the number of articles or books which have already been devoted to it, one point remains relatively hazy, albeit fundamental. And that is the very definition of housework, of the object of study.

The definition of housework remains hazy not because of an unresolved debate, but, on the contrary, because a tacit consensus exists as to its content. Housework is never formally defined, but the examples cited show authors adopting uncritically a 'commonsense' definition of housework (which is also the one used in time-budgets surveys). This takes housework to be the work done within the house by the wife: cooking, washing, ironing, sewing, shopping, cleaning and servicing (i.e. housewifery in the restricted sense of 'doing the housework'), and care of children. But is this empirical definition adequate? Is it accurate? And is it compatible with the economic attributes of housework identified above?

The empirical content given to housework is inevitably affected by the theoretical interpretation given to the subject. It seems to me that a great many of the dead ends in which the debate on housework currently finds itself could be avoided if there was agreement on its principal characteristics. This implies that there should be a formal (and not an empirical) definition of the object of study, i.e. of the content of housework; and, conversely, that important features of housework will be found only when it is studied empirically from the point of view of its structural and economic characteristics.

Such a procedure might be taxed with being arbitrary, or the argument could be dismissed as circular, in that the economic (structural) characteristics attributed to housework at the start might be the ones one wanted to retain at the end as essential traits. The difficulty can best be avoided by taking as the point of departure *only* those characteristics of housework on which there is universal agreement: that is, its character as *work*, and its character as *unpaid* work.

This done, we can pose two questions. Does the commonsense content, the empirical definition of housework, cover all its economic characteristics? And, conversely, do these characteristics cover all its content? Putting this in other words:

1   is it only *housework* (in the commonsense usage) which is *unpaid*?
2   and is *all* household activity unpaid work?

I shall try to show, on the one hand, that the defining economic characteristics of housework cover a great deal more than the classical contents and apply also to 'work' which is supposedly not 'of the house'; and on the other, that these economic characteristics do not apply to all household activity in the technical sense.

To this end, I shall make a detour via a subject which seems at first sight foreign to housework: the production which national accounting lists under the heading of 'for self-consumption by households'. I shall restrict myself to describing production for self-consumption in agriculture (i.e. that of small farm households) because this is both quantitatively the most important in much of Europe and also the best researched.

Production for self-consumption on farms

The fact that agricultural households/enterprises produce for their own consumption is well known and could indeed constitute a definition of contemporary small farms as a social stratum ('peasants'). Many authors consider that 'self-sufficiency' is the trait which most differentiates small farmers from the 'rest of society', whose members cannot directly consume what they produce. Further, this self-sufficiency makes this sector relatively independent of the exchange which necessarily unites the members of a society with a marked division of labour.

I believe this self-sufficiency, which is often presented as a major characteristic of the classical and atemporal peasant, to have been largely exaggerated. None the less, the quantity of agricultural produce which is directly consumed by its producers is substantial. According to Milhau and Montagne (1968): 'French agriculture retains at least 25% of its gross produce for its own needs, and the proportion is much higher still in other countries.'

This high percentage should be treated with reservations, however, because of the ambiguity introduced by the term 'gross product'. This makes it appear as if some intermediary production may be included; and even if we accept that the percentage consists solely of what the household appropriates from its final product, there is a further difficulty. The figure gives us an *average* rate, and in the actual situation of French agriculture, where there are enormous variations, an average, of whatever it may be, tells us next to nothing.

If we take the classical division of agriculture into three sectors:

1 (so-called) subsistence agriculture;
2 (so-called) artisanal agriculture (holdings which are traditional in production structure, but mechanized and of medium size); and
3 (so-called) capitalist or industrial agriculture,

it is clear that the extent to which products are commercialized, and hence the extent to which self-consumption is possible, must vary enormously between sectors. In the 'agribusiness' of Beauce or Soissonnais, specialization in cereals is combined with the whole product being commercialized. This holds true generally for purely cereal holdings: they produce nothing except for the market. Households on such farms, like urban households, buy all the products which they consume in the market.

But it is not the scale of the holdings, be it in area or in total amount of business, which provides the appropriate criterion for dividing holdings which produce for their own consumption from those which do not do so. The extent of *specialization* is more to the point. Holdings specializing in fruit growing, market gardening, factory farming of pigs or chickens, or vineyards are all in the same position as the big cereal farmers.

At first sight, it seems that monoculture by its nature limits the possibilities for self-consumption. You cannot live exclusively on grapes, or pork or peaches or whatever. But this explanation is less 'obvious' than it appears, for in fact specialization of holdings itself results from an economic choice, from a decision to adapt to, or to orientate exclusively towards, the market.

Non-specialized holdings, on the other hand, those subsistence or artisan farms which make up the majority of France, are said to be 'general' farms. This term tends to confuse because it leads to – or derives from – two received ideas which do not correspond to reality. One is that these holdings have several types of market speculation: that they offer various types of produce on the market, whereas specialized holdings or monoculture offer only one. Second, that production for self-consumption, sometimes seen as the principal *aim* of traditional agricultural production, is also the *consequence* of 'general' production: it results from the production of diverse goods for the market.

In reality, general farm holdings usually have only one market specu-lation: stock rearing, either for milk or for meat. The growing of plants – which is what makes it mixed or 'general' farming – is an intermediary production. The plants do not reach the market. They are consumed in the process of producing market animals. Thus, so far as the market is concerned, to call such farms 'general' is misleading. There is however good and plentiful general farming on these holdings, but contrary to what Milhau and Montagne assert, this diverse production is not (or is no longer) motivated by a concern to reduce risks by offering several products on the market – to secure oneself against fluctuations in prices. It is for self-consumption.

It can thus be seen that it is not specialization as such which prohibits self-consumption, for general farm holdings are, from the point of view of the market, in the same situation as those which are specialized. Both offer only one final product, and the specialized holdings could, just as well as those in general farming, have diversified cultivation for their own consumption. In so far as they do not do so, it is because of their economic attitude. They calculate in terms of profitability, and this calculation leads them to choose commercialization at the expense of self-consumption. Similarly, the self-consumption typical of general farms does not result from a diversification given by what is produced – a diversity which exists prior to a choice to produce for self-consumption. On the contrary, a choice is made in favour of production for consumption at the expense of production for the market.

Production for self-consumption in agriculture is taken into consider-ation when national accounts are constructed. This production, although non-market in essence, is included in the gross national product and the gross national revenue. However, since, in the strict sense, it has no value – not having been the object of exchange – to be included it has to be attributed one. How is this value determined?

The very fact of including a pig, produced and eaten by a household, in the GNR, follows from two presumptions:

1   that the household, if it had not eaten the pig, would have been able to sell it; and
2   that the household, if it had not produced the pig, whould have had to buy one.

These two propositions are equally legitimate. However, from an accounting point of view, they are not equivalent. According to which you choose, the pig has a different value. National accounting outside France chooses the first proposition and calculates the loss of earnings to agriculture. It invoices the pig at its selling price. French national accounting has favoured the latter proposition since 1963 and calculates the saving in spending for the household. It invoices the pig at its retail price. The latter is greater than the former.

According to the experts, the French solution presents some drawbacks because

it is the price of production which represents the cost of the consumption in question . . . commodities consumed on the farm do not carry the expenses of transport, the profit margins of intermediaries, and the taxes which encumber the retail price . . . evaluation at retail price . . . consequently includes . . . the value of services which have not in fact been provided
    (Marczewski 1967).

Despite these drawbacks, the French national account changed tack because, although this method makes a supplementary production appear (that of transforming agricultural produce into the products of the agricultural and foodstuffs industries) which, according to Marczewski, hasn't been effected, in other respects the augmentation of the gross internal product of the holdings (and thus the gross national product) is counterbalanced by the attribution of a debit of equal amount to the disposable income of households. Thus, according to our expert 'the balance of accounts is not affected.' In addition Marczewski admits that, if it is 'certainly not true' that agricultural households and holdings fulfil some commercialized functions (whose value is included in the retail price), it is 'partly true that they fulfil for themselves the functions of transforming agricultural products'.

This admission is welcome, because if Marczewski had held to his first position, according to which agriculturalists do not carry out *any* transformation of agricultural products, we would have to suppose that they consume the same raw product as they sell, and thus that they devour pigs running on their four trotters.

Some of the transformations which are necessary to make agricultural products consumable are thus accounted, but only some. The products are valued at their retail price. The pig is (happily) killed, skinned and cut into joints, so French farmers cannot be taxed with eating live animals. But the national account stops there: at a point when the pig is still far from being consumable. The last necessary operations – preparation, cooking and serving the pig – are not taken into account. Once again agricultural households must be suspected of uncommon feeding habits – for example, a taste for eating raw meat directly off the slab – unless of course we want to suspect those who construct national accounts of being arbitrary.

But the arbitrariness of the national account is not surprising. For what are the transformations which continue to be invisible, what are the things which are not thought of as being done? Those which correspond to some of the operations covered by the term 'housework'.

Housework as production

It is often argued that housework is unpaid (free) because it is not productive, and that it is not productive because it 'does not enter into the system of values', i.e. it does not pass through the market. Not only is this a poor explanation, it is above all a curious definition of productivity, because as we have just seen, some non-market products, consumed by their producers, are accounted and treated as productive. The absence of passage through the market (or not having been exchanged) is thus not the reason for the status of domestic work. The previous discussion has shown that housework is productive if we adopt the terms of national accounting, which are legitimate in that they define as productive all work which increases wealth. Accordingly, housework should be considered as productive along with other production accounted under the title of 'for household self-consumption'. The process of production for one's own consumption is a whole: either all the operations which lead to the final consumption are productive, or none of them are.

So we could ask why the French national account in particular makes such an arbitrary division within this process? If the prevalent principle in evaluating production for self-consumption made explicit reference to the lack of monetary gain – hence to the fact of goods not reaching the market – then the exclusion of the transformations to make food consumable – but of all the transformations to make it consumable – would be comprehensible (that is to say, if the principle stated that the value accounted was the sale price of the pig 'on the hoof', because only the potentiality of sale makes it a production). But such is not the case. On the one hand certain transformations *are* accounted, and, on the other, reference to potential marketability would in any case *not* justify the exclusion of housework.

We have seen that the only part of self-consumption which is accounted for is the value of goods in the state in which households usually purchase them on the retail market (i.e. before the final housework transformations). These final transformations, which are not counted in agricultural households, are not counted in any other households either. Only agricultural households raise pigs, but chops are cooked in all households. Consequently *all* households, and not just agricultural households, produce for their own consumption. Hence the sum of services and values which the national account ignores is substantial. To understand how and why this institution establishes this arbitrary cut, and to say why reference to marketability also does not justify excluding housework, we must make a new detour. At the end of the detour we will have the answers to these two questions and, moreover, will be able to reply to the first question posed: is housework the only unpaid work?

The difference between occupational work and household work on farms

On agricultural smallholdings, women take part in all production, as much in that destined for the market as in that destined for the accounted aspects of self-consumption. This is true for men too. But women also do some additional unaccounted work which men do not do, whose products are consumed by the household. This work is designated 'housework'.

Time-budget studies of the wives of small farmers distinguish their 'housework' from their 'occupational work'. Most of the authors of such work say how difficult it is to distinguish the two, and they underline the concrete overlap of tasks. Becouarn (n.d.) and Bastide and Girard (1959) deem that the wives of small farmers do an average of four hours of farm work a day; Allauzen (1967) raises this figure to five hours.

But what criteria distinguish housework from occupational work? Apparently the distinction between 'holding' and 'house'. This itself recovers, or rather applies to the agricultural holding, an opposition between business and household; which itself hides another opposition, between production and consumption, without which the first has no meaning. But this cannot be used to single out housework alone, precisely because on farms, part of what is produced by the 'business' is directly consumed by the household. The distinction between exchange-value and use-value (between production for the market and production for consumption) which may be being referred to implicitly, is also not relevant either. If it *were* used, it would not separate 'housework' from 'occupational work', but rather 'housework-and-some-occupational work' from 'the-rest-of-the-occupational-work', because 'occupational work' covers all the holdings' production, and a substantial part of this is self-consumed (i.e. constitutes use-values).

How, then, is the *holding* itself defined? It is neither a place (because many occupational activities take place inside the house) nor a business (because it does not produce exclusively for the market). In which case, how is occupational work to be defined, since 'occupational work' refers back to (is the work associated with) the 'holding' and no definition of holding exists?

In the absence of definitions, we have to look and see what the empirical objects are with which these terms coincide. We then see that, in actuality, the term 'occupational' is applied to activities which have as their object *accounted production*; and as we saw in the last section, all the household and holding production is accounted – except for the part called 'housework'. Housework is itself implicitly defined in opposition to, or rather as what is left when, occupational work is subtracted. It is what is *not* occupational work.

We thus arrive at a reasoning of remarkable circularity, and certainly at a theoretical dead end. There is no formal, economic, definition of occupational work or the holding. (Since these two terms refer back to one another, if one lacks a definition so must the other.) Likewise occupational work, having no economic definition, has no features which distinguish it formally from 'housework', which at the same stroke has no definition either. These two terms certainly relate to one another, but, in the absence of definition, not as two concepts but as two empirical objects. They are opposed, but in some way other than in the economic logic from which they are deemed to arise.

We therefore have to look once again to the empirical world to find our way out of the impasse; or rather, to see in what domain these two types of 'work' are defined. We can then establish that rural researchers call 'housework' certain tasks which are in fact in no way distinguished on the economic level from the other tasks carried out by the wives of small farmers. The only thing which distinguishes these tasks from the others carried out by the same women, is what does not distinguish them from tasks carried out by women in non-agricultural households. What distinguishes housework on farms is that it is not specifically agricultural. It is done elsewhere as well. In sum, researchers call 'housework' work which is not specific to agricultural production for self-consumption, i.e. which is common to all production for self-consumption.

'Occupational work' on farms in turn is thus nothing – it cannot be anything – other than what is left once 'housework' has been subtracted. The definition of 'occupational work' depends on housework, defined as a package of tasks; and the only sociological characteristic of this package is that it is work for self-consumption which is done by non-agricultural households as well as by agricultural households.

To sum up, the definition of accounted self-consumption on farms seems to be: all agricultural production for self-consumption less the production for self-consumption common to all households, rural and urban. This definition might seem to show that urban criteria are applied improperly to agricultural households: that production is counted when it is done outside the household, while all that is done inside the household is counted as non-productive, even though on farms it is productive.

But the problem goes far beyond making categories of industrial accounting adequate to agriculture. For in fact, even though the urban household is held to be non-productive, in reality it *is* productive. It could be argued that not only occupational work in agriculture, but also occupational work as such, is empirically defined as what remains once housework is eliminated. The only justification in fact for declaring the work done in non-agricultural households non-productive would be if all work for self-consumption were declared non-productive, including therefore all the production for self-consumption in agriculture which is officially accounted.

Housework as unpaid work

The reason why housework is not considered to be productive and why it is not accounted is because it is done, within the confines of the home, for free: because it is not paid, or exchanged in the general fashion. And this is not because of the nature of the services which make it up, because one can find any and all of them on the market; nor is it because of the nature of the people who do it, because the same woman who cooks a chop unpaid in her home is paid when she does it in another household (see The main enemy, Chapter 4). It is because of the particular nature of the contract which ties the female worker – the wife – to the household of her 'master'.

But, you may say, the non-remuneration of work is not specific to housework. It is true of all the work people do for their own consumption. No one gets paid for work they do for themselves and their families.

Some authors, however, including Dalla Costa (1972), have argued that housework – which they extend to cover all the work women do to reproduce themselves and their families (which I would call production for self-consumption) – is unpaid, in the sense of it being productive and necessary work which *should* properly *be* paid. Dalla Costa, and the group which formed around her work, have concluded that *all* housework, including the housework done by single women for themselves as much as the work of wives, should be paid for by the state. They have demanded wages for housework.

As I see it, they make an intellectual slip, due to the same lack of theoretical rigour as is shown by other authors who define housework as a series of tasks. They call work, and hence unpaid work, all the services you do for yourself (including the work single men do for themselves). They do not define the social conditions of production which would qualify an activity's being treated as *unpaid* work. I believe only services furnished *for others* should be so designated.

To take again the example of self-consumption in agriculture, let us suppose that a small farmer (who could be a man or a woman) makes his or her own bread. This activity is considered productive even by the national account. If the farmer does not eat the bread, he or she can sell it; if they had not baked it, they would have had to buy it. Should this accounted activity also be paid for? (Is it 'unpaid'?) If farmers bake bread, should they be paid for the baking? Of course not. It is held, and rightly, that they remunerate themselves: that if they did not bake their own bread, the baking should certainly be paid for, but by them, to the baker. If they do bake, they collect the price of baking in being thrifty. This is why it is legitimate to add this value to the national product. A loaf has effectively been baked. That the producer has consumed it forthwith (or almost) in no way detracts from the fact that the bread has been well and truly added to the overall total of individual and national wealth. That the bread does not pass through the market means the values of transport and commercial services are not added – but it changes nothing about the production of the bread itself. It is legitimate to *add* the value of home-baked bread to the income of small farmers because they profit from this added wealth. If they had sold it instead of eating it, they would equally have found themselves richer by the value of a loaf.

To consider that, not having been *paid* (in money) for work, an individual has performed *free* work, is a gross error. He or she has been remunerated, whether in saving the baker's service or in consuming an extra loaf. In either case, they have been remunerated. It may be well or badly, in terms of monetary calculation (when the saving made is compared to the time spent, for example), but this matters little, for the individual has chosen his or her own remuneration.

It is thus not contradictory to say, both, that work is productive, and that it should not be remunerated by an external source, in so far as productive work adds an element to the riches of its producers, and thereby carried its own remuneration. To pay for such work would be absurd. It would be to pay for it twice: to add a second remuneration to the first. Similar reasoning could, and should, be applied to all the services that you do for yourself. They could, and should, be accounted, but since you then consume them, they are remunerated. We could even skip the transition 'since you then consume them', since by definition you consume a service you produce for yourself. Indeed it is often consumed by you at the same time and in the very act of its production (e.g. combing your hair).

Work is certainly being done, and appropriated, but by you. It is work which is remunerated even though it is not paid. It is work precisely because it 'profits' someone, but because it is rendered to yourself, it carries its proper remuneration in itself: it is not unpaid, it is not 'free' work. It follows therefore that the only work which should be called 'unpaid work' is work which is both *unpaid and unremunerated*. This can only be work done for someone else. In sum, work can be:

1 accounted and remunerated (e.g. the work done by a peasant farmer who bakes bread for him or herself);
2 accounted and *not* remunerated (e.g. the work done by the wife of a farmer who bakes bread for her husband);
3 *not* accounted and *not* remunerated ('housework').

The fact that particular work is noted by those who construct national accounts does not imply that it is remunerated, nor does it induce it to be remunerated. On the other hand, the fact that certain work is not remunerated certainly does induce (lead) to its not being accounted. The national account's differential treatment of work which is *equally* non-remunerated (e.g. the butchering and cooking of pigs), if it makes no difference to the objectives of the national account (i.e. to balancing the accounts), certainly does introduce a division into the work for self-consumption done within households.

The national account takes the household as a unit. It does not want to know *who* has done *what*, nor under what conditions (of remuneration or unpaidness) within it. It is the 'household' which 'produces' for itself and which consumes. By definition things are handed over to the outside by the household and vice versa. Nothing goes on inside this cell. For the national account there are no individuals, nothing is exchanged or extorted from anyone, within households, and consequently there are no modalities (of exchange or non exchange) to be studied, since nothing takes place. From the point of view of individuals, however, their relations of production are fundamental. Housework therefore cannot begin to exist as a subject of study until we pass the barrier of the household as a unit.

Conclusion: the definition of housework

On the basis of the arguments above, we can begin to specify what we mean by saying that housework is 'free' or unpaid. We mean that it is work which is not paid, and which is not remunerated either, since it is done for others. From this point onwards, housework can no longer be defined as either this or that or the other *task* , or even the *totality* of the tasks of which it is composed. It must be defined as a certain *work relationship*, a particular relationship of production. It is all the work done unpaid for others within the confines of the household or the family. From this point of view, there is no difference at all between 'housework' and all the other work of the wives of small farmers, nor between their work and the work of wives of artisans or businessmen or wage-workers. Nor is there any difference between the work of wives and the work of other unpaid family workers (male or female) – called in France 'family helps'.

This doubtless explains why the wives of small farmers can only draw a distinction between their 'household' activities and their 'occupational' activities with great difficulty, and at the behest of sociologists. One of the reasons why the distinction is difficult to make is certainly that the different tasks overlap concretely, and women pass incessantly from one to another within the same hour. But this 'reason' is itself determined by the underlying and principal reason why they do not draw a distinction, which is that the work-of-the-holding and the work-of-the-house are carried out *within the same relations of production*. Although they may consist of different tasks (each whole, 'occupation work' and 'housework', being itself disparate and constituting a lot of separate tasks), they constitute but one and the same *job*: the job of a wife.

While it is legitimate to look at certain tasks women perform in order, for example, to compare or re-evaluate the techniques used now and in the past, as soon as we start to interpret the economic nature of housework, we must adopt an economic definition. This in turn requires that we take into account all the work of wives, that we treat all the work done within the same relations of production as a whole.

To talk of the structural characteristics of 'house work' while continuing to define this as a collection of tasks, is a contradiction in terms. If the purpose is to explain (or at least to interpret) the unpaid nature of 'housework', then all unpaid work (both 'work' and 'unpaid' having been defined) must be taken into account. Only then can the boundaries of the object of study be drawn. At present the limits have been set in advance, and empirically. In other words, the empirical object itself has yet to be *theoretically* determined.

This is why, since the characteristic relations of production of housework are not specific to it, or are not restricted to it, but also characterize other types of tasks and work (e.g. wives' 'occupational' work on farms), I propose that we henceforth substitute the concept of domestic[3] work for that of housework – for the object of study is certainly free work carried out in the *domus* in the wide and sociological sense.

The defective definition of housework, or rather the contradiction between its common practical definition and the study of its relations of production, has, I believe, greatly limited the latter. The demand for wages for all household *tasks* is a proof of this by absurdity. It is not, however, the most serious manifestation of this limitation. But that is another matter.

Notes and references

1   Among the first publications appearing in 1970 were those of·
    Benston, Larguia, Delphy, Olah, and Mainardi. Since then many
    others have followed, too numerous to mention.
2   For my reasons for talking of 'women wives', see below p. 00.
3   When I originally wrote this article in 1978 I used the term *domestic*
    work, deriving from *domus*, to stress that the other participants in
    the debate in fact misused 'domestic' and did not distinguish it from
    housework. *Domus* has many connotations of *place*, and I now believe
    that 'familial work', which would connote mainly *relationships*, is the
    better term.

6. Continuities and discontinuities in marriage and divorce*

Studies devoted to divorce in the past have presented it as the sum of individual divorce situations, they have not defined it (e.g. Goode 1956; Kooy 1959; Chester 1973). This is doubtless because the definition of divorce and its sociological significance are taken for granted; divorce means the breakdown and failure of marriage. These are the words used by the individuals concerned and sociologists have implicitly approached the problem from the same point of view. Even if they have apparently (but not always) refrained from direct value judgements and emotionally laden terms such as 'failure', they have still considered that the definition of divorce as the end of marriage, its revocation, or as the opposite of marriage, was a satisfactory one.

By contrast, a great deal of attention has been paid to the individual causes of divorce, and here it is evident that sociologists have not limited themselves to the reasons advanced by the protagonists, nor to their psychological 'motivations', but have included in their studies more objective data: for instance, social characteristics such as class origin and educational level. They have, however, always directed their attention to the 'couple' or the individual union. This method may have enabled them to pinpoint the differences (if indeed there are any) between couples and/or individuals who are divorced and those who are not; but it cannot teach us about the institution of divorce, for this is not just a multitude of individual accidents.

Were a similar method of analysis to be applied to marriage as has been with divorce (and indeed this has unfortunately often been the way sociologists have approached marriage, unlike anthropologists) we would look for – and would in all probability find – differences between

---

* First published in D. Leonard Barker and S. Allen (eds.), *Sexual Divisions and Society: Process and Change*, Tavistock 1976.

married and non-married individuals. But marriage is an institution and merely to look at those who enter or leave it, cannot shed light on the institution or why it exists. Similarly with divorce. Divorce is an institution which follows certain rules, it is codified and subject to control, ranging from implicit but unformulated social control to penal control.

Furthermore divorce is organically related to the institution of marriage. In an old American film the heroine asks what the grounds for divorce are in the state where she lives, and the lawyer replies, 'being married'. But I would go further and argue that not only is marriage the necessary condition for divorce; but also that divorce is not inconsistent with marriage. For while a divorce signifies the end of *a* marriage (marriage meaning here a particular union), it by no means implies the end of *marriage* as an institution. Divorce was not invented to destroy marriage since divorce is only necessary if marriage continues to exist. Indeed, it is often argued that the increase in the incidence of divorce can be interpreted as proof, not that the institution of marriage is sick, but on the contrary that it is thriving.

Further, divorce reveals and throws into relief certain institutional aspects of marriage, and it makes clear what is otherwise latent. Conversely marriage sheds light on divorce. Not only do certain aspects of marriage make the institution of divorce more intelligible; what is more noteworthy is that they are carried over and perpetuated in divorce.

The institution of marriage is, of course, complex and it is imperative to specify which aspect and which function is being studied. This paper will focus attention exclusively on the economic aspect of marriage, and to make clear what this means, I will first summarize briefly the approach that is used. (For more details, see Chapter 4.)

A theory of marriage

My proposition is that marriage is the institution by which unpaid work is extorted from a particular category of the population, women-wives.[1] This work is unpaid for it does not give rise to a wage but simply to upkeep. These very peculiar relations of production in a society that is defined by the sale of work (wage-labour) and products, are not determined by the type of work accomplished. Indeed they are not even limited to the production of household work and the raising of children, but extend to include *all* the things women (and also children) produce within the home, and in small-scale manufacturing, shopkeeping, or farming, if the husband is a craftsman, tradesman, or farmer, or various professional services if the husband is a doctor or lawyer, etc. The fact that domestic work is unpaid is not inherent to the particular type of work done, since when the same tasks are done *outside the family* they are paid for. The work acquires value – is remunerated – as long as the woman furnishes it to people to whom she *is not related or married*.

The valuelessness of domestic work performed by married women derives institutionally from the marriage contract, which is in fact a work contract. To be more precise, it is a contract by which the head of the family – the husband – appropriates all the work done in the family by his children, his younger siblings, and especially by his wife, since he can sell it on the market as his own if he is, for example, a craftsman or farmer or doctor. Conversely, the wife's labour has no value because it cannot be put on the market, and it cannot be put on the market because of the contract by which her labour power is appropriated by her husband. Since the production intended for exchange – on the market – is accomplished outside the family in the wage-earning system, and since a married man sells his work and not a product in this system, the unpaid work of women cannot be incorporated in the production intended for exchange. It has therefore become limited to producing things which are intended for the family's internal use: domestic services and the raising of children.

Of course, with the increase of industrial production (and hence the number of wage-earners) and the decrease in family production, many women-wives now work for money, largely outside the home. They are none the less expected to do the household work. It would appear that their labour power is not totally appropriated since they divert a part of it into their paid work. Yet since they earn wages they provide their own upkeep. While one could, with a touch of bad faith, consider the marriage contract as an *exchange* contract when women work only within the household, with married women providing domestic work in exchange for upkeep, when married women earn their own living that illusion disappears altogether. It is clear then that their domestic work is given for nothing and the feature of appropriation is even more conspicuous.

However, the modes of appropriation differ depending on whether the woman has a paid job or not. When she does not, her total work power is appropriated, and this thus determines the type of work she will do – if her husband is a doctor she will make appointments for the patients; if he has a garage she will type the bills, etc. It also determines the nature of the relations of production under which she operates – her economic dependency and the non-value of her work – for while she may accomplish exactly the same tasks as her well-to-do neighbour, the upkeep she receives will be different if her husband's financial status is not as good. When she has a job, however, she recuperates part of her labour power in exchange for the accomplishment of a precise and specific type of work: housework. Legally any woman can now choose the second solution, although in France the law requiring a husband's authorization for his wife to work outside the home was abolished only some ten years ago. In point of fact, however, it seems reasonable to suggest that the only women who work outside the home are those whose husbands give their consent if they consider that they do not need all their wife's time. Equally, in France, the obligation to do housework is not written in any law; all that is said in the *Code Civil* is that the wife's contribution to the 'household charges' can be in kind if she has no dowry or independent income. But this obligation is inscribed negatively, so to speak, in the sense that failure to assume it is sanctioned.

Some of the possible sanctions are social worker intervention or divorce (see Dezalay 1976). When social control agents intervene, whether it be in the person of the children's judge, the social worker, or the court, and if a divorce ensues or the family budget comes under the control of the social workers, the obligations of marriage are officially expressed and in particular the differential duties of the husband and the wife. This precision and differentiation contrasts markedly with the vague legal formulation of marriage contracts, which suggest an apparent reciprocity in the respective duties of the partners (notably the wife's contribution in kind and the husband's in money are represented as having the same value and producing a similar status for both partners).

Conclusions following from this theory of marriage

It is clear that the position of women on the labour market and the discrimination that they suffer, are the result (and not the cause as certain authors would have us believe) of the marriage contract as we have described it.[2]

If we accept that marriage gives rise to the exploitation of women, then it would be logical to suppose that pressure is brought to bear on women to persuade them to marry. Of course there are various sorts of pressure – cultural, emotional-relational, and material-economic – and one could argue that the last is not the most important, or that it is not perceived as a pressure at the time of marriage, or that it is not operational at this time. However, if we compare the standard of living to which a woman can aspire if she remains single and the standard which she can reasonably expect from being married, it seems certain that relative economic deprivation will be experienced by single women as time goes on. We are confronted with a paradox: on the one hand marriage is the (institutional) situation where women are exploited; and on the other hand, precisely because of this, the potential market situation for women's labour (which is that of all women, not just those who are actually married (see Barron and Norris 1976)) is such that marriage still offers them the best career, economically speaking. If the initial or potential situation is bad, it will simply be aggravated by the married state, which becomes even more necessary than ever. The economic pressure, in other words, the difference between the potential 'single' standard of living and the actual 'married' standard of living, simply increases as time goes on.

Marriage as a self-perpetuating state

When women marry or have a child they often stop working or indeed studying; or even occasionally among the middle class – the American model is becoming general in France[3] – they stop studying in order to put their husband through college, by means of a job that has no future, and they stop working as soon as their husband has obtained his degree. If they continue working, they do so at the cost of enormous sacrifices of time and energy, and even then they are still not as free to devote themselves to their work. As a result they cannot aspire to the promotion which they might have had if they had not had to look after a husband and children materially as well as themselves. Ten years after the wedding day, marriage is even more necessary than before because of the dual process whereby women lose ground or at best remain at the same place in the labour market, while married men make great progress in their work as they are not hampered by household obligations. Of course, individual husbands are not responsible for this situation, but all men benefit from a situation that is taken to be normal. A 'normal' day's work is that of a person who does not have to do his own domestic work. But even though this is the norm, it is none the less made possible only by the fact that the household tasks are assumed by others, almost exclusively by women. It is evident that the career of a married man must not be compared for our purposes with that of other men, but with the life he would have led if he had remained single, or if he had had to share the household tasks including the raising of children. This dual process is particularly evident in the case where the wife gives up her own studies in order to finance her husband's. Here, even though both begin in more or less the same position (not taking discrimination into account), marriage results in the wife moving down the economic ladder and the husband moving up, and these changes combine to create an important gap between the economic possibilities of the two partners.

Thus it can be said that, from the woman's standpoint, marriage creates the conditions for its own continuation and encourages entry into a second marriage if a particular union comes to an end.

In this respect statistics are ambiguous, or, more precisely, are difficult to interpret. There are generally more divorced women at work than married women (annual statistics from the Ministère de la Justice 1973). This could be taken as confirmation that their economic situation, notably the absence of an independent income, discourages full-time housewives from getting divorced. But on the other hand many women begin to work just because they face a divorce – they start the moment they decide to get a divorce, long before the decree is issued. This explains why they are registered as 'working' at that particular time. Having a job enables some women to envisage divorce, while others in the same situation but lacking a job have to 'make a go' of their marriage. A large number of women who are divorced or about to be divorced come on the labour market in the worst possible conditions (as do widows), with no qualifications, no experience, and no seniority. They find themselves relegated to the most poorly-paid jobs. This situation is often in contrast with the level of their education and the careers they envisaged, or could have envisaged, before their marriage, the social rank of their parents, and not only the initial social rank of their husband but, more pertinently, the rank he has attained when they divorce, some five, ten, or twenty years after the beginning of their marriage. In addition, those with dependent children have to look after them financially, and this new responsibility is added to the domestic work which they were already providing before divorce. For the majority of women, the contrast between the standard of living that they enjoy while married and that which they can expect after divorce simply redoubles the pressures in favour of marriage or remarriage depending on the circumstances.

The state of divorce as a continuation of the state of marriage

The fact that the material responsibility for children is assumed by the woman after divorce confirms the hypothesis concerning the appropriation by the husband of his wife's work, but it suggests as well that the appropriation which is a characteristic of marriage persists even after the marriage has been dissolved. This leads me to contend that divorce is not the opposite of marriage, nor even its end, but simply a change or a transformation of marriage.

At the beginning of a marriage this appropriation is legally masked; it is a matter of custom in the sense that the legal framework which underlines it is vague and unused and even useless. It only begins to operate – by means of the intervention of the judicial system – when the marriage comes to an end. Even then its apparent purpose is not to burden the wife with the entire responsibility for the children nor to exempt the husband totally. It *permits* such an outcome, but by omission rather than by a positive action. There *is* positive action, however, in the official guideline of considering 'the child's interest'.

Unofficially custody of the children is considered to be a privilege and even a compensation for the woman who may be left badly off in other respects. A real battle is staged to make the two spouses turn against each other and to keep them uncertain as to the outcome of the conflict for as long as possible. The custody of the children[4] becomes the main issue, and at the end of the battle the spouse who obtains this custody considers that he or she has won the war. But in fact when the children are young they are almost always entrusted to their mother. Officially both parents share the responsibility for the cost of looking after the children, but the woman's income after divorce is always very much lower than that of her former husband, and the allowance for the children decided by the courts is always ridiculously low.[5] The woman's financial contribution is thus of necessity greater in absolute value than her husband's, even though her income is lower. As a result her participation and her sacrifices are relatively much greater. Furthermore, 80 per cent of all allowances are never paid (Boigeol, Commaille, and Roussel 1975). Even if the official directives are respected and the allowance is paid, the amount agreed never takes into account the woman's time and work in the material upkeep of the children.[6]

Thus the courts ratify the exclusive responsibility of women both by positive actions, granting custody to the mother and assigning a low allowance for the children; and by negative action, failing to ensure the payment of the allowance. The 'child's interest' makes it imperative for him or her to be entrusted to his or her mother, be she poor, 'immoral', or sick, as long as he or she requires considerable material care: as long as there are nappies to wash, feeds to prepare and special clothes, toys, medicaments, lessons, etc. to pay for. As soon as the child reaches the age of 15 the courts usually regard the father more favourably than the mother:[7] she is thought to be unable to provide the child with as many advantages as the father, who is better off (for very good reasons). A child who has been entrusted to his or her mother can then be handed back to his or her father, again in the 'child's interest'. And yet, curiously enough, this aspect of the child's interest – the parent's wealth – did not come into play when the child was younger. Objectively the child's interest[8] has served to make his or her mother poorer and his or her father richer, creating thereby the conditions in which it will be 'in his/her interest' later on to return to the father.

Two conclusions can be drawn: in divorce, as in marriage, the work involved in raising children is carried out by the woman unpaid and the husband is exempted from this charge as part of the normal process. Furthermore, the financial care of the children, which was shared by the couple or assumed by the husband alone in the marriage, is thereafter assumed predominantly or exclusively by the woman.

In compensation the woman no longer has to carry domestic responsibility for her husband. This casts a special light on the marriage contract. Indeed, when the married state is compared with the official as well as the real divorced state, it becomes clear that the material responsibility for the children is the woman's 'privilege' in both cases; while in marriage, in contrast to divorce, the wife provides for her husband's material upkeep in exchange for his contribution towards the financial upkeep of the children.

Marriage and responsibility for children: a question of theoretical antecedence

An overriding concern in this paper so far has been to rethink the economic aspects of the institution of marriage and to give them the definition that they have lacked. Comparing marriage to divorce, it seems that the material upkeep of the husband by the wife is related to the participation of the husband in the financial upkeep of children. This provides grounds for viewing marriage differently. This approach is consistent with the contention that whereas marriage sheds light on divorce, the reverse is also true. So far this has meant only that divorce reveals the nature of the marriage contract, but it can also be taken to mean that divorce can shed light on what made this contract possible in the first place.

I contend that these conclusions allow us to see childcare (from the analytical not the empirical point of view) as separate from the rest of domestic work. The obligation of childcare may have to be viewed as not so much perpetuating the husband's appropriation of his wife's labour, as making it possible in the first place. Or, to put it slightly differently, these conclusions compel us to consider the possibility that the continuation of the obligation of childcare is a continuation of the marriage contract, *in so far as* the appropriation of the wife's labour includes the obligation of childcare; but that this obligation, while *carried out* in marriage, does not necessarily *stem* from it; that it might be antecedent to it, and might even be one of the factors that makes the appropriation of wives' labour – the free giving by them of the rest of housework – possible.

If marriage is considered as giving rise to the appropriation of the women-wives' work, the position of married women who work outside of the home suggests that this total appropriation can be transformed into a partial appropriation, bearing no longer on their time or work power as a whole but on a specific task, the household work, that can eventually be replaced by an equivalent sum of money.[9] This evolution of the system of appropriation of wives' labour may at first sight call to mind the evolution of the appropriation of the labour of slaves between the Roman Empire and the late Middle Ages. The appropriation by the seigneur of the slave's total work power became a partial appropriation, approximately half of his time, three days work per week (Bloch 1964), when the slave became a 'serf' and was 'settled'. He then worked part-time for his own profit on a piece of land which he rented from the seigneur. The time debt to the seigneur was later itself transformed into the obligation to accomplish a specific task, the *corvée*, which later on could be commuted into a money payment.

However, this way of formulating the problem is perhaps false because the partial appropriation of the married woman's labour on this analogy should be counterbalanced by the woman partially recuperating her work power, when in fact she pays for the freedom to work outside, and to have an independent income, with a double day's work. It cannot be said that she recuperates either a period of time or a value. On the other hand she does partially escape from a relationship of production characterized by dependency.

Furthermore, if marriage as a state is characterized and differentiated from divorce by the 'contract' of appropriation, marriage and divorce can be considered as two ways of obtaining a similar result: the collective attribution to women of the care of children and the collective exemption of men from the same responsibility.

Seen from this angle, not only the married and the divorced states but also the state of concubinage, in short all the situations in which children exist and are cared for, have similar characteristics and are different forms of one and the same institution, which could be called X. The situation of the unmarried mother can be taken to be its extreme form, and at the same time its most typical form, since the basic dyad is the mother and child. Marriage could be seen as being one of the possible forms of X, in which the basic couple is joined by a man who temporarily participates in the financial upkeep of the child and in return appropriates the woman's labour power.

This view is similar to that of those anthropologists (Adams 1971; Zelditch 1964) who criticize Murdock (1949) and say that the family defined as a trio proceeding from the husband and wife couple (taken to be the fundamental dyad) is not a universal type, whereas the mother–child association is. This point of view may become a new element in the study of western societies, where it has generally been taken for granted that the family is patrifocal. This element may be new, but it is not contradictory; for if the family, considered as *the place where children are produced*, can be viewed as matrifocal, even in our own societies, it remains none the less true that as an *economic production unit* (for exchange or for its own use) it is defined, as during the Roman era (Engels 1884), as the group of relatives and servants who give work to the head of the family: the father.

Going a step further, the state of marriage-with-children appears as the meeting place for two institutions: on the one hand the institution relating to women's exclusive responsibility for child-care, on the other the institution relating to the appropriation by the husband of his wife's labour power.

Indeed if one considers marriage alone, it appears that the care of children, their upkeep, which is no different from the material upkeep of the husband by the wife and which is carried out in the same manner – the execution of work in exchange for maintenance (financial upkeep) – partakes of and flows from the appropriation of the wife's labour power by her husband. As long as there are two parents it can be postulated that the children, in accordance with the legal terms, are their common property, possession, and responsibility. In this case, in the marriage situation half the work involved in the upkeep of the children is appropriated by the husband-father, and continues to be so after the divorce. But children do not always have two owners. In the absence of the father, their upkeep by the mother, or even half of this upkeep, is obviously of no benefit to any particular man. Besides, even in marriage or divorce it is doubtful whether the parents are the only ones, excluding society as a whole, to benefit from the children, and consequently it is not at all certain that the husband-father should be considered as the only one to benefit from his half of the work involved in looking after the children, or as the only one to appropriate his wife's work, since he does not carry it out with her. If this is accepted, then the raising of the children will have to be considered apart from the woman's family work (household or other) and the exclusive responsibility of women concerning the children will have to be treated as a relatively autonomous institution with respect to marriage.

If the relationship between marriage and divorce is viewed in this way, it appears slightly differently from what was suggested at the beginning of this paper. The husband's appropriation of his wife's work then ceases, in part or completely, as soon as the marriage comes to an end (depending on whether or not the husband is considered as continuing to benefit from the children, and from their upkeep, either partly or not at all). In this view divorce is not the continuation of marriage. However, the situation after divorce, in which the responsibility for the children is an important aspect, constitutes a strong economic incentive to remarriage for women.

When there are children, the responsibility for their care continues to be borne exclusively by the woman after divorce, and this burden is increased by the financial cost. However, rather than considering that this illustrates a continuation of the husband's appropriation of his wife's work, it would now seem more exact to say that it illustrates a new form of women's responsibility for children, which exists before the marriage, is carried on in the marriage, and continues afterwards. This responsibility can be defined as the collective exploitation of women by men, and correlated with this, the collective exemption of men from the cost of reproduction. The individual appropriation of a particular wife's labour by her husband comes over and above this collective appropriation. It is derived from, or at least made possible by, the collective appropriation which acts in favour of marriage, since if the husband appropriates his wife's work power, in return he contributes to her financial upkeep and the children's, and in this way he 'lightens' her burden by partially assuming a responsibility from which society exempts him. In other words, the institutional exemption from which he benefits allows him to claim his wife's total labour power in exchange for his contribution to the children's financial upkeep.

Notes and references

1   I use the expression woman-wife to stress that the one is a person and the other a role. This ontological distinction is blurred by the fact that the social role is so widely associated with a biological category that they have become equivalent.
2   The thesis of Blood and Wolfe (1960), for example, is that no model exists, let alone a patriarchal one. If more married women do the housework than married men, it is because they have more time to do it and their husbands less since they work outside (!). And if married women are of less weight in making decisions, it is owing to the fact that since they do not work outside (this being compensated by the extra time they have to do the housework) so their contribution to the domestic economy is less important.
3   See, for example, couples where the husbands are at business school (Marceau 1976).
4   This is a legal notion which officially denotes official responsibility and, unofficially, the right to dispose of and enjoy as one may dispose of and enjoy any possession.
5   In a study I was involved in, we found in one provincial court that the ex-wife was awarded a *mean* of £10 per month per child. In general, courts in France will never instruct the ex-husband to pay more than one-third of his income to his ex-wife and children.

6 I distinguish the financial and material upkeep of a family. The first is the part of the consumption that is bought. The second consists of services, or labour applied to goods bought by the wage.

7 This is based on statistics from the Ministère de la Justice (1973) and oral communications from a lawyer.

8 That this is a mere legal fiction is clear if we consider the result to which it leads, and that from the very beginning it is the judges and not the children who talk of their 'interest'.

9 When for example the woman buys off her obligation by paying for a nurse or a public nursery, etc. out of her salary.

7. Our friends and ourselves: the hidden foundations of various pseudo-feminist accounts*

I. Neo-sexism or masculine feminism

We have some good friends among men. We flee them like the plague, and they try to force our interests. Who could fail to recognize in this the marks of true friendship!

All these friends, all these masculine partisans of women's liberation, have a number of things in common:

1 they want to substitute themselves for us;
2 they actually speak instead of us;
3 they approve of women's liberation, and even of the participation of women in this project, so long as liberation and women follow and certainly do not precede them;
4 they want to impose on us their conception of women's liberation, which includes the participation of men, and they want to impose their participation so as to control the movement and its direction: the direction of women's liberation.

So well meaning are our masculine friends that they cannot help bending their ears to us from time to time. They understand what the women's liberation movement is about to the extent that, because it is only open to women, they can say 'Of course the oppressed must liberate themselves', and in so doing they distinguish themselves from, and show themselves to be superior to, the vast majority of men, who do not understand, and whom they can virtuously repudiate. They thus show an 'open' attitude. They try to understand because they are keen political brains, the type who can tell which way the wind is blowing

* First published in *Questions Féministes*, No. 1 (1977). The first English translation was by Linnie Price, mimeo 1978.

before anyone else. But it is precisely their duty as keen political brains to produce keen political analyses, and this inevitably leads them to spot here and there points which have been neglected by women (who remain, don't forget, the principal agents of their own liberation). And, having located these points, it would be dishonest, nay unfriendly, of these keen brains not to point out to us the factors we have neglected. And point them out they do, kindly but firmly.

But where do these men get their clear views, not only of what feminism ought to be, but of what it *is in essence* – an essence of which the existing movement is nothing but a chance incarnation in their eyes: nothing but a reflection and, according to them, a very approximate, if not frankly unsatisfactory, imitation of what it could and should be?

The fact that they do not participate in the actual movement, that they do not follow the discussions and contradictory debates which take place within it – in a word, the fact that they are not the individuals directly and primarily involved – does not seem to be an obstacle to them. Indeed they think that their opinions are not only just as valuable as those of the thousands of women who have been considering these various problems for years, but rather that they are *more* valuable. These men seem to conceive of their inevitable non-involvement, their status as observers, not as a handicap, but, on the contrary, as an advantage. However this (generally implicit) idea quite obviously goes against their own political principles and against those which they accept in accepting the women's liberation movement.

So why is there this flagrant contradiction? First, because our friends do not believe that women are oppressed in the same way as other groups. They would not dare 'advise' the Blacks, the people of the Third World, or the Palestinians on how to lead their struggle against us, i.e. against western whites – still less to 'rectify' their 'errors'. They would not dare imply of these oppressed people what they constantly imply of women: that we are partial, 'both prosecutor and judge', whereas *they* are impartial and will only appraise. In a word, they do not really believe that *they* oppress us.

Second, and related to this, the 'friendship' of friends is *paternalism*: a benevolence which necessarily involves a good measure of scorn. Indeed, a benevolence which can only be explained by scorn. They meddle in our affairs because they think we are incapable of dealing with them.

But this is not all: the truth – another truth – is that they who are first in everything cannot resign themselves to not being first here too. Yet obviously they cannot be first here. Their benevolence is nothing but an attempt to secure a place, an attempt not to be left out. There is certainly an objective and a major reason for their attempt to control the direction of the women's movement, which is the fear that things will go against them. But there is also a tendency, imprinted in them since birth, which has become second nature, and which is stronger than they are. And that is that any place must be *their* place, and that their place is *in front*.

This was seen in a spatial way at the first large women's demonstration in France in November 1971 for free abortion. If a third of the men were at the back as arranged, the other two-thirds were at the front, hiding the women and behaving as if this were a normal demo; that is, a men's demo. No exhortation could persuade them to move, if not to the back, then at least into the ranks. They knew it was a women's demonstration, but their conditioning went against the practical consequences of this fact. They had to be there, as usual, in the front line of what was happening, even at the risk of harming the political objective they were supporting.

So what is the difference between these friends and our declared enemies, those who drag us in the mud and cover us with ridicule? It is a difference of means and not of ends: a matter of tactics and not of strategy. Our enemies attack from the front and frankly (honestly?) acknowledge their objective: to stay in their place (and thus to keep us in ours). Our friends, however, have chosen to keep their place in a more subtle, but also a more thorough way. Our enemies are excluded at least from the feminist ranks, which matters little to them since they still have the rest of society; but our friends envisage nothing less than *maintaining their power even within the small bastion of resistance to that power*.

One such friend is Claude Alzon, Professor of Sociology at the University of Vincennes and self-proclaimed feminist. In recent years he has written a number of leading articles in *Le Monde* on women's liberation. Various activists in the WLM asked to be allowed to write similar articles but without success. Alzon has never written a single article in *Le Monde* on any other subject; and he was given space only because he was talking about women. He would not have been able to publish on this subject ten years ago. It was the emergence of the WLM and the demand for speech *by* women which created a demand for speech *about* them. But male power not only dissociates these two exigencies, it in fact uses one against the other. It is not enough to refuse to allow women to speak; it is necessary, the better to re-establish order, to have men speak about women. Alzon speaks *doubly in our place*: he speaks about women, indeed about our liberation; and he speaks about it in places which would not have existed but for the WLM, but from which women are excluded. Our friends can give voice thanks to us, and, to make matters worse, they do so by withholding it from us. While writers like Alzon, and film makers anxious to make a name and a career, jump with both feet and open arms into the new domain of women, editors and television producers anxiously await something even better than women's silence: men talking.

The friends of women's liberation have many a time revealed that their understanding stops short at the point where our real liberation begins. How else, in the circumstances, could they claim to be our allies without some forfeit?

They do not claim to be our allies for long, anyway. It is not hard to see that the benevolence they display, and which they claim distinguishes them from other men, simply disguises the same contempt as is shown by the hostility of the majority. They soon abandon the carrot for the stick: 'Take care', they say, 'not to alienate those men who *are* well-disposed towards you.' But why should we be careful not to alienate men? Haven't they agreed woman's liberation depends upon women? Their warning reveals that our friends, who claim to believe we are the agents of our own revolution, are merely mouthing our words as a tactic. They do not believe a word of it. They think that the 'support' of a minority of men is more important for women's liberation than raising the consciousness of the majority of women.

We hope that the support of some men – or rather, of some individuals who have *abandoned* the privileges of their position as men in so far as they can, since if they keep them they will still be enemies – will be useful from time to time. But to say that the support of class enemies is always useful is going a bit far, and to suggest that it is determinant, that it is an indispensible condition for the success of a revolution, is both historically untrue and politically inept.

It is therefore perhaps not surprising to find Alzon continuing his confusion to its logical end and maintaining that 'the opposition is not between men and women, but between feminists and anti-feminists'.

Class position and the way of thinking about it – the materialism which he claims as a marxist – are here completely absent. He suggests that all that is needed is a bit of good will, and pow!, we can thumb our noses at the social (sex class) structure.

I am always amused to hear 'marxists' assert that it is all a question of values; or, going further, that it is all a question of declarations of good intent. I am amused to hear them say that revolutionary struggles are not conflicts between concrete groups with opposed concrete interests, but rather, as (scholarly as well as popular) idealist philosophy has been telling us repeatedly for two thousand years, that conflicts arise between groups supporting different ideas, and that the fact that one group benefits from and another *suffers* an oppression is not the point at issue! On those occasions when our friends do suggest that which side you are on actually does make a difference, they are referring not to the reality of oppression (which is, after all, the reason for wanting a revolution) but rather to the values you hold; whether you are sexist or racist. And then, lo and behold, it appears that feminists stand accused of sexism because they refuse to allow men into the WLM.

Racism, sexism, non-mixed organizations and heterosexual couples

Turning the accusation of sexism or racism back onto the victim is a classic defensive reaction, and a classic reactionary defence. We are, of course, quite used to seeing *women* accused of sexism by people who do not even know the meaning of the word, but such people at least have the excuse of not claiming to be 'revolutionaries', still less 'feminists' or friends. To accuse women of 'inverse sexism' (or Blacks of counter-racism) is not only unfriendly, it is reactionary, because it posits a symmetry between oppressor and oppressed. To decry or exclude those who oppress you is not symmetrical with decrying or excluding those whom you oppress. It is therefore incredible that anyone who claims to be up to date with Black or feminist struggles, let alone a friend or a 'specialist' in the area, should demonstrate such ignorance.

The 'concept' of 'counter-racism' has long been shown for what it is: an attempt to intimidate and to prevent an oppressed group organizing on its own behalf. This demystification was the work of the Black Power movement in the USA, which began in 1965 with the *exclusion of whites* from the 'civil rights' organizations. This revolution ended fifty years of reformism on the racial problem – fifty years of white paternalism.

The functioning of the liberal race relations groups was based on a denial of reality, on a constant pretence. They pretended that the situation in which the whites were oppressors and the Blacks oppressed had no influence on the functioning of the civil rights groups: neither on their politics, nor on the power structure within the groups. They proceeded as if the intrinsic inequality which characterizes relationships between Blacks and whites was annulled as soon as they entered the organizations' headquarters. Liberals denied that the whites brought with them superior political resources – their better knowledge of, and access to, the power structure – and that they had what, for want of a better word, can be called superior 'psychological' resources. Since one cannot struggle against something one is unaware of, something whose existence is denied, these factors played fully and without check within the groups, with the inevitable result that the whites occupied privileged positions even within the organizations dedicated to 'improving the lot of the Blacks'. But the white presence had even more fundamental consequences than their occupying every dominant position in the hierarchy of the group itself. It affected even more important areas. It affected the definition of the objectives of the movement, which is linked to the definition of the struggle – i.e. it affected the definition of the oppression against which the movement was supposed to be fighting.

1 Blacks could not recognize their own oppression in the presence of whites. They could not denounce the dominant position of the whites in the group itself, even if they recognized it, since the dogma (the official representation of the group's functioning on which the existence of the group as a mixed group depended) denied from the start the possibility of the whites being dominant in the group.

2 In addition, whether or not the whites in a group individually had dominant positions, their presence reinforced the tendency to adopt the dominant definition (that is, the *white definition*) of what the Blacks were 'suffering'. This definition by the oppressor of the nature of the oppression, which was general in the society outside and therefore internalized by Blacks and whites alike, was personified by the white members of the group. They expressed it sincerely, and it was therefore all the more difficult for the Blacks to begin to oppose it with their own definition of what they suffered. Their own definition could not really exist so long as the whites' definition was the official one. The opinion of the whites

within the group was therefore sustained both by the wider culture in which the Blacks also participated, and by the whites' own individual prestige.

3   Not only did the whites' prestige prevent the Blacks finding their own definition of their oppression, but the presence of the whites also prevented the Blacks fighting the prestige which whites had in Black eyes. Blacks could not be with whites without seeing them in a positive way: they could not *not* admire them and not want to be like them, since this is one of the manifestations of their oppression and one of the means by which it is maintained. Being in the presence of whites meant accepting a positive image of whiteness and accepting what underlay this, the condition necessary for this positive image: a negative image of blackness. This negative image of blackness thus not only existed, it was also sustained and at work inside what was supposed to be a struggle for Black liberation.

It was no chance then that the exclusion of whites from the anti-racist struggle coincided both with the 'Afro' fashion – which is much more than a fashion, or even than a therapy – and with the slogan 'Black is beautiful'. Being non-mixed was the logical and historical condition for the struggle against self-hatred, which was why the new feminist movement adopted a similar practice. The concrete facts – the concrete history of the struggle of both Blacks and women – like the logical implications of the proposition that the liberation of the oppressed is mainly, if not solely, the work of the oppressed, leads to the same conclusion: oppressors cannot play the same role in the liberation struggle as the oppressed.

Our friends, however, do not see this. They usually attribute the non-mixed character of women's groups to the 'after effects' of the 'trauma' that 'male authoritarianism' has produced in women, and treat it as a passing phenomenon. They thereby demonstrate their total and general incomprehension of the processes of liberation, and not just of the liberation of women. For they reveal a view of liberation struggles which is both static and idealist.

It is static in that they see the oppression women suffer as already known and accepted. However the major obstacle to struggling against an oppression is not feeling oppressed. Hence the first moment of revolt for women consists not in joining the battle for change, but rather in discovering themselves to be oppressed. It involves discovering that oppression actually exists, and discovering its *extent*; and then slowly looking further, searching here and there, getting deeper and deeper.

The feminist struggle consists as much in discovering unknown oppressions, in seeing oppression in an area where it was not recognized before, as in struggling against known oppressions. This is not obvious. It is necessary to have lived this dynamic to understand it, to realize how far a representation of liberation as a single battle is false. This static view of liberation implies that a map of women's oppression already exists, with the bearings marked and the contours clearly delineated. There is thus no concern other than to advance across the map to win victories. But, on the contrary, liberation consists precisely in filling in the map, because the more you advance the more you realize how hazy and distant are the outlines of the territory. This process and our progress is not just horizontal and territorial, for each new territory annexed to the problematic of oppression is additionally and inextricably a new dimension, in the sense of meaning added to, and thus transforming the very definition of what we are fighting against. To suggest that the non-oppressed (or rather the oppressors) can participate equally with the oppressed in exploring the nature of the oppressed's suffering is absurd.

Our friends' view of women's liberation is also idealist because they seem to see achieving our freedom as merely a process of overcoming a number of purely psychological or ideological obstacles – using these terms as opposed to 'objective' obstacles, as epiphenomenal is opposed to structural, and, in the end, as 'imaginary' is opposed to 'real'. Consequently they see the oppression women experience as relatively easily cured, since, like all subjective factors, they see it as changeable. Once the weights which have been put on women are lifted and our trauma has been cured by a period of rest (for this is how they see and justify non-mixedness – as the half-time when the players dress their wounds), we shall be able to start fighting our known oppression side by side with men.

Alongside the view that the oppression suffered by women and exercised by men is psychological is a view that it is interpersonal. Some of our friends suggest that the only obstacle to men's participation in women's liberation is the authoritarianism men exercise, which, they claim, can be lifted with men's goodwill. They suggest that oppression can be avoided in individual interactions between men and women, and in heterosexual relationships; and as evidence they often claim to have avoided it in their own interpersonal relationships.

They thus affirm, like the man in the street, and the typical oppressor, that 'sexism', the ideological expression of institutionalized oppression, the surface aspects of patriarchy, constitutes *all* the oppression there is. They deny the existence of the institutional *structures* which *cause* 'sexism', and they deny that the psychological structure which relays the institutional structure via the production of 'prejudices' and the said 'sexism', and which, like them, is its creation, is as concrete and objective and as external to individual action as the institutional structure.

Authoritarianism is not, however, a psychological trait which we merely need to become aware of to be able to get rid of it. As a concrete psychological trait, it cannot be 'abolished' by an act of pure will, any more than a bridge can be leapt simply by wishing. And even if this trait could be suppressed (obviously by other means than simply volition) its suppression would not abolish what caused it in the first place and what continually reinforces it. What is really in question, and what should make us doubt whether the means to suppress the psychological trait actually exist, is the real (i.e. the institutionally and materially established) authority which men possess – without having to want it and whether or not they are 'authoritarian'.

This material base on which the 'psychological constitution' of individuals grows, and which reinforces and is reinforced by it, brings us back to the social structure. This constrains everybody. It is both external to interpersonal relations and is the framework in which these are set. Whatever my 'opinions' or 'attitudes', whether or not I hold racist beliefs, I profit from the oppression of immigrant workers. Their exploitation is one of the conditions of my material existence. Whether I am a 'revolutionary' or not does not alter the matter: I live as I live because, among other reasons, Africans are exploited in France and the West exploits the Third World. It is not a question of moral subtleties, nor a matter of whether I feel guilty or not. I have contributed nothing towards this exploitation individually, and it is not as an individual that I profit from it, but as a member of a group which I did not choose. However I personally treat immigrants when I meet them, and whatever my subjective reactions to their exploitation, it exists. To the extent that I am exempt from a type of exploitation, I benefit from it, willy nilly, and in two ways. First, because their exploitation increases my income (perhaps in a minimal way in so far as this benefit is in turn taken back from me by others who exploit *me*); and second, and principally, because when others do certain work, I do not do it. Without even mentioning positive benefits, I profit from the exploitation of others simply to the extent to which I am exempt from it.

In the same way, all the efforts a man may make to treat his wife as well as possible, and I am prepared to be optimistic about this, will neither hide nor abolish nor even mitigate the fact that he owes his material situation (and here, to simplify, let us speak only of his occupational situation) to the discrimination which women – the group to which his wife belongs – suffer in the employment market. We cannot separate the situation which men – and hence this particular man – occupy, from the situation which women – and hence this particular woman – occupy in the market.

The interpersonal relationship of a man and a woman is not an island, contrary to what our friends would have us believe. Even if a husband and wife or two lovers do not work together, their respective situations in the labour market, as members of differently treated groups in this market, are part of their overall situation – and therefore of their relationship, even though the latter appears to have nothing to do with labour or the market. The involuntary benefits the man in a couple derives from his group membership on the 'occupational' scene, are not absent from the loving, relational, conjugal scene, whatever you call it. They are part of the objective resources which he brings to it, whether he wants to or not, simply in bringing his person. The non-benefits of the woman in the couple are also part of what she does, or does not, bring into the relationship. An individual man does not need to lift a finger to have an advantage over women in the labour market; but nor can he help being so advantaged, nor can he renounce this advantage. In the same way, he may not necessarily take active advantage of his institutional privileges in marriage, but he still has them.

Even accepting that a man may not seek to take full advantage of his benefits at all levels, and of the disadvantages at all levels of the woman he has in front of him; and accepting that he wants to set the relationship up as egalitarian, what does this mean? At most that he does not pursue his advantage voluntarily, that is to say, that he does not voluntarily use his *initial advantage* to obtain *others*. But he cannot renounce this initial advantage because he cannot suppress it single-handedly. He cannot destroy what is not of his making. And for the same reason he cannot suppress the institutional disadvantages of 'his' woman.

Benefits and advantages tied to group membership (to one's 'sex') do not play their most important role in one's heterosexual relationships directly. Rather they are factors which make the more immediate power relationships possible, because there is, institutionally, no symmetry between the 'partners' in any conjugal or paraconjugal relationship (and every 'love relationship' between a man and a woman comes into this category). The directly economic constraints and the general social constraints in such an association are infinitely stronger for women than for men, and the penalties attached to refusing such relationships are infinitely worse for them. Thus the association of a woman with a man does not have the same objective meaning for him as it has for her, which reflects the ideological norm that marriage and 'human relations' are women's affair, and that they are a 'real woman's' major preoccupation; which in turn reflects the different subjectivities of men and women (the importance of love and the emotions in general in women's consciousness). Arguably discrimination in the labour market exists only to turn and return women to marriage, precisely in so far as marriage constitutes their objectively most profitable, or least bad, 'career' (ideologically: their 'destiny', their 'whole existence').

This asymmetry manifests itself on the occasion of *a* marriage, within a given union, because of the interpersonal tensions which then emerge, but it is not caused by this union. The asymmetry pre-exists the union: it is the reason for its unequal and eventually conflictual *form*. But above all it is the reason for the very existence of the union: for 'heterosexuality' in Adrienne Rich's usage.

In short, not only is it not necessary for a man to be a voluntary oppressor for a woman to be oppressed in heterosexual relationships, but the general oppression which precedes any particular relationship itself determines the very existence of the relationship. The particular individual man does not play a personal role in this general oppression, which occurs before his appearance on the scene: but, reciprocally, no personal initiative on his part can undo or mitigate what exists before and outside his entrance.

Only a view of human relationships which involves splitting individuals from society, which considers them as two distinct, albeit linked, orders, which sees a split between what goes on inside and outside people's heads, and inside and outside particular relationships, and between the 'political' and the 'personal', could postulate that interpersonal relationships are a matter of choice and 'emotions'. Only such a view could suggest that any of these choices and emotions are asocial in nature, and that they are not all affected by social determinants. Only such a view, which is idealist or indeed naturalist, could produce the belief that asocial islets of egalitarian personal relations can exist inside an oppressive structure.

It is not surprising that we frequently come across such idealist and individualistic arguments, since these are the dominant ideologies of our society. Idealism impregnates our whole lives and all our most everyday concepts.

What *is* surprising is that many of our male friends who produce them are left intellectuals – self-styled marxists and materialists – yet they use idealist arguments about women's oppression. Why should they abandon materialism there?

Perhaps it is because they cannot participate in the production of new materialist explanations – not being part of the political movement which is fighting for women's liberation, and not occupying that social position which has an objective interest in unmasking the ideology, i.e. not being victims of the oppression. On the other hand, this does not explain why they do not adopt the points of view produced *by* the victims. Perhaps we need to resort to a more cynical explanation for our friends' abandonment of materialism; to look to the fact that, under the circumstances, materialist thought is in contradiction with their objective class interests, and to recognize that it certainly serves men's interests to apply ideological thought to women.

It then becomes interesting to note the ways in which these objective interests are translated: the various ways in which our friends think about women, and what this reveals (betrays) about their attachment to their own class interests, since what they say and do often contradicts (betrays) their avowed political purpose. Time and time again they affirm support for the *women's* movement, yet they do not support *all* women, and indeed they seek to divide women against each other.

I shall look again at the work of Alzon for examples of this, and particularly at the article he was asked to write by the radical publishers Maspero for their journal *Partisans*, and which they subsequently published as a short book entitled *The Ornamental Woman and the Useful Woman* (1973).

Dividing women 1: feminists from antifeminists

We have already encountered Alzon's proposition that the dividing line is not between men and women but between feminists and anti-feminists. This clearly implies, on the one hand, that men can play the same role as women in women's liberation, and on the other, that feminists can, and should, treat non-feminist women as enemies.

It is highly possible that this pseudo-thinking is motivated solely by the former 'implication': that the whole discourse is aimed at encouraging acceptance of men's equal participation in women's liberation. If so, it is particularly odious that a self-declared feminist man like Alzon does not hesitate to use this line to divide women in order to force his way in. This fact alone should prove, were proof necessary, that his concern and his purpose is not the liberation of women. He is prepared to weaken, or attempt to weaken, women's liberation if he thinks this is the price which has to be paid to gain himself a place.

In order to prove that men (and Alzon himself) can participate in the women's movement, he has to prove that the fact of being a man does not automatically justify his exclusion. This for him excuses asserting the symmetrical proposition: i.e. that all women are not automatically involved. Of course it is a gamble to try to prove that membership or non-membership of a group does not count in matters concerning the group, and it is easier to proceed negatively, by dividing women, than positively, by proving that men are taking as much part as women in the latter's liberation.

Alzon therefore argues that we should treat antifeminist women like antifeminist men. Once this point is established, he thinks it will mean that feminist men will be treated like feminist women. Unfortunately, there is no shadow of the symmetry he postulates. The antifeminism of men corresponds to their objective interests, and nothing further need be said on the subject. On the other hand, the antifeminism of women differs radically from that of men; it is diametrically opposed to their interests. What is racism for the oppressor is self-hatred for the oppressed. It is normal for women to be antifeminist: it is their being feminist which is astonishing. Gaining consciousness, 'becoming feminist', is not a sudden and brutal Pentecost. Feminist consciousness is not acquired once and for all, it is a long and never-ending process – and painful with it. We must constantly struggle against the 'evidence': against the view of the world presented to us in a variety of ideologies, and against ourselves. The struggle against self-hatred is never ending. There is thus no abrupt rupture between feminist and 'antifeminist' women, but rather a continuum of points of view of the same situation; because, whatever their 'opinions', women *are* oppressed. Since anti-feminism is (1) an obstacle to women becoming aware of their objective interests, and (2) more directly, the reflection in our subjectivity of our oppression, it is therefore one of the means by which our oppression is maintained.

Whereas the antifeminism of men comes from the oppression they *exert*, the antifeminism of women comes from the oppression we *suffer*. In no way can feminists see antifeminist men and antifeminist women as the same, nor can they call the latter their enemies. Antifeminist women are not separated from us by objective interests but by false conscious-ness. Furthermore, false consciousness does not really separate us because we have all had it, and we all still have at least some of it. It is our common enemy. When we are struggling against their 'opinions', we are not struggling against antifeminist women, but against this common enemy – and thus *for* them, and for ourselves.

Dividing women 2: the threat of 'bourgeois women'

The other side of Alzon's demonstration – his other attempt to divide women – consists in waving the red flag to make conditioned cows charge. Having claimed that liberation does not *interest* all women, he goes on to claim that oppression does not *involve* all women. He tries to show that one category of women is indeed not involved in the women's movement, on the grounds that the criterion of gender is thus no longer salient, and so feminists of the masculine gender can be part of the movement. The movement will, of course, then be emptied of its political content, because what becomes of a movement for the liber-ation of women if gender is no longer pertinent? But no matter. Alzon knows what he is up to. The keystone to his second attempt at division is the magic phrase 'bourgeois women'.

The question of bourgeois women has long concerned and divided the women's movement, and continues so to do. One is therefore sure to spread trepidation by raising it. Quite why is not clear, but it definitely has more to do with women's guilt than with reality, for in fact nobody knows any of the 'bourgeois women' of whom people speak – neither the feminists who insist bourgeois women must be excluded from the movement, although none of them has so much as knocked at our door; nor outside experts like Alzon.

So who are they? Who has seen the frightful privileged women who are our class enemies? Where do we find them and how do we recognize them? What is the operational definition of a bourgeois woman? Nobody even seems to inquire.

Debates within the WLM around the subject of bourgeois women have always been abstract and have shown marked illogicality – associated as a rule with great emotion. Thus it has been said that 'bourgeois women' 1 are not oppressed and 2 are our enemies, because 3 'they rally behind their men'. The contradiction between 1 and 3 has not seemed to bother anyone; nor has the fact that women have spoken here for women other than themselves. It has also not been noticed that the speakers attribute to bourgeois women behaviour – rallying behind their men – which each speaker denies is true of herself (though in fact the very existence of the Trotskyist groups from which these contradictions were hurled confirms that women *will* so rally). Perhaps the greatest irony in the affair has been the fact that the women who make these accusations within the movement define *themselves* as 'bourgeois' (or 'middle class'). The contradiction between this self-definition (the fact that although 'bourgeois' they not only feel themselves to be oppressed, but also that as individuals they constitute part of the women's liberation movement) and that they are prepared to forecast what will be the sentiments and behaviour of other women, has not seemed to disturb them at all.

An obvious example of the mythical character of the 'bourgeois threat' is given by the fact that the only concrete reference to bourgeois women in France used to consist of a horrified evocation of Madame Pompidou. Now she obviously does not constitute a category in herself, nor has she ever, so far as we know, shown the slightest interest in joining the movement, let alone in subverting its revolutionary goals. From the tenor of some of the discussions in the past it might, however, have been believed that this was imminent and that it constituted the greatest danger that the movement could ever face. What was interesting was that the objective economic situation of Madame Pompidou – reputedly an extremely exploitative capitalist – was never actually discussed. For American groups, Jackie Kennedy, whose personal economic situation was different, played exactly the same role. It is clear from the choice of a single individual in both cases, and from the choice of the same individual, the wife of the head of state, again in both cases, that these women were used as *symbols*. What is *not* clear is what they symbolize. In my opinion they were selected because of the convergence of a number of ideological processes.

The 'threat from bourgeois women' is in part purely and simply a reflection of masculine ideology, of sexism. This produces, and is manifest by, among other things, the displacement of hatred of the oppressor – the capitalist – on to his servants and possessions. The 'bourgeois woman' is the favourite target of male 'revolutionaries'.[1] She is hated much more than the real oppressor, the bourgeois man. This in turn corresponds to three distinct but non-contradictory processes.

1 It is precisely the real power of the oppressor, the bourgeois man, which makes him *unattackable*, or at least not attackable without enormous risks. It is easier, and also more rewarding, to attack him through his possessions; to attack the people who participate in his power. On the one hand, these women make this power manifest, and to attack them is to attack this manifestation; and on the other, they do not possess it, which minimizes the risk of reprisal.

Eldridge Cleaver expressed his hatred of white men's power over him by raping their women. White women's participation in white power consists in receiving crumbs, scraps from the white man's table, but it also and mainly consists in being *under their protection*. Even if the risks of reprisal are smaller, it might seem paradoxical to attack those who are nothing but the delegates of a power which lie elsewhere, who are not its principal holders. But it is there precisely that the blow wounds because:

2 Holding power is all the more, and never less, provocative than when this power (however little it may be) is perceived as *illegitimate*. In this sense, the fact that the scraps of power held by the white men's women, or the wives of bourgeois men, is delegated, and not possessed by them in their own right, works not in their favour, but to their disadvantage. The very thing which should make the wives of bourgeois men exempt from attack – the fact that they hold their bit of power in an indirect fashion – renders them particularly odious to other oppressed people. The authority which bourgeois wives are able to exercise – over taxi-drivers and housekeepers, etc. – is perceived as illegitimate *precisely because it is indirect*.

3 This perception reveals two things:

a   that this authority is perceived as going against their rightful status: it prevents them from being *treated as they should be, i.e. as women*. This in turn reveals that women's status should by rights be incompatible with *any* such authority; and

b   that this authority is perceived as contradictory, thus illegitimate, because *it is derived, not from the classic source of authority*, which is considered normal – economic control – *but from its opposite*; from their status as the possessions of bourgeois men.

Thus precisely because they are possessions,

1   the authority of bourgeois wives is invalid; and
2   their private appropriation by bourgeois men is one of the examples of class inequality and oppression of the proletariat.

Abducting their women lets the bourgeois men know that their monopolization of the world's goods is not acceptable, and is itself a fresh start at redistribution. Equal access to women continues to be an implicit demand in popular (men's) communist sentiments a hundred years after Marx denied it, believing, in his innocence, that this senti- ment was held only by bourgeois men. This concept of egalitarianism is still rife, and it continues to show that women are considered to be *goods*, objects.

Attacks on 'bourgeois women' thus reveal in negative the popular conception of what the social order should be. The indignation of communists, proletarians, Blacks, and Algerians – in short, of all oppressed men and those who support them – when this order is not respected, reveals what it should be.

1   Women should be shared equally; and
2   There is no reason why their 'condition' of being the possessions of certain men (which is shown by their being monopolized) should in any way detract from certain aspects of their 'normal' condition.

For a man to put his hand on the arse of a 'bourgeois' woman, as on that of any woman anywhere, is seldom a *sexual* pleasure or compulsion. It is a way of recalling her and of reminding himself, of the true hierarchy. For arse-touchers, and for men in general, membership of a sex *should* outweigh membership of a class. This is what is shown by the indigna- tion provoked by the instances where it does not happen: where a woman, by virtue of being married to a bourgeois man, gives orders to a man. It is also shown by the insults, written or spoken, which are addressed to these women. The indignation provoked by the mitigation of sexual status by class status shows that gender is conceived as outweighing class – by Alzon, by certain feminists, and by the left in general. It is thus clear that the hostility towards 'bourgeois women' is due to a feeling that they are *out of their place*, that they are usurpers (as well as being wrongfully appropriated objects). This hostility is therefore based on the opposite of what the theory which rationalizes it says.

In the theory, the wives of bourgeois men are 'bourgeois women' (i.e. they are oppressors) rather than women (i.e. oppressed), and they are hated in the same way as their male homologues because their class – their condition of being enemies – outweighs their gender. But, on the contrary, if the 'power' of 'bourgeois women' causes indignation, it is not because they are seen as bourgeois, but because they are seen as *not* bourgeois, as not being *allowed* to be bourgeois. The fact that they exercise, or seem to exercise, certain bourgeois prerogatives arouses indignation because they are seen as doing this unjustifiably, i.e. they are usurping a position. And not only are they usurping it and posing as bourgeois (thereby escaping their 'normal' treatment), but it is precisely because they are the property of bourgeois men (because they are possessions and *not* bourgeois) that they can pose as bourgeois and deny the fact that they are possessions!

Thus the attacks on 'bourgeois women' mounted in the name of 'class' consciousness – which say that class outweighs gender – reveal a diametrically opposed consciousness. They reveal that:

1   the wives of bourgeois men are seen (correctly) as not belonging to the same class as their men (women belong to it not as subjects but as objects);
2   the wives of bourgeois men are seen as 'women' rather than as 'bourgeois women'; and that
3   gender – the subservience owed to all men by all women – should outweigh class.

If we acknowledge the guilt – the oppression – which underlies the 'bourgeois woman myth' for women, we must realize just how odious it is of men to support it or even to use it. But then Alzon for one is not really free to take it or leave it. He needs the masculine version of the myth for reasons not of self-hatred but of hatred of others. He needs it to attack feminists. We therefore find in his analysis all the attitudes revealed above.

Attacks on (bourgeois) women disguised as love of the proletariat

The first indication that we are dealing with a myth is the total *irrationality* of what one would not dare call an argument. Drawing on a personal reading of Engels, Alzon in his book introduces a quite arbitrary distinction between 'oppression' and 'exploitation'.

It is not that we have not heard this one before, but rather that we know that it would not be worth saying were it not that it allows the person saying it to put in terms he or she considers polite, their view that the oppression of women is 'secondary'. This distinction is therefore a kind of refined insult. What is unexpected is that Alzon produces a whole *pamphlet* based on, and consisting solely of, variations on this theme.

Alzon defines neither of the terms, which makes distinguishing them difficult; but then he does not care about this since he does not even try to justify the distinction. One might have thought that this distinction, that this 'idea', good or bad, proven or not, must underpin what follows and must run through the whole 'proof ', since it opens, introduces and justifies the existence of the entire pamphlet. But no. He abandons it as soon as he has mentioned it and does not bring it up again. Why? Because it has served its purpose. It has produced a fake theoretical formulation: a fake division between 'bourgeois' and 'working-class' women.

That it is a myth is also shown by the fact that he never refers to any concrete social group. Who are these 'bourgeois' women, what do they *do* and *where* are they to be found? It appears that they are not the wives of 'bourgeois' men in the marxist sense, since their husbands not only work, but get their income from work. It is thus not a matter of the owners of the means of production collecting the surplus value. Indeed, surplus value has disappeared so far as I can see, or else Alzon is using 'bourgeois' to mean managers, with no excuse and no explanation. But perhaps his excuse is that he has other fish to fry?

Bourgeois women, he says, do nothing; absolutely *nothing* – except go to cocktail parties. Here we have the familiar account of the idle rich, but I do not recognize anyone I have ever met, being socially excluded from these circles, like other petit bourgeois people. For a start, sociologists (and therefore myself and also Alzon) have no hope of being able to penetrate or investigate the circles where these fabulous creatures might be found; and so long as our sources of information are no better than those of everyone else (that is, the *News of the World*, *France-Dimanche* and the odd nineteenth-century author) we would be wiser, not to say more honest, if we kept quiet. In addition, what little we do know leads me to believe that those women who do absolutely nothing do not exist, especially as most of them have children, for the simple reason that this is *impossible* (even if they have one or even more servants) – as those involved well know and would say *if they were asked*.

But what does this lack of information about these mythical creatures matter to Alzon? Does it even matter that there is no proof that they actually exist? What matters to him are the observations which he is going to make about this mythical group, at the expense of flesh and blood women. For example, their husbands are defined as *workers*, yet the wives are '*bourgeois women*'. Does this contradiction matter? What counts is that we note the difference between husbands who *toil*, and *idle* wives; that we see the first *supporting the latter by the sweat of their brows*. (This is undoubtedly why they have been decreed 'workers': if the above-mentioned husbands supported their wives by the sweat of their dividends, Alzon's conclusion would be singularly lacking in impact.)

We can recognize here the popular theory according to which women 'at home' are supported 'in idleness'; which says that they do not earn their living; in short, that they are not worth their keep. Feminists have dealt a rude blow to this view of things. We have shown that housework is work, and that the support such women get is far from being a gift; that it is an inferior form of remuneration to a wage – not in quantity but in kind. But for the moment let us keep to the first subject. The important thing is that without having understood what feminism says about housework, Alzon accepts it. Why? Because by accepting it, by 'granting' that certain women are exploited – gee, thanks mister – and by refusing to accept that others are, he finds a new, cleverer, more 'feminist' basis for the same old project: dividing women. To be sure, his 'refusal' to grant that certain women are exploited originates in part from his failure to comprehend what domestic exploitation is; but it stems mainly from his political purpose (which in turn is the cause of his failure to comprehend). He admits the theory of domestic exploitation only in order to divide women by denying that it applies to some. On the subject of 'bourgeois women' he resorts to the ideological view, according to which the support furnished by the husband is a gift; it is given in return for nothing. This takes no account of the fact that when talking about 'working-class women' he sees their exploitation in quantitative terms: as consisting of the difference – the deficit – between the money value of their maintenance and the money value of the wage which they might receive. (Where and how?) The wife works more than the husband and consumes the same amount, so the wife is 'robbed'. This is exploitation for Alzon. Consequently if, all things being equal, women were to eat more than their husbands, the problem would be solved. But either 'maintenance' is always an ideological concept or it never is, it cannot be *half* demystified.

But, once again, what does it matter to Alzon, since his approach leads him to this veritable pearl: bourgeois women exploit their husbands! (By this reckoning, children 'exploit' their parents, conscripts 'exploit' the army, and the elderly 'exploit' the hospital.) He does not explain how husbands who are 'dominant' can also be exploited, which is a logical paradox and if it were true would be an absolutely unique occurrence in the history of humanity. (If such men *do* exist, I think they deserve what they get because they are really too stupid. If I were in their place I would use a little of my power to put a stop to such intolerable exploitation.) But this enormity is a trifle in the eyes of one who has transformed the economic dependence of women into an exploitation exercised by them. Furthermore, Alzon is not going to solve the mystery. Having mentioned it, he carries on, because his purpose is not to justify aberrant and thus unjustifiable propositions, but simply to find new insults to throw at 'bourgeois' women.

But alas for him, his passion is too strong. It drags him further than he would wish. It makes him show himself in his true colours. In order better to prove his point about the idleness and hence, according to him, the non-exploitation of 'bourgeois women', Alzon compares them to high-class prostitutes. He thus reveals just how far he understands women's oppression (for him it is not, as we had thought, the client, who exploits the prostitute, *but the prostitute who exploits the client*) and the quality of his 'feminism'. To say that 'bourgeois' women are high-class prostitutes is, for feminists, to say that these women are exploited like the rest. For Alzon it is to say the opposite (since it is the kernel of his 'theory' according to which women exploit their husbands), for he uses this comparison to prove that they are different from other women. However, it is certainly not as *prostitutes* that 'bourgeois' women differ from other women. Why then should Alzon believe this to be a decisive argument? High-class prostitutes do indeed differ from other women from a certain point of view; but not from a feminist point of view. Alzon thinks he can 'prove' that these women are not exploited and so are politically inferior to others by treating them as high-class prostitutes. But it is precisely on this point that they are *like* the others. He thus reveals that his point of view is not only not feminist, but anti-feminist.

The point of view which sees women in a pejorative fashion is the point of view of the worker who calls a 'bourgeois' woman a 'slut'. Alzon is saying the same thing in 'academic' terms. He is saying that whatever they may think, those women to whom I have no access, those whom I cannot oppress, they are tarts just like the rest! The only perspective from which Alzon's assertions on 'bourgeois women' are comprehensible, and the only perspective from which they could have been uttered, is that of sexism. From a sexist perspective it is inadmissible that certain women have, or seem to have, escaped, even in part, from their common fate. This is the perspective of men who are indignant to see their sexual privilege – in particular, their sexual access to all women – held in check by the privileges (or more exactly the *protection*) of class. The very *worst* thing for them is knowing that these 'privileges' are derived from, that they are obtained by, sexual oppression: by prostitution, the very thing from which they had hoped to benefit, but which is here reserved for men of the dominant class. This is not the point of view of someone who is calling for an end to the oppression of women. On the contrary, it is that of someome who, like the majority of men, is calling for the total application to all women without distinction, exemption or mitigation, of the fate of the most oppressed. It is the point of view of the sexual 'sharers', of those who want the unequal distribution of women to stop.

This hatred of 'bourgeois women' is obviously not provoked by a love of women and a desire for their liberation. It is not even a hatred limited to a particular category of women. It is a hatred of all women. It is not particularly aimed at 'bourgeois women', except in so far as they seem partially to escape opression, or certain oppressions, or oppression by certain men. In practice the active hatred is certainly reserved for 'bourgeois women', for it is they who appear to benefit from an exceptional status, who are allowed a scandalous exemption. But the fact that this supposed status and exemption arouses indignation and hatred with regard to these 'beneficiaries', shows what is in fact the only condition deemed suitable for *all* women.

The only condition for women which does not awaken hostility in the likes of Alzon is a situation of total oppression. This reaction is classic in the annals of relations between dominant and dominated groups, and it has been amply studied in the American South in particular. The benevolent paternalism of whites towards Blacks who 'know their place', and who stay there, is curiously transformed into a murderous fury when the Blacks cease to know their place. The American feminist movement has also analysed masculine reactions to 'uppity women' (literally women who do not lower their eyes). The famous 'bourgeois women' are not among these 'arrogant' women: they are not those 'women's libbers' who contest their role. They are rather women for whom a classic submission to men pays off when their man belongs to the superior stratum of his sex; when the man they belong to dominates other men as well as women and can protect them against these other men. This is experienced by the other men, as I have said, as an anomaly, as a transgression of the ideal rule, which is the submission of all women to all men. It is the more outrageous for being the result of obeying the rule. Left intellectuals are rarely conscious of their attachment to this norm; even more rarely do they put it into words. It is only revealed negatively, in the indignation which its transgression excites in them.

II. Self-hatred as the basis of 'left feminism'

It is within this context that the moral debates in certain strands of the women's liberation movement, and the 'politics' adopted by certain groups, must be understood. The debates do not relate to any description of actual women's situations, nor do the positions adopted derive from either an analysis of the concrete situation of concrete categories of women, or an analysis of the political implications of this or that position for actual engagement in the liberation struggle. The debates are simply an expression of the guilty consciences of those who participate; a conscience which, needless to say, is both the product and the sign of their oppression.

Many women (like most men) think that class outweighs gender. Not only do they evaluate their own class membership incorrectly, identifying themselves with either their husband or their father (if classed themselves, by their own position, they would realize that almost none of them is bourgeois), they also believe their 'class membership' puts them in a category of superiority or 'total non-inferiority' *vis-à-vis* certain categories of men. They then project their bad conscience – in the form of hostility – on to a mythical category of women whom they feel exemplify this anomaly.

This guilty conscience is particularly articulated and systematically expressed in 'leftist' ideology: in the positions adopted by groups within the WLM which are aligned with groups in the male extreme left. But this is not the source of the guilt. It is merely found there in a pseudo-theoretical formulation, and is accepted by male leftists as a 'revolutionary' rationalization of their male interests. But for women, this theoretical formulation has no structural relationship to the ideology or the movement for a socialist 'revolution'. Rather, women's involvement in the 'proletarian' struggle, the leftist struggle (whose proletarian character remains to be verified)[2] implies that 'bourgeois' women must be excluded. They cannot be among the people who form the revolutionary vanguard and do the liberating.

Leftist women reproduce in their women's groups the guilty conscience of the petit bourgeois members of the male left *vis-à-vis* the 'masses', i.e. the proletariat. They feel guilty about their comfortable life-style and they pretend to be part of the working class so as to justify leading the class struggle. But for women it really is a reproduction – an imitation – in the sense that it is based on their identification with 'their' men. It is only by identifying with men that these women can feel themselves to be fully 'privileged' and therefore 'guilty'.

This identification has many aspects. On the one hand, there is an identification with the 'personal' oppressor, taken as a model (i.e. the classic feminine alienation), and on the other, there is false consciousness. Following close behind is a *really* guilty conscience.

The identification is produced by women's desires to believe in, and to produce belief in, similarity across the barrier of the sexes. It is a typically magical reaction, a way of annulling in dreams the oppression which cannot be suppressed in reality. Like any recourse to magic, it brings its own contradiction, its annulment, since *identification* is pre-emptive proof of non-identity. You cannot identify with 'your' man if you are not distinct from that man. From this identification follows the belief of women born of, or married (legally or not) to, bourgeois men that they are themselves 'bourgeois'. This is false consciousness. They do not participate in the privileges of their men's class, whatever they may think. These women then feel *really* guilty in relation to proletarians, partly through false consciousness (because they wrongly believe themselves to be in the same situation and with the same objective relation to the proletariat as their 'blokes'), but also because they feel that the class privileges which they think they exercise as their men do, are, for them, usurped. They feel they have even less right to power and privileges than their men. This second feeling is analytically distinct from the first, even though the two usually go together.

To explore this further, let us distinguish a number of class situations for women which are often lumped together as their being 'bourgeois'.

1   That of the woman who is really bourgeois, that is, a capitalist and owner of productive property. In France there are eleven thousand women who are classified in the census as 'employers in industry and commerce'. Since this category includes both the Rothschilds and the corner-shop, and given the number of small shops owned by women, we can assume that the majority of these eleven thousand 'employers' are closer to grocers than to the Rothschilds. Few of the bourgeoisie in the strict sense are women.

2   That of a woman married to a bourgeois man and benefiting from a certain amount of delegated power.

3   That of a woman with a professional job of her own (some left feminists).

4   That of a woman married to a manager or a professional man and benefiting from next to nothing (some other left feminists).

For the left, in cases 1, 2 and 3 the privileges women derive either from their class membership or from being the possession of men of the bourgeois class are stained with guilt, doubled in the second case by the way in which they are acquired (the prostitution for which proletarian men reproach them with such virtue).

In cases 2 and 4, there may be certain privileges: almost all the privileges are imaginary in 4, and in 3 imaginary ones may be added to privileges which are derivative but real. In other words, bad conscience works in all cases: all these women feel they have power and privileges which they ought not to have. Guilty conscience is doubled in the second case, that of the classic 'bourgeois women', by awareness of the cheating which provokes masculine indignation. In the fourth case, however, the troubled conscience is due solely to false consciousness.

False consciousness can also function very well in the second and third case. When you have a few morsels of power you can very easily think you have it all – indeed, it is hard not to.

Left women share with their men the guilt of having class privileges; but for women the left adds to this the guilt of having these privileges improperly, being women. That is to say, it adds to the class oppression (which the women *think* they exercise) *a reversal of the normal sexual hierarchy*. The pangs of conscience due to this reversal have two aspects: first, the women feel that *nothing* should put them in a position to oppress any men; and second, they feel that they are not really in the same situation as their men, that the oppression that they force the proletarians to 'submit to' is not founded on the same basis as that of their men: *that it is even less legitimate*. These two feelings are, ironically, contradictory. The first is guilt for *being* bourgeois, the second is guilt for *not being bourgeois*, but for possessing privileges none the less.

This guilty conscience, then, is systematized in political form – it is expressed in 'theoretical terms' in certain left women's groups, as we have said, though it is also utilized as a means of control in non-left groups (e.g. in the Psychoanalysis and Politics groups in France)[3]. The pretext is an attempt to 'reconcile' the class struggle with the women's struggle. This implies that they have been put at daggers drawn. But instead of this 'reconciliation' being derived from an actual analysis of the articulation of the class and woman's struggles (which their motivation renders them incapable of making), it derives from magic.

They do not try to analyse how the oppression of women, as such, articulates with the oppression of the proletariat as such. To do this would first of all necessitate knowing what the oppression of women consists of, and this they do not want to know. The articulation is therefore effected, or rather is felt to be effected, at the level of concrete groups. They put the accent on *proletarian woman*, or rather on the wives of proletarian men, since they do not draw a distinction between the two (which says a lot about their analysis of the class position of women). They thus substitute for an analysis of connections and contradictions a *factual coincidence*, incarnated in an empirical situation.

They believe that they have articulated class and gender because they concentrate on a group which is oppressed by both capitalism *and* patriarchy. But the existence of such a group does nothing to clarify the question of the relationship between the two *systems*, and the glorification of this group does not replace an analysis which remains to be developed. Furthermore, the contradiction mentioned above is still intact: the women who support this position are not among the women they dignify with being 'saved', since according to their own analysis, left feminists *themselves* are (petit) bourgeois, or middle class, and hence, in their theory, not oppressed.

Left women's hatred of 'bourgeois women' is thus the result of three mechanisms of oppression:

1   It is primarily and objectively a hatred of oneself, since these women define themselves as bourgeois. It is even possible that they so define themselves in order to find an 'objective' basis for the self-hatred they share with all women;
2   It is a product of women's false consciousness: their erroneous belief that they possess the same privileges as the men 'of their class';
3   Above all it originates in their guilty conscience. They feel that they usurp whatever privileges they have. They feel they are improperly in a 'bourgeois' situation, since, contrary to what they say, they think this is reserved for men – as is proven by their feelings of guilt.

Women's worthlessness and left accounts of working-class women's oppression

This hatred shows guilty conscience yet again. Not content with feeling themselves *particularly unworthy of oppressing others*, left women feel themselves *unworthy of being oppressed*. They never refute radical feminist arguments that women form a class with theoretical and logical arguments, but always brush them aside in an emotional fashion. What this emotion reveals is a deep refusal to consider themselves on the same footing as other oppressed groups, in particular as equal to the typical oppressed group, the proletariat.

Why? Because the 'working class' (but also the 'Blacks') are represented by *men*, and images show them as men in particularly 'virile' attitudes: wearing helmets, armed and shaking their fists. This image is the one with the highest status for 'revolutionary' women.

To think of yourself as a class is primarily to think of yourself as a *man*, and, furthermore, to think of yourself as a man of the most *glorious* category. It is to raise yourself to the rank of the cultural heroes. But this, in its double claim, is psychologically impossible and unthinkable for the majority of women. It would be a double sacrilege, a double profanity: it would defame the dignity of men and the dignity of the proletariat. (However, since this dignity extends to the oppressed, who are not necessarily proletarian, just because they are men, in the circumstances I am inclined to think that it is *virility* which lends prestige to the proletariat.) Here again, women's feeling of unworthiness leads them to fear that they are usurping power, and it is this feeling which invalidates the account which tries to rationalize their feelings. This account rests on the opposite premises; it explains their refusal to see themselves as equally oppressed on the basis of the pre-eminence of class over gender; but their refusal itself rests on the pre-eminence of gender.

Another example of this feeling of unworthiness in women is their acceptance of the various masculine theories of women's oppression in the family. In one such theory, women's oppression in the family is caused by capital's need for the reproduction of submissive personalities: by the necessity for children to be brought up to be docile workers. It is argued that because of this, everyone – including women – must be sexually repressed so that their libidinal energy is channelled towards work (W. Reich). Another similar theory suggests that women are oppressed by their husbands because their husbands are oppressed by their bosses. In order that male workers shall be allowed a sense of pride, so that they will not rebel and direct their anger against their bosses, men are allowed to dominate someone in their turn: i.e. men are allowed to dominate their wives and children.

What strikes one about such theories is that *even the oppression of women is not aimed at them*. The role of the family is either purely ideological: it is there to form a certain type of personality; and this character formation is but one of the means or the products of the exploitation of the proletariat. Thus the material and very concrete oppression of women is nothing but a means or a consequence – in any case nothing but a by-product – of an *ideological* oppression which itself is but a means to the real aim: the exploitation of these selfsame workers.

In such theories women are twice removed from the objective – from what is posited as the ultimate end – of the process which oppresses them. Not only is their material oppression not an end in itself, but it is an almost accidental consequence of another oppression; and not only is this other oppression again not an end in itself but only a stage towards the real oppression (the exploitation of the proletariat); and neither of these moments – neither the stage nor the end – concerns *women as such*.

Not only are they exploited, but they are only exploited to the extent that their exploitation serves *another exploitation*.

In other words, it is clear that women are perceived as *unworthy even of being exploited*. Their oppression can only be explained, given theoretical status, if it is put forward as mediating another oppression. This clearly means that they are *no more thought worthy of being exploited for themselves than of living for themselves*. Their exploitation, like their existence, must be justified by something other than itself: by its usefulness for the lives of men or for exploitation by men.

That women are in theory not the subjects of their own exploitation reflects the fact that in society they are not the subjects of their own lives. That the theoretical status of women's exploitation should be mediated by men, well reflects the fact that their actual status in society is mediated by men. The deeper meaning of this 'theory' is that if men were not oppressed, women would not be oppressed. This means that the question is put in the following terms: why oppress women if not in order to oppress men?

The desperate concern to 'articulate' women's oppression with the oppression of the proletariat recovers the barely hidden enterprise of attaching the women's struggle to the class struggle, there being no shadow of symmetry in this 'articulation' (i.e. no concern to link the class struggle to women's liberation). The worst of it is that this haste to integrate women's oppression into capitalist oppression, without even knowing what the first consists of, comes not from a bad but from a good political intent. It comes from a concern to establish the reality of women's oppression, to render it visible.

What it shows is that for many women, and men, if the oppression of women is not 'attached' to that of men it will tend to vanish before their very eyes, being quite denuded of meaning. For them only the oppression of men has a meaning in itself, and if the oppression of women is not linked to a self-justifying oppression, it is *insane*.

The inverted image of women's class position

What is shown by the reaction of many women (and men) to the suggestion that women are oppressed in and of themselves; what is shown by the shared but different hostility of women and men towards 'bourgeois women'; and what is shown by the very construction of this scapegoat myth, is what is also unveiled by objective analysis. It runs like a watermark through the very positions which deny it. It constitutes their hidden foundation. This is that *the wives of bourgeois men are not 'bourgeois women'*. They owe their 'class position', which is held to outweigh their status as women, to this very gender status.

This is the point made in Chapter 2 in this book: the fact that popular, like academic, sociology attributes women the class *of their husbands*: that for women we use a criterion of 'class membership' which is different to that used for men (hence for husbands). For women, and only for women, marriage on the one hand replaces a position in the processes of production as the criterion of class membership; and, on the other, even when women have their own place in the capitalist mode of production (i.e. when they work for wages outside as well as unpaid within marriage), marriage nevertheless outweighs their paid work. 'Bourgeois women' are, thus, so called, and identified with their bourgeois spouses, not because the same criteria are used to class them as to class their husbands, but, on the contrary, because a criterion is used *which distinguishes them*: that of marriage.

What distinguishes bourgeois men from 'bourgeois' women in the class process, is precisely what unites 'bourgeois' women to 'proletarian' women, who are also classified by the class of their husbands. We therefore cannot speak of class *differences* between women – which it seems is the source of eventual political *divisions* – except by first treating them in the same way: by determining their 'class' by their relationship to a man. These differences of classification are thus based on what all women have in common – the fact of being 'someone's daughter and actual or potential wife/woman'.

The fact that this attachment is used instead of actual class member-ship shows that *dependence* – the status of being women, synonymous in French with that of being a wife (*femme*) – outweighs class membership, i.e. their position in capitalist production. It outweighs it in classifica-tion because it outweighs it in reality: because women either have no position in capitalist production, or else this position is less important for their material existence than their patriarchal dependence. It is the latter which constitutes their main (or sole) relationship to production and their main (or sole) class membership, *both being non-capitalist*.

Hostility towards 'bourgeois women' thus rests, in the final analysis, on the correct perception that women do not really belong to the bourgeois class. This hostility reveals that gender membership, an individual's patriarchal class, is perceived as outweighing, and furthermore as rightly outweighing, their 'class membership'. If we find the same thing in an objective analysis as we found in the 'political' (or emotional) positions adopted, it is because this political analysis rests implicitly and in an underhand way on the objective positions. The political analyses are held all the more strongly for being based on a reality which is in absolute contradiction to the manifest argument. If the reality which serves as the basis for the argument is denied by the argument, it is because the argument is designed to justify reactionary positions about this reality. In order that these reactionary views do not appear as such, reality is inverted in the argument, so that we shall no longer see that it is the positions which are upside down.

The differential methods by which the general oppression of women operates, the different forms taken by an oppression deriving from a common basis, still, however, remain to be found and defined. I suspect this will necessarily open up a redefinition of oppression, and not only that of women. But this research cannot proceed with the concepts which are currently in use, i.e. from the problematic of the division of women along traditional class lines, for the reason shown. In reality these divisions are based not on what differentiates women but on what is *common* to us all. The current perception of these 'divisions' is due not only to women's material dependence, but also to our guilty conscience – these being the lot of women. Far from being an analysis, still less a 'revolutionary' analysis, the current perception is a manifestation, and a further proof of, oppression. It will therefore be *from somewhere else*, from a different analysis and politics, from a totally different problematic, one which knows and recognizes this fundamental community of women and which does not derive from guilty conscience (i.e. from a properly *feminist* problematic) that this research can be undertaken. It will be a research of liberation.

Notes and references

1   Up until 1972 (when I stopped reading them) the typical theme of the strip cartoons drawn by *Hari-Kiri* and *Charlie-Hebdo* was the humiliation of a 'bourgeois woman' by a reputedly revolutionary male. Or rather the fact of putting down such a woman alone sufficed to designate him as a revolutionary.
2   Everything I said on pages 110–17 about whites and Blacks

applies *mutatis mutandis* to the relationship between left and proletarian groups.

A critique of the extreme left, of its avant-garde pretensions which are aggravated by – and alas caused by – its (nearly) exclusively petit bourgeois composition, is not my purpose here. It remains to be made. We can, however, mention that the women's movement practice has added to the criticism that this 'proletarian' struggle is neither directed nor even followed by proletarians, another symmetrical, but not identical, criticism: that the fight of revolutionary petit bourgeois men does not stem from their own oppression. This makes clearer a note which should logically have come at the end of the first part of the paper, in response to the question which will inevitably be asked, 'Is there then nothing men can do in the anti-patriarchal struggle?'

The reply to this question is to be found in the practice of certain men who, instead of giving women advice, work on themselves, on *their* sexist problems; who, instead of calling on women, interrogate themselves; who, instead of pretending to guide women, seek their own way. These men look for the ways in which the anti-patriarchal struggle directly concerns them in their everyday life. And they find such concerns without difficulty, needless to say, because it is not recognizing them which is difficult.

3   For further discussion of psychoanalysis and politics see Douglas 1980 and Kandel 1980.

8. Patriarchy, feminism and their intellectuals*

The term 'patriarchy' was little used until the early 1970s, i.e. until the renaissance of feminism in western societies. The term was, however, part of everyday language, but it was used principally in the form of the adjective 'patriarchal'. It was above all literature, and particularly the literature of the nineteenth century, which made it familiar. The human sciences, in contrast, ignored it, and still ignore it for the most part.

Curiously, authors such as Bachofen, Morgan and Engels, whose evolutionist vision of the history of human societies rests on the very dubious presumption of an original matriarchy which was later 'overturned', did not consider it useful to call the stages which followed this overthrow 'patriarchal'. And when Marx uses the word it has the same atemporal, in a word poetic, connotations as are found when it is used by Victor Hugo. This adjective for them, as for almost all authors who use it, has an eminently positive connotation. It is generally followed by the word 'virtues', and the greatest patriarchal virtue is 'moral simplicity'. In what do these 'simple' morals consist?

On examination, we find the poets who speak of patriarchal 'virtues' evoking the same sort of society as those sociologists who, like Tönnies and Durkheim at the beginning of the century, got excited about *Gemeinschaft* (olden communal society) and 'organic solidarity', in contrast to *Gesellschaft* (modern, atomized society) and 'mechanical solidarity'. In the same way contemporary anthropologists, generally marxists, are inclined to oppose primitive societies (which are supposedly classless and with no exploitation) to modern stratified and exploitative societies. These oppositions, more or less clearly mythical,

---

* First published in *Nouvelles Questions Féministes* 2 (October 1981). An earlier version was presented to the 'Jornadas de estudio sobre el Patriarcado' held at the Autonomous University of Barcelona in April 1980.

nevertheless all say the same thing. They show a nostalgia for a 'golden age' of humanity, based on consensus and not conflict. This utopia is directly associated for them with an image of a human group where family organization is simultaneously the principal concrete base and the model for all social relations.

These myths – whether they are recognized as such or credited with an appearance of science – all reveal the same belief: that peace, social cohesion and the absence of hierarchies between 'classes' – meaning between men – require that familial hierarchy, which is good and natural (good because natural, in fact called natural because judged good) be established and accepted.

The introduction of the noun 'patriarchy' and its widespread use, however, are due to the feminist movement of the 1970s. And the feminist movement introduced this term not on the literary or the university scene, but in the place where such movements must situate themselves: on the political scene. Before the new feminism,[1] the term 'patriarchy' had no explicit meaning, and above all no explicitly political meaning. This is not surprising. It is of the nature of patriarchy – as of all systems of oppression – to deny that they are such. Thus feminists in some ways invented the term, in the frequent and favoured use they give it, and above all in the role they had it play. And, obviously, for feminists its connotations are no longer positive, but, rather, negative. It is no accident, however, that they (that we) have chosen this word to designate what is responsible for our oppression. A systematic content analysis would doubtless reveal that all the explicit meanings which feminists give to the term 'patriarchy' were present in embryo in literary and commonsense (i.e. in patriarchal) usage of the adjective 'patriarchal', as I have tried briefly to show.

The renaissance of feminism in the late 1960s can be characterized in many ways. The new feminism sought a marked break with what remained – in worn-out, degenerate and reformist form – of earlier feminist movements, and with other contemporary political movements. It introduced simultaneously a new way of understanding women's situation, and hence the situation of all social groups, and a new way of doing politics. As a corollary, it introduced a number of new concepts necessary to express its different visions. For both these aspects, i.e. its conception of the 'feminine condition' and society on the one side, and its conception of politics and revolution on the other, 'patriarchy' is without doubt one of the most, if not *the* most important concept.

Variations in the use of 'patriarchy' in the WLM

However, the usefulness of patriarchy as a concept is not unanimously accepted among feminists. The role which has devolved on to it in different analyses reveals the deep splits which exist within the movement. In France the division is clear. The use of the term 'patriarchy' neatly divides the radical feminists from the socialist feminists (called 'Tendance lutte des classes'). While the opposition between these two currents has been present since the start of the WLM in all countries, various changes have taken place over the last ten years. The women's movement has changed. And in France, as elsewhere, it has, as a whole, become radicalized. This radicalization is attested to by the more and more frequent usage of the term 'patriarchy' by socialist feminists. It has not, however, reached the point where the term has ceased to be problematic, nor has patriarchy ceased to be the rallying cry of the radical tendency. In Paris on 8 March 1980, the radical feminists marched behind the banner saying 'We struggle here against patriarchy', which clearly showed that they were not sure that this held true for all the demonstrators.

I shall presume sufficient familiarity among readers with the situation of the women's movement, and with the disagreements between the two main groupings, for it to be unnecessary to elaborate at length here on the reasons why patriarchy is a controversial notion. For socialist feminists, the oppression of women is due, in the last analysis, to capitalism, and the main beneficiaries are capitalists. For radical feminists, on the other hand, women's oppression is mainly due to a different, earlier, system, which although it is tightly intermixed with capitalism in the concrete society, is nonetheless not to be confused or identified with it. It is men who benefit from this system, and the system is patriarchy.

The basic reason why patriarchy was transformed from a description of society into a major *concept* in a theory of women's position was because feminists perceived women's oppression as a system. This perception itself flows from the first and common postulate underlying the whole of the new feminism: that women's oppression is not an individual phenomenon and not a natural phenomenon. It is political. This perception has different implications however in different analyses. Socialist feminists do not deny that the oppression of women is part of a system, but they think the determinants of this system are to be found in capitalism. They think that the system which oppresses women is at base the same as the one which oppresses male workers.

This position has a number of shortcomings which are revealed by the fact that socialist feminists have never been able to produce an analysis of a single aspect of women's oppression which relates exclusively, in the final analysis, to capitalism. It is doubtless because of this, as much as because of an authentic radicalization (which elsewhere cannot be denied) that they are obliged more and more to resort to the term 'patriarchy', or to the qualifying adjective 'patriarchal' (as in patriarchal capitalism). If this recourse is evidence of the weakness of the position which says there is but *one* system of oppression, it shows even more clearly that the *term* patriarchy is not synonymous with the *concept* of 'patriarchy'. Indeed, the way in which some socialist feminists use the term shows clearly that they still refuse to consider patriarchy as a system. Using the term is thus not a theoretical panacea. It does not guarantee a radical feminist analysis.

On some occasions when socialist feminists use the term 'patriarchy' it appears simply to be a way of reintroducing distinctions which radical feminism has thoroughly questioned, e.g. between the public and the private spheres, or between the natural and the social. For instance, in one of the first writings by socialist feminists in which the term appeared (e.g. Bland *et al.* 1978), it was used as a coverall. It certainly had no theoretical status. There was no knowing if patriarchy described a global system of social relations (as in radical feminist analysis), or if it was part of a system, or it could possibly have been an ideology, or even a psychological trait. It was a *deus ex machina*,[2] which came from who knows where to account for whatever orthodox marxist concepts had failed to explain. A *deus ex machina*, but also a dustbin, wherein were consigned all the anomalous bits and pieces which wouldn't fit orthodox marxist theory.

In socialist feminist usage, patriarchy has been thrown back above all on to the side of 'ways of thinking'; but not on to the side of 'ideas attached to a particular social system', but rather to the side of fundamental and ahistorical 'mental patterns', in a word, to the side of 'human nature'. In the article by Bland, Brunsdon, Hobson and Winship mentioned above, there are in fact just such connotations of the classic (i.e. pre-feminist, i.e. biologistic and psychologistic) use of 'patriarchal'. In such usage, patriarchy is some kind of simultaneously inexplicable and irreducible core of 'human nature'.

It was Juliet Mitchell, however, who gave the most explicit formulation of such a recuperation of the term 'patriarchy' in her *Psychoanalysis and Feminism* (1975). She, like others, uses the term while denying the feminist definition, and hence the theoretical utility, of the term; i.e. while denying its nature as a *social system*. Her definition of patriarchy has been criticized in detail elsewhere (McDonough and Harrison 1978, and Beechey 1979) so it need not be repeated here. I want merely to underline the fact that her work caricatures all the theoretical and analytical inconsistencies, and all the reactionary implications, of the use of the term.

Mitchell sets patriarchy (explicitly) within the superstructure, where she calls it not an ideology but The Ideology. According to her, not only is a material oppression (that of women) caused purely by an ideology, but this ideology is, curiously, that of capitalism. But not only of capitalism, however, since she says patriarchy is also the ideology of pre-capitalist societies as far back as pre-history, or even as the (unknown and unknowable) 'origins' of humanity. Thus while on the one hand she suggests patriarchy might arise from history, since it is called an 'ideology' (which presumes a precise social system), on the other she equally and at the same stroke de-historicizes it because she sees it as an ahistorical mental structure, produced not by one or by some concrete societies, but by Society. She in fact presents patriarchy as being the very base of the constitution of society as such.

The political implications of Mitchell's analysis are clear. If patriarchy is the corollary, or better the condition, of the passage from nature to culture, it is not only inevitable, but also desirable. Patriarchy is dictated by the nature of the social, which is itself dictated by physical nature. The passage from nature to culture in this vision necessarily implies the oppression of women, because of the respective anatomies of men and women, or rather of males and females. Thus the advent of patriarchy and its subsequent maintenance appears doubly inexorable and justified. It is inevitable and just, on the one hand, because of biology, because of the animal nature of the human species; and on the other, because of the social, because of what is strictly human in our nature.

The concept of patriarchy can be co-opted, it can be emptied of the meaning of 'social system', in other ways too. For instance, the concept can have reinjected into it elements of patriarchal ideology itself. In particular it can contain the nebulous and typically ideological distinction between 'production' and 'reproduction'.

The feminist debate in Anglo-Saxon countries is more and more orientated in this direction, as also is some of the research on domestic work in France (Bourgeois *et al.* 1978). Those of us who are materialist radical feminists find this dangerous. However, it has to be admitted, and it is not the least of the paradoxes of the history of radical feminist ideas (and of the history of ideas, full stop), that among those who claim to have re-invented as a marvellous discovery what they have in fact inherited from patriarchal ideology, there are some radical feminists. Indeed, the theoretician who is considered by many in the USA and in England to have founded radical feminism, Shulamith Firestone, is outrageously biologistic, since she sees the oppression of women as deriving from the 'natural handicap' of pregnancy (Firestone 1971). Socialist feminists have long opposed her theory, with good arguments though for bad reasons. In denouncing Firestone's biologism, they used to reject the primacy which she gave to the struggle between the sexes, so they could reaffirm the equally doubtful principle of the primacy of the class struggles. Not being able to explain totally the oppression of women in terms of capitalism, they nowadays, as I said, deny the latter arguments. Instead they now talk of 'patriarchy', but they identify this with a new concept, that of a 'system of reproduction'. It is not at all clear what this term covers, except that it is linked to the physical role of the sexes in procreation, on the one hand, and explicitly opposed to the concept of a 'system of production' on the other. In using this concept they make clear the underlying biologism with which their analyses have always been tainted. If until recently they were pre-occupied with only the 'capitalist' oppression of women, this was precisely because this is the only thing they see as social, all the rest being, by implication, natural. In addition, by identifying a 'system of reproduction' when, to their way of thinking, the system of production remains the motor of history, they are only leading back, in different words, to the doctrine according to which the women's struggle is secondary in relation to the anti-capitalist struggle.

Stranger still, what they now support is obviously the same analysis as is proposed by some radical feminists, such as the English revolutionary feminists, but which leads the latter to absolutely opposite political conclusions. The revolutionary feminists in fact retain from the division between production and reproduction only the irreducibility of the one system to the other, and they therefore argue the priority for women of the anti-patriarchal fight. While it must be admitted that there is no perfect equation between analyses and the political strategies which are held to 'derive' from them, this disparity is bizarre. It does make clear, however, that the biologism which those of us who are materialist feminists see as an essential dividing line between analyses, is not an essential divide from the point of strategies. It is not the perspective on biology which divides radical feminists (for whom patriarchy is the enemy) from socialist feminists (for whom capital is the enemy).

Feminists must accommodate to the paradox that the road to exactly the same political conclusions, far from being the same for all, can in fact take divergent and even opposite paths. This requires us to look more closely at the relationship between theoretical analyses and political strategies; and it suggests also that it might be advisable to look at the biologism of radical feminists and of socialist feminists to see if they have exactly the same content – though I cannot undertake this here.

Those of us who are radical feminists and also claim a materialist approach, have, after years of thought, arrived at the provisional conclusion that to understand patriarchy it is necessary *radically* to question the whole of patriarchal ideology. We must reject *all* its presuppositions, up to and including those which appear not to be such, but rather to be categories furnished by reality itself, e.g. the categories 'women' and 'men'. Sketching in our current work very briefly, we think that gender, the respective social positions of women and men, is not constructed on the (apparently) natural category of sex (male and female), but rather that sex has become a pertinent fact, hence a perceived category, because of the existence of gender.

For most people, including many feminists, anatomical sex (and its physical implications) creates, or at least permits, gender – the technical division of labour. This in turn creates, or at least permits, the domination of one group by another. We believe, however, that it is *oppression which creates gender*; that logically the hierarchy of the division of labour is prior to the technical division of labour and created the latter: i.e. created the sexual roles, which we call gender. *Gender in its turn created anatomical sex*, in the sense that the hierachical division of humanity into two transforms an anatomical difference (which is in itself devoid of social implications) into a relevant distinction for social practice. Social practice, and social practice alone, transforms a physical fact (which is in itself devoid of meaning, like all physical facts) into a category of thought.

This is obviously a hypothesis, and it will be some years before it is proved (or disproved) since it runs directly counter to what now appears as incontrovertible evidence – namely, that the different roles played by males and females in procreation *could not but* possess an intrinsic importance for society as a whole, whatever form is subsequently constructed on this difference. To show that the process is in fact the opposite of this, and that this difference (i.e. the meaning given to it) is the end result of social practice and not the basis of social practice, is a gamble, but it is nevertheless the bet we wish to place.

This approach is for us the logical follow-up to the initial common vision of the women's movement, i.e. seeing men's domination as a political phenomenon. This starting point has lead us to put the accent on the *relationship* which establishes women and men in two groups which are not only different, but above all, and from the first, hier-archized. That is, it has led us to adopt a class problematic. In such a problematic it is not the content of each role which is essential, but the relationship between the roles, between the two groups. This relation-ship is characterized by hierarchy and it is the latter which explains the content of each role, and not the reverse. In this problematic, therefore, as we see it, the key concept is that of *oppression*, which is, or ought to be, the key concept of all class problematics.

This has consequences not only for what is contained in the analysis of the situation of the oppressed and for the strategies aimed at ending this situation; it also has implications for ways of thinking about oppres-sion: for the role of theory itself, and of theoreticians, in the struggle.

The role of theory and intellectuals in class struggles

This paper was first given at a conference held to discuss patriarchy, and held within a university. Yet up to this point there has been no mention of either particular disciplines or of academia as a whole in relation to the concept of patriarchy, and this is not by chance. It is because universities have played no role whatever in the creation of this concept, nor indeed in the creation of any other political concept, just as they played no role in the emergence of the social movement, feminism, which developed the analyses and concepts. However, academia has obviously played a role in promoting debates around the various theories and concepts. The question is, *what* role precisely?

One of the things which distinguished the WLM from the ultra-left from the start – the left which remains its opponent and its privileged interlocutor – is the relationship between the subject and the object of their discussions and 'revolutionary' practice. For left groups fight for liberation and for the coming to power of a proletariat of which they are not part, *for people other than themselves*. The contradictions which result from this situation are foreign to feminism. We are not fighting for others, but for ourselves. We and no other people are the victims of the oppression which we denounce and fight against. And when we speak, it is not in the name or in the place of others, but in our own name and in our own place.

This identity of victim and champion, of subject and object of struggle, gives us a revolutionary legitimacy which the petits bourgeois who make up the ultra-left cruelly lack. That women, because they are fighting for themselves, should have this direct legitimacy seems plain. But is it a plainnness or a semblance; or rather, is it directly a reality, or is it simply a potentiality?

Women, like all oppressed people, hate feeling they are women, because we, like all human beings, hate feeling oppressed. This is a major obstacle to women getting involved in the women's movement, because to join in the fight is to recognize that one *is* oppressed, and recognizing one is oppressed is painful. For many women, the only possible mitigation of the oppression they endure consists in fantasy, in a denial of this oppression, since they cannot escape it in reality. This denial leads to a refusal to accept the relevance for them of the feminist struggle.

But there is also another form of denial. This consists in saying, or implying, in words or in actions, that, sure women are oppressed, but only other women, or principally other women. I think here of the practice which has been maintained for a long time by a whole section of French socialist feminists. For them the women's struggle consists in fighting precisely and exclusively against the exploitation of working-class women, which they are not. This obviously corresponds, to the ultimate degree, to the remit of their mixed organization, and reflects the 'workerism' ranging in this sort of extreme left group. But I think this remit also meets needs in the women; and the need is not to be confronted with the fact that *they* are also women. Paradoxically, the fact of pursuing what they call a 'women's cause' (*boulot-femmes*) distances them radically from a consciousness of being women – or at any rate it has held back their feminist consciousness rather than raised it. Either way, the practice of consciousness raising, a fundamental element in the new feminism, was condemned as 'petit bourgeois' in such groups and explicitly forbidden. I think also of the Yugoslavian university women who, in 1978, organized a seminar on the situation of women and talked all the time about 'them'. To say 'them' when it is no longer possible to keep quiet altogether, is the last defence of those faced with the fearsome perspectives opened up by the word 'us'.

These two examples recall moments in feminism's evolution, whether they have been or remain to be overcome. But is there no possibility of going backwards, especially if we think this time of the collective level? Does a *movement* always go forward?

Feminism had entered the university, in the US more than in Europe, in England more than in southern Europe, in Spain more than in France. No one denies that 'women's studies' are a good thing. But again it depends on how they develop and, even more to the point, what relationship they maintain with the political movement which instigated them and which feeds them. The development of women's studies in the United States is such a vast topic that it is neither my purpose nor within my competence to deal with it here, except to say that certain aspects of its development disquiet, reasonably it seems, more than one American feminist.

The problem which we have to face is what role in the struggle can, and should be played by feminists who are also intellectuals, or intellectuals who are also feminists? Academia is not a neutral location and the revolution is not, to my knowledge, over. This is a question which concerns not only universities and feminists, but the intelligentsia in general and political struggles in general.

There are in fact several orders of problem. I will start with the most obvious, the one which faces all revolutionaries and the whole intellectual class. (To forestall any criticism let it be clear that I am using class here in a very loose sense.) Some think that being women we are only women, and hence absolved by our quality of victims in this regard from our privileges in any other. But we materialist feminists, who affirm the existence of several – at least two – class systems, and hence the possibility of an individual having several class memberships (which can in addition be contradictory); we who think that male workers are not, as victims of capitalism, thereby absolved of the sin of being the beneficiaries of patriarchy, must refuse this way out. It is too easy to be honest. How can those of us who have an institutional bond to the intellectual class make sure that academia serves feminism and not feminism academia? The latter seems totally improbable at first sight, but it isn't.

Take for example the role played by marxists in French academic life and in French intellectual life in general. If in the US marxists intellectuals can be counted on the fingers of one hand and take risks in declaring their politics within their work situation, this is not the case in France. Marxism is largely accepted in French university life. I do not doubt for a moment the good faith and the goodwill of our marxist thinkers. They are sincere in calling for the revolution they desire and they work hard for it in their disciplines. But what is the end result of all their efforts and all their labours? Is the revolution further ahead in France than in the US, or than in Spain, where marxism had until recently a smell of sulphur and was certainly not compatible with a university career? The analyses of our marxist intelligentsia are astonishingly revolutionary. The only problem is that they are written in language which can only be understood by a ridiculously small proportion of the population. They certainly denounce the reactionary presuppositions and ideology of capitalism wherever they see them. But above all they like to unmask them in other scientific work, rather than in ideological production aimed directly at the general public. It follows that their denunciations are very convincing . . . when you can understand them. And in general only their colleagues can understand them. From this comes the paradox that they are understood and appreciated by those they consider their political opponents, i.e. their reactionary colleagues, while those they claim to defend at best ignore them, and at worst see them as mystifiers, hence as enemies. Whatever their intentions, what is the objective outcome of their work? In so far as they address right-wing intellectuals and exclude the non-intellectuals of the left, their work objectively helps the cohesion of the intellectual class as a whole, all political positions taken together, over and against the non-intellectual ranks of the population.

This is not due solely to the contradiction from which women escape: the fact that they do not in reality belong to the class they support. If as feminists we do not have this initial handicap, if we are both subjects and objects of our analyses, we are none the less as members of universities, members of the intellectual class, even if low-ranking members. The oppression of women could become one object of study among others, without questioning either the methods of the disciplines or the role of academia and science as privileged locations for ideological production, and hence for the maintenance of oppression – of all oppressions. This is what has happened to orthodox marxism, perhaps because of the petit bourgeois origin of marxist theorists. But then again we could ask why it has been precisely the petit bourgeois who have monopolized marxist theoretical accounts.

In the hands of intellectuals, marxism has undergone an enormous perversion. Marxist analysis of society is presented, in the orthodoxy, as being *the source* of class consciousness and of perceptions of oppression. Indeed, in this orthodoxy it is marxist analysis and it alone which can disclose oppression and, in the last inversion, it is marxist analysis which confirms oppression, which gives a 'certificate of oppression' to a group to enable it to rebel in a legitimate fashion, i.e. with the approval of the marxist establishment. At any rate this was the sort of argument that leftists used when trying to invalidate feminism at the start of the WLM. But such treatment isn't reserved for women alone. Many intellectuals believe that it is marxist *analysis* which establishes the reality of proletarian oppression, a belief which is both historically and logically absurd.

I cannot expand at length here on how Marx himself in fact started from already *authenticated reports* of the oppression of workers; how he could not have done otherwise; how, far from trying to prove its existence, the certainty of its existence was for him a basic given; how, without this *a priori* he would have had no reason, either subjective or objective, to try to demonstrate the mechanisms by which the oppression was obtained; and in short, how you cannot study something which does not exist.

This perversion of revolutionary theory, of the conception of the origins of revolt and class consciousness, effected by orthodox marxism, also lies in wait for feminism. This perversion can take other forms, but don't imagine that we shall be preserved from danger either by magic or by our ovaries. In any case we shall certainly not be saved by the fact that we are intellectuals, because it is part of the objective interests of the intellectual class, of which we are *also* members, part of the logic of its maintenance as a class, to claim to hold all the lines of social movements, up to and including their origins. This is why this class gathers everything, including revolution, together into its private domain: analysis and theory.

Let us make no mistake. Analysis and theory have their limits. They can tell us how, and in a strict sense why, oppression exists; but they cannot pretend to authorize revolution, which comes from a consciousness of oppression. And they cannot establish the reality of oppression since they themselves only begin from the moment when this reality is established. Otherwise the theory would have no object. Oppression is a reality and at the same time an interpretation of reality: a perception of reality as intolerable – as precisely oppressive. This perception of reality as oppressive cannot be founded 'in reason', based on a theory which at the start ignores it and then 'discovers' it. On the contrary, different theories of society, of reality, start from pre-existing perceptions of what is tolerable and what is not; of what is just and what unjust. There is no Science which can tell us that we are oppressed. Oppression is the experience of being unjustly treated, which becomes objective because it is shared. It has no more scientific base than ideas of justice or equality. We must always be aware of this. We must always remember that theories cannot substitute for revolt, and that, on the contrary, theories themselves derive from revolt and can originate *only* from it.

If we accept that all intellectual practices are rooted in a class position, whether consciously or not, it follows that no analysis has any strictly scientific value. There is no Science with a capital S. This is for me the inevitable corollary of a materialist position of any consequence. An analysis has value only from a class position, in so far as it serves this position. (This means of course that reactionary analyses are not 'wrong' in the absolute. They are correct from the point of view of the dominants.) If there is no Science, there is also therefore no neutrality. This means that once an analysis no longer serves a particular class position, it does not therefore become neutral, still less 'objective'. It deserts the first position, but, being unable to be outside class, it then serves *another* class position.

This has a whole series of implications for our work, which I have far from fully explored and concerning some of which I have at the moment no more than a few intuitions.

One of these intuitions is the primordial role which must be played in our work by anger, *our* anger, in the way we approach the problem of the relationship between our membership of the intellectual class and our revolutionary usefulness. This is not an exclusively feminist problem: it has been broached by others. It has been an extremely painful contradiction for all those who have realized really sharply both their objective function in serving the power of the intellectual class *and* the need for revolution. It has led those such as Sartre to wish 'to destroy myself as an intellectual'. This position shows great moral and political integrity; but it does not resolve the problem of the existence of the intellectual class and its role. We live this role every day. Academia produces knowledge which is both necessary for the revolution and withheld from its protagonists. It can produce knowledge only in a form which makes it incomprehensible to the masses and which at the same stroke alienates them from it. Production of knowledge (which is frequently useful) is, under present conditions, inseparable from the production of a *learned* discourse which is defined in opposition to 'popular' language – i.e. that of the group which is dominated. The progress of knowledge thus itself reinforces, in a seemingly inexorable way, the exclusion of the masses, and their increasingly radical separation from intellectual tools: from ways of thinking about their oppression.

Feminists also face this problem. Concretely, what use should we make of the instruments of knowledge given us by academia. How far will our feminism undermine academia? How far, on the other hand, will it be recuperated by the latter, for its own ends? For example, when we criticize the sexism of the work of our male colleagues, it is obvious that we do it with the intention of forwarding the feminist struggle. But how will we, how can we, do it in such a way that the critiques can be used by feminists as a whole, since this presupposes first and foremost that the critiques should be *understandable*. But, depending on the language we use, our critiques may be understood by feminists – and disdained by our learned colleagues; or else they may be understood by these selfsame colleagues, who we thus convict of sexism in the eyes of the scientific community, but with whom we thereby establish a much more fundamental complicity – a complicity based on the exclusion of all non-intellectuals, in which group are also to be found the majority of feminists.

I have no ready answer to this question, no miraculous remedy to a problem which no one has managed to resolve up to now. I have only an awareness of certain definite dangers. If the critique of sexism in scientific disciplines is important, it is important only in so far as the accounts of these disciplines are the learned version of popular patriarchal ideology. *That* is what matters to us, *that* is what our critiques must reach. What must interest us is not the arguments of our masculine colleagues in and of themselves, but the fact that they give a guarantee of 'science' to the dominant ideology; it is because the mystification of Science redoubles the mystification of popular ideology that we must analyse these learned accounts. But we tread a fine line. If other women do not understand our critiques, if they cannot use them, if they mean nothing to them, then we will in fact be addressing ourselves to our male colleagues; we will have confirmed our solidarity with the mystifying institution over and above having been useless to the feminist battle. We will thus be doubly traitors to the class of women.

To use academia in the feminist battle necessarily leads to a denunciation of the academy, to a denunciation of the double mystification of learned discourse: the first mystification being that it does nothing other than paraphrase and reiterate the dominant ideology; the second that it gives legitimacy to the myth of Science: Pure, Neutral, Universal. The sole fact of individual feminists, or feminists' concerns, entering academic life does not guarantee that the resources of academia will be recuperated by us, i.e. used against the role of the intellectual class and for the revolution. When a feminist question, for example that of housework, becomes an academic subject, when it is treated as such, i.e. as under the jurisdiction of Pure Knowledge (a patriarchal and bourgeois myth), then feminism is, wittingly or not, betrayed. The only valid reason for studying housework, since we are in the privileged position of being able to *study* it, is that thousands of women, every day and every second, suffer in the flesh from being 'only housewives'. To make this into a mere academic problem is to deny, worse to insult, this suffering. It is to take the part of the intellectual class against the oppressed, against housewives, and to reify the latter a second time.

The only way to avoid this involuntary reversal of alliances is to always keep this suffering in one's mind and to know that it is the only valid reason for studying housework. Likewise to remember that the only value of theory lies in the contribution it may make to ending this situation. The only way not to forget the suffering of others is to start by recognizing your own. That this isn't easy goes without saying.

The admittance of feminist questions to the rank of academic questions often appears as progress for the feminist struggle itself, not only because academia thus gives us a warrant of 'seriousness', but also because university circles assure, indeed require, a non-emotive approach to problems. This passionless approach seems to guarantee a more rigorous, calm analysis. This is a devil's trap. That is to say, it is part of the dominant ideology which has created a myth of Science. If we succumb to this all too easily, it is because this dispassionate approach also attracts us more directly, i.e. affectively. Without even looking at the interests of Science, it is clear it gives us protection against our own anger. Contrary to what is commonly thought, it is not easy to be, and above all to *remain*, angry. It is painful, because to remain angry is to keep permanently in mind the cause of this anger; it is constantly to remember what we want to forget, at least from time to time, to be able to survive – i.e. that we too are humiliated and offended against.

But for us as intellectuals to forget this, even for an instant, is to loose the thread which connects us to our class as women. It is the railing which prevents us tipping over on to the side of the institution, to the side of our oppressors. We tend to see anger as something we can get beyond, and also as a disagreeable feeling; as something temporary, which ceases at some time to be useful; and even as something of an encumbrance, which we should leave at the university door so as to be able to work in peace.

But our only weapon against the potential treason written into our status as intellectuals is precisely our anger. The only guarantee that we will not, as intellectuals, be traitors to our class, is our awareness of being, ourselves, women, of being among those whose oppression we analyse. The only basis for this consciousness is our revolt; and the only foundation for this revolt is our anger.

Notes and references

1 Veronica Beechey (1980) has suggested that 'first wave' feminists in England, such as Virginia Woolf, Vera Brittain and the Fabian Women's Group, already used the term patriarchy.

2 'A god from a machine' was a device in Greek theatre. A god was elevated above the stage and provided solutions to problems mortals could not resolve – or interesting twists to the plot.

9. A materialist feminism *is* possible*

The first issue of *Feminist Review* (January 1979) contained a review of my work by two English sociologists, Michèle Barrett and Mary McIntosh. I replied to this three issues later and sought to show, first, the various ways in which they had misrepresented what I had written; second, what I think the concerns of feminist criticism should be; and third, and most important, the various ways in which Barrett and McIntosh fundamentally misconceive marxism. It is not necessary in this collection to include the first part of the article, since the collection itself makes the relevant articles available in English, but the latter two parts are significant because they expose the widespread theoretical schizophrenia of the left on the subject of women's oppression. The contradictory analyses Barrett and McIntosh produce are due, I believe, to a desperate desire to continue to exempt men from responsibility for the oppression of women.

Marxism misunderstood: abused and used

Barrett and McIntosh's article rests on a set of attitudes which are common in intellectual circles:

1 a religious attitude to the writings of Marx;
2 an assertion that marxism constitutes a whole which one must take or leave;
3 a confusion between the materialist method, used for the first time by Marx, and the analysis of capitalism which he made using it; or rather the reduction of the first to the second;
4 a confusion, voluntarily perpetuated, between these two things and

---

* A version of this article appeared in *Feminist Review*, no. 4 (1980).

the interpretation which 'marxist' sects make of contemporary society; and

5   a presentation of this triple confusion as the whole (to be taken or left) of 'marxism', which is in its turn not only presented as a science, but as The Science having all the characteristics of this pure essence: in particular, neutrality and universality.

The religious attitude builds Marx into an object of study in himself. 'Marxologists', as their name indicates, are interested in Marx *qua* Marx. They lose sight of why Marx is important; or rather they invert the order of priorities. They judge Marx not in terms of politics, but rather they judge politics in terms of Marx. This talmudic attitude may at first sight seem contradictory to the very varied interpretations to be found among the different marxist sects (in itself no bad thing) and the fact that their analyses, all supposedly 'marxist', diverge radically among themselves. But in reality the reverence for the letter of Marx, the constitution of this into the ultimate, quasi-divine reference, the dogma of infallibility, serves to construct the *authority* with which later 'marxists', whoever they may be, adorn themselves. Recourse to *argument from authority* – I am right because I'm a Marxist – is by no means peculiar to marxists, but that doesn't make it any more excusable.

Marxism is erected as the value of values and is seen as not only above the struggles, but outside them. The ultimate perversion, and one which is moreover widespread, is that people then come to judge real oppression, and even the very existence of oppression, according to whether or not it corresponds to 'marxism', and not marxism according to whether or not it is pertinent or not to real oppressions. This perversion is not, of course, a simple diversion of the intellect, devoid of political meaning. For to stress in a revolt, like a women's revolution, only that which is consistent with their interpretation of marxism, allows people eventually to decide that a revolt is invalid or unimportant ('what matters is to be a marxist, not to make a revolution').

In so far as these two linked attitudes incarnate 'marxism' today, it is more than understandable that most of the oppressed, including most feminists, refuse to call themselves 'marxists'. Like them, I stress those things in marxism which are consistent with women's revolt. I won't shed one tear for marxism if it has to be abandoned because it is seen to be useless in analysing oppression. This is an essential difference between my approach and that of Barrett and McIntosh because it seems to me that the very meaning of marxism rests in its political utility. People who do not have a specific political interest – who are not part of an oppressed group – have diverted this meaning by making marxism into an object in itself. Or rather, in so doing they have revealed that they are not politically engaged. But what does this mean? Is it even possible? Nothing is outside the field of politics: one is simply on one side or the other. If you are not on the side of the oppressed, you are on the other side; and your intellectual approach will show it.

Marxism and the politics of knowledge

Subordinating political validity to theoretical 'truth' is a typically reactionary procedure (and, additionally, one contrary to the spirit of marxism). Theoretical truth – whatever theoretical truth it may be – simply does not exist. For where does a theory draw its truth from? In what can it be more or less true than another theory, if not in that it serves a class; that it is true or false from a *political* point of view, from a given position in the class struggle (in the wide sense)? To what 'absolute truth' can one refer to decree a theory 'correct' without making reference to the class struggle? I do not know; or rather, I know only too well. This absolute truth is what bourgeois science pretends to possess; and it is precisely this pretention that materialism deflated. Marx precisely denounced it in saying that all intellectual production is the product of a real situation and practice. Science, capital S, does not exist, and what does must be called 'bourgeois science'.

It is therefore strange to see some 'marxists' (like Louis Althusser) rehabilitating the notion of Science and laying claim to an absolute truth, but this time for marxism. This status is simply not compatible with the very theory – marxism – for which it is claimed, at least in so far as marxism does not break with the approach which engendered it – materialism. But it is more than contradictory, it is disquieting, because the pretention to universality, to the absolute, is precisely the mark of intellectual products coming from dominant positions. Only dominants claim to be above the mêlée, and they must claim so to be since all their knowledge, their Science, tries to claim that this mêlée does not exist; or – in a secondary fashion – to deny the class struggle. From this it would seem that any claim to universality, in knowledge of no matter what, hides a dominant perspective (of the dominant group in whatever inter-group antagonism is at stake, and varies from case to case).

But Barrett and McIntosh present as a criticism the fact that:

it is clear throughout her work that Delphy's theoretical position is closely related to her political stance, and indeed she has argued that 'each is indispensable to the other'.

They thereby imply not only that *their* theoretical position is *not* related to their political position, but further that this is a good thing: that theory can be independent of the social and/or political position that one occupies, and that it *should* be. In the article which they cite (see p. 211) I say that theory should not be independent of politics, but that anyway it cannot be, even should it want to be. In so doing I am only reaffirming what has been said elsewhere by many other authors, starting with Marx, and which is the basis of the materialist approach. All knowledge is the product of a historical situation, whether it knows it or not. The idea of a neutral science – of a theory which is not related to a social/political position – is not in itself a neutral idea; it does not come from an *absence* of socio-political position, since such an absence is inconceivable. The idea that knowledge does not have a foundation in the social position of its producers is, on the contrary, the product of a very precise social position: the position of dominance.

So, when Barrett and McIntosh see the rooting of a theory in a political position as a weakness, they reveal at the same time that they adopt a notion of knowledge and hence of marxism which is not only profoundly anti-marxist, but above all profoundly reactionary and hence antifeminist. Two of the most serious practical political implications of this situation, which are visible in their article, are that on the one hand it justifies their not revealing the political position from which they speak, and on the other, it implies that people *other than the oppressed* – theorists, scientists – may talk about the oppression. This stance is directly linked to the reactionary content of the political position they are hiding.

We have seen that the reification-deification of Marx serves to construct the *authority* from which the imposition of 'marxist' theses is then *argued*. This is simply a way of evading the discussion: of dispensing, or thinking one is dispensing, with the need to prove the internal coherence of an argument by calling on a principle of authority. It justifiably horrifies feminists – and others – and it distances them from marxism.

Marxism and the analysis of capitalism

There are many 'marxist' theses. They all have, however, one point in common: all the different parties and schools which call themselves 'marxists' today agree to perpetuate, under cover of the authority which their talmudic studies have conferred on Marx the man, an unpardonable confusion between the principles of materialism and the analysis which Marx made of the capitalist mode of production (and which in turn they interpret liberally and diversely). Although inexcusable, this reduction of the former to the latter is today so widespread that most 'marxists' – and plenty of others – think that capitalism 'invented' exploitation, that capitalism *is* exploitation, and that exploitation *is* capitalism. Here again, it is not just a matter of simple 'error' or 'ignorance' striking by chance. This 'error' has a political meaning which feminists have clearly recognized: it makes the antagonism between the proletarians and the capitalists – which is one of the possible forms of exploitation – into the principal conflict wherever it exists; into the model for all oppression; and finally into the very definition of exploitation. This is evident when 'marxists' say:

1   either that feminism cannot use marxism: 'no concept of relations of production developed on the "model" of Marxism . . . includes the necessity of sexual division' (Diana Adlam (1979) in a review of *The Main Enemy*);
2   or that the exploitation of women does not exist since marxism is indifferent to sexual division (Mark Cousins (1978) in *m/f*).

Both here confuse marxism – the method – with the marxist analysis of capitalism – one of the possible applications of this method.

The concepts used for the marxist analysis of capitalist exploitation (or *Capital*, to simplify) cannot actually account for the exploitation of women, for the same reason that they cannot account for the exploitation of serfs, or slaves, or indentured servants, or prisoners in labour camps, or African share-croppers. The simple reason is that the concepts used to account for exploitation *by wages* – and it is this which is the subject of *Capital* – cannot account for the exploitation of the unwaged. But the concepts used in the analysis of capitalism are not the whole of marxist thought. On the contrary, they are themselves derived from more general concepts. How, otherwise, would Marx have been able to analyse non-capitalist modes of production and exploitation, such as slavery and feudalism? The concepts of *class* and *exploitation* do not come from the study of capitalism; on the contrary, they pre-exist, it, permit it, and are at the origin of the notion of capitalism in its marxist sense, i.e. as a *particular* system of exploitation. These more general concepts – class and exploitation – not only in no way require that sexual divisions be ignored, but on the contrary are eminently useful in *explaining* them. And I mean here 'explain' in the strong sense: not just in describing it, not in describing only what happens after the division exists, but in accounting for its *genesis*.

These concepts are the key concepts of materialism to which I see two foundations. For me, the first foundation of materialism is that it is a theory of history, one where history is written in terms of the domination of social groups by one another. Domination has as its ultimate motive exploitation. This postulate explains and is explained by the second foundation of materialism: the postulate that the way in which life is materially produced and reproduced is the base of the organization of all societies, hence is fundamental both at the individual and the collective level.

Marxism and women's oppression

Marxism is, by all the evidence, materialist. To this extent it can be used by feminism. In so far as materialism concerns oppression, and inversely if we accept that to start from oppression defines among other things a materialist approach, a feminist science will tend inevitably towards a materialist theory of history. To me materialism is not one possible tool, among others, for oppressed groups; it is *the* tool precisely in so far as it is the only theory of history for which oppression is the fundamental reality, the point of departure.

This had been hidden across the years by people who have appropriated marxism and, in so doing, have not only reduced materialism to the analysis of the capitalist mode of production alone, but in addition have evacuated the very materialism of this analysis because they have made it one academic analysis among others, and in competition with the others on its 'intellectual merits' alone. They have thus dropped the deep meaning which propels marxist analysis and which distinguishes it as an approach far more than its content – the explanation of and struggle against *oppression*. It is therefore clear that the non-recognition of sexual division in the analysis of *Capital* in no way prevents the application of materialist concepts to the oppression of women. However, this non-recognition poses a problem – not for women, but for the analysis of the capitalist mode of production. It is in fact not so much a matter of non-recognition as of non-problematization. The analysis Marx made of wage exploitation is not, as Mark Cousins pretends, indifferent to the division of the sexes, or at any rate it is not so in the sense that Cousins (and others) understand. They think that in the analysis of capital, the positions described – or the classes constituted by the analysis (capitalists and workers) – can be indifferently occupied by men or women. The fact that they are above all occupied by men is seen as an external factor, and one which removes nothing from the validity of the analysis. This implies that the latter would be the same if the classes were constituted in equal parts of women and men. But this is false: the analysis of the capitalist mode of production is indifferent to the sexual division in the sense that the fact that the positions *could not* be occupied indifferently by men or women is not even perceived as a problem. Their theory is indifferent to the problem, certainly, but in the opposite sense: it takes the sexual division as given, it recognizes it and integrates it: it is based on it.

Hence a materialist approach cannot be content with adding the materialist analysis of the oppression of women to the analysis of the oppression of workers made by Marx, and later marxists. The two cannot be simply added together, since the first necessarily modifies the second. Feminism necessarily modifies 'marxism' in several ways: first, because it is impossible for it to accept the reduction of marxism solely to the analysis of capital; second, since the struggle between workers and capitalists is not the only struggle, this antagonism can no longer be taken as the unique dynamic of society; and third, because it also modifies the analysis of capital *from within*. The recognition of the existence of patriarchy – or, for those who are shocked by this term, of sexual division (which no one can deny and which for me is one and the same thing) – makes it apparent that 'the working class' described by marxists and characterized by them as 'theoretically asexual' is well and truly sexed, and not only in an empirical and contingent fashion. It is concerned entirely with only the male part of the working class. All the concepts used by Marx, and then by the others, take as a structural and theoretical definition of the worker's condition the lot of the male worker. Women workers are invisible, they are absent from the analysis of the labour market on the one hand, and their domestic work and its exploitation is taken as given on the other. Thus not only the reduction of marxism to the analysis of capital, but the very content of this analysis, makes it impossible to apply *this* marxism to the oppression of women. But, still further, taking account of the opression of women – which is what it means to be feminist – makes, or should make, it impossible to accept this analysis even as it concerns capital.

Two objectives: the extension of the principles of marxism (i.e. of materialism) to the analysis of the oppression of women, and a review of the analysis of capital from the viewpoint of what has been acquired in feminist analysis, are what should define a marxist feminist or feminist marxist approach, if the words have any meaning. But it is the very possibility of such an approach which Barrett and McIntosh try to deny (or rather to forbid) by affirming that their conception of marxism is the only one, and in claiming, in addition, that I would be contradicting myself if I were to 'attempt in my use of marxism' to do what I say is impossible: 'to abstract technical concepts from their "reactionary context".' Noting in passing that they here qualify marxism as a 'reactionary context', I maintain that this is true of all the overall theories of society or humanity we possess. General accounts of the world, whether they are anthropological, sociological or psychoanalytic, take the oppression of women as given, are unable to explain it, and above all are unable to help in overthrowing it. This applies equally to marxism as Barrett and McIntosh understand it (i.e. to the conventional analysis of *Capital*); and that it would be 'illusory to claim to arrive at different results with the same conceptual tools' is abundantly proven by the failure of the 'domestic labour debate'. This is indeed why I do not use this analysis and why I deem that they should not use it either. *But* this is not true of materialism as a method, and this is why a feminist materialist approach is not only possible, but also necessary, whatever they may say.

Polemic and feminist criticism

This set of attitudes to marxism is the basic problem in Barrett and McIntosh's approach. This is why I have dealt with it first, leaving aside temporarily their polemic . . . on polemic. For polemic is certainly one of the things at issue in their polemical article. They criticize me for doing something which they themselves are busy doing. I could, of course, have fallen for it in making a reply, and perhaps I should have contented myself with mentioning this irony and let them have the benefit of the doubt: I could have accepted that they did it intentionally, to be funny. But I want to profit by the occasion to tackle the problem in depth and to look at the questions of polemic and feminist criticism.

Barrett and McIntosh reproach me:

1   for writing polemical and not theoretical articles;
2   for being 'locked in . . . political combat with enemies found within the women's movement itself', that is of setting myself against other feminists; and
3   for hating marxism, the proof being my opposition to socialist feminists.

They use polemic in a pejorative sense; at first intellectually pejorative, later politically pejorative. The intellectual line signifies nothing, as regards my articles. It is simply a way of putting one's opponents down by suggesting that they are ranting. But, in a more general manner, it is absurd to oppose polemic to theory for a very simple reason: no new idea appears in a void. In the place where it wants to establish itself there is always already another idea on the same question, an *accepted* idea, which it is therefore necessary initially to demolish. Theoreticians have always been polemicists; one of the greatest, Karl Marx, was also one of the most tenacious polemicists of his epoch. It is present in all his work, even those pieces which are not explicitly polemical, even those whose title is not *Critique of. . . .* He could not have constructed a materialist theory of capital except in opposition to, and after initially demolishing, liberal economists' theories about the selfsame capitalism.

Thus on the ground of the facts of intellectual history, this opposition – between polemic and theory – has no meaning at all; but on political grounds it has one, and it is dangerous. They aim to convict me of non-sisterliness. They say I find my enemies within the movement. I dispute this at the level of facts and of principles.

On the factual level, I will say, since they force me to make the distinction, that my 'main enemies' are outside the·feminist movement: that I am concerned with 'feminist' men – like Alzon, whom I denounced in 'Our friends and ourselves' (p. 106) – or women like Annie Leclerc – see 'Protofeminism and antifeminism', (p. 182) – who *refuse* to be called feminists. However, although it has not been my practice to polemicize within the movement, I do not for all that think that it is illegitimate, and for an obvious reason. The movement is not an island, feminists are not born by spontaneous generation, they do not live on another planet, they are not outside this society. The ways of thinking outside the movement are also in the movement. If not it would be so easy!

If not, why should one of the first slogans of the movement have been 'get rid of the phallus/man in your head'? To rid ourselves of the dominant way of thinking is a priority, and a collective task, which requires the freedom to criticize. To deny ourselves this is to prevent our advancing. It is more than a sterile attitude: it is dangerous, because, as Juliet Mitchell says (citing from memory), 'The danger from the outside consists not so much in its opposition as in its influence', and as Monique Plaza says in her preface to a critique of the way of thinking exemplified by Lucy Irigaray, to forbid criticism under the pretext that it concerns 'the discourses of feminist women' is to individualize and moralize a problem when:

what interests us in a feminist critique of a discourse is the location of its *social determinants*. . . . What holds us back . . . is the envelopment of the author in rules and schemes external to her
    (Plaza, 1977:90).

This is even more true when we criticize other feminists.

In these quotations I think that the objectives, but also the *conditions*, of a feminist critique are well enough defined. Feminist criticism is, first, and this may seem tautologous, feminist; which is to say it attacks not an individual, of course, but a way of thinking. Above all it atacks what is *not* feminist in a way of thinking, and in doing this it is necessarily in solidarity even with the woman attacked. A feminist critique is always aimed, even within the movement, at the exterior. Further, a critique, even one made from within the movement, if it does not aim at the outside but on the contrary comes *from* the outside (i.e. from external arguments, theories, or interests) is not feminist. Let us, therefore, look more closely at what Barrett and McIntosh see as 'within the movement' and as 'marxism'.

On the one hand they take my disagreement with certain socialist feminist positions as necessary and sufficient proof of my 'hostility to marxism'. Thus socialist feminists and marxist feminists are held to incarnate marxism in the least of their words. On the other hand, socialist and marxist feminist positions are represented as coming from 'within the movement': socialist/marxist feminists thus represent feminism. Now I think they must make a choice: either these positions are effectively marxist, and, since we know marxism was not invented by feminists, these positions are not *particularly* feminist. As marxist they are not either more or less feminist (nor more or less antifeminist either) than any other position coming from outside. An attack on them is not in any case an attack within the movement; or these positions are purely feminist and they owe nothing to marxism, in which case I cannot see why an attack on them indicates an hostility to marxism.

In either case, there is no reason not to criticize marxist positions, nor some feminist positions. Quite the contrary, as mentioned above. And if Barret and McIntosh violently attack the freedom to criticize marxist positions and feminist positions, it is precisely in order to arrive at a double censure which results in a double validation and a privileged position for certain theoreticians – the marxist feminists.

If we accept the principle of the authority of 'marxism' which they defend, and the corollary that this must not be attacked on the one hand, and if we accept the myth that feminist solidarity prohibits criticism 'within the movement' on the other, then marxism validates certain 'feminist' positions, but, even more, *feminism validates marxism.* According to Barrett and McIntosh, marxist feminist positions are unattackable because they are 'marxist': to attack them is to be 'hostile to marxism'. But even if one breaks this taboo and scorns being taxed with 'hostility to marxism', it then becomes impossible to be hostile to marxism because, in the devilish logic of Barrett and McIntosh, the movement comes forward and covers 'marxism' with its maternal wing. When marxism is defended by marxist feminists it becomes 'feminist', and to attack it is quite frankly to take on one's sisters.

What a marvellous example of a double bind! Here is a move which, if it succeeds, puts those who call themselves marxist feminists in a position of absolute control over the whole movement, since they will become immune to all criticism. Happily, such an attempt is condemned from the start by the transparence of the syllogism which it uses. But beyond the naïvety of the intellectual procedures at work, the Machiavellian intention remains – to control the whole movement. And to control it in the name of what?

The 'marxist feminist' position which they claim to defend does not exist; or rather it is unjust to join the epithet of marxist feminist to it. I have described above what a position which could call itself marxist feminist should be. It would consist in doing two things which they precisely do not do: applying materialism to the oppression of women, and looking again at the analysis of Marx's *Capital* from an analysis of patriarchy.

In what then does their position consist? Just the simple juxtaposition of two political interests: the anti-capitalist interest and the anti-patriarchal interest. We could then ask which women in the movement are not both anti-patriarchal and anti-capitalist, and therefore why some of us need a particular name? This is such an important question that I cannot deal with it within the framework of this article. But the simple juxtaposition of these two interests is not enough to justify the use of the term 'marxist feminist', for such a term denotes a fusion of the two, leading to one unified vision applying to all problems. They do not have such a vision, and they cannot have it, because of their refusal to effect this fusion and particularly to do the two above-mentioned things which are the prior condition for it. Their conception of each of the terms of this juxtaposition, and their conception of marxism in particular, condemns them to not being able to come to such a unification. In fact, from their position, when feminism encounters marxism it is as a *boundary*. For them marxism is equal to the conventional analysis of capital, but in this analysis the capitalist conflict is the fundamental dynamic of society. Women, as we have seen, are doubly excluded from this dynamic; first, because the conventional analysis cannot account for their oppression, and, further, because this analysis *incorporates* the oppression of women as given.

Thus their position – which Barrett and McIntosh assert is the 'marxist feminist' one – has as its logical implication the necessary and inevitable subordination of the oppression and struggle of women to the anti-capitalist struggle. Is this really what they want? At this stage – i.e. basing myself solely on what they say and not taking account of the history of the movement – I can only put forward a conjecture.

This conjecture derives from the gulf which exists between the anger my work arouses in them and the reasons they give for it: from the disproportion between their objective of totally discrediting my approach and the arguments which they invoke against it. The evidence suggests to me that something *other* than what they say provokes their anger; something they do not say, and it is this I have searched for.

The two-pronged attack on materialist feminism

The fact that they do not dare to indicate their true position, that they never write down in so many words the theory which they oppose to mine – which is none the less the reference theory from which they criticize me – already gives *one* indication of its nature. It indicates that the political premises and the implications of this theory risk being disagreeable to the women's liberation movement. This suspicion is confirmed by the fact that they use not *one* but two lines of argument to reject my materialist analysis of the economic oppression of women, for remember, it is to this and this alone that I apply myself. I wrote explicitly, and in my very first article (see p. 74–5), not only that I did not pretend to explain *all* the aspects of the oppression of women, and even more precisely that all the aspects attached to sexuality are as important and as *material* as economic oppression, but that they were outside the field of my analysis. Thus the allusions of Barrett and McIntosh to the fact that my theory does not explain *everything* leave me cold, since it was never my ambition to explain *everything*.

What is curious about the use by Barrett and McIntosh of two separate lines of argument against my analysis is that these arguments are not complementary, but rather logically incompatible with one another. However, they must have something in common, if only that they are used to the same end, and it is a good bet that it is what they have in common, and not their specific contents, that will indicate their real meaning. One is based on the analysis of domestic work, and thus accepts as legitimate the study of the economic oppression of women. The other, on the contrary, is based on the rejection of all study of economic oppression, such an approach being called 'economistic'. The logic of the passage from one to the other, if we can manage to disclose it, must constitute the *real* message – however hidden – of their article.

Domestic work: the economic oppression of women

The part of the Barrett and McIntosh critique which attempts to deal with the economics of women's oppression reveals a total incomprehension of the type of approach I myself and others are aiming at. After having accepted that the topic of my work is all domestic work, they seem in the space of one paragraph to decide that I see only farmers' wives as being exploited, and conclude that since farmers' wives are only 10 per cent of women in France and are even fewer in England, my analysis is not very relevant to France and not at all to England. Now my 'theoretical edifice' does not 'rest' upon the proportion of such women in the general female population. I use the example of the work of farmers' wives, which although producing goods for the market is still unpaid, to prove the falsity of the theory (still favoured by some marxist feminists, such as Sue Himmelweit (1977)) which says that it is because domestic labour produces only 'use-values' and not 'exchange-values' that housework is not paid. I seek to stress that wives do productive work for their husbands within the labour relationship of marriage. The tasks they do vary with their husbands' needs and desires. The actual number of farmers' wives is therefore immaterial to the argument. Even if there was only one of them, and she lived 10,000 miles from the English shore, as long as women in England still did the washing-up, and I have been led to believe that they do by biased informants, my analysis will have no problem in crossing the Channel.

Barrett and McIntosh also reproach me for looking 'at only one half of the family production, that of the housewife', and for not looking at 'the man's relation to his subsistence', which would enable me to see that the 'man's principal productive activity is in the social sphere of wage labour'. Thus it appears from their article that I have not seen what I never stop shouting from the roof-tops – i.e. that men and women have different relations of production. But obviously Barrett and McIntosh aim *not to see* these differences, since their goal is to try and annul them by speaking of the 'domestic economy' as a whole, indissolubly consti- tuted of the wife's work and the man's wage. This is the same as the way in which liberal economists treat the market economy as constituted indissolubly of the alliance of capital and labour. The fact that this mutual dependence is not exactly reciprocal and that this allows one of the indissociable elements to dissociate its interests from those of the other element enough to exploit it, is not something they want to see.

What does this reconciliation of the couple, this negation of sexual antagonisms within the 'domestic economy', this refusal to look at the internal functioning of the family, mean? It means they adhere, as they mention in an aside, to the theory proposed by the English participants in the domestic labour debate, according to which domestic work serves only to lower the overall level of wages. This means that the economic exploitation of women not only benefits capitalism, but benefits only capitalism. In no way can it benefit any man, since far from benefiting husbands, the domestic work performed by wives is used to exploit their husbands further by lowering their wages.

Another of their arguments is to say:

1 that my analysis 'offers no distinction between the situation of wives and that of women in general';
2 that if 'offers no account of the category of mothers';

3   that my use of the term 'patriarchy' is 'ambiguous' because 'at times it refers to the system by which husbands appropriate their wives' labour, at other times . . . to the domination of the father over his family';
4   and finally, that my analysis does not say anything about women who 'like Christine Delphy herself, ourselves and many other feminists, are not signatories of the marital labour contract'.

All these criticisms stem either from failure to understand or, I fear, bad faith. The power of the husband and the power of the father are not opposed; they are both the power of the head of the household, and that power accounts for the appropriation of the labour of the children as well as of the wife, and that of unmarried female or male relatives and other dependents.

The absurdity of which they accuse me – 'are we to see children and the old and disabled as exploiters?' – exists only in their heads and because they have so little grasp of the concept of appropriation that they are unable to distinguish between the person for whom a service is performed and the person by whom the labour incorporated in the service is appropriated. Clearly, services applied *to* children are not appropriated *by* them, but by the person who would have to perform (half of) the work if his wife did not provide the totality, i.e. the husband. Even though I have not dealt explicitly with the unpaid work performed by unmarried women for their aged parents, for example, the concept of appropriation does give the means to find, or at least indicates the direction in which to look for, the real beneficiaries. How this concept can account for situations outside of marriage I have shown in my analysis of divorce by demonstrating that the labour of ex-wives continues to be appropriated by their ex-husbands after the marriage proper has been dissolved.

I have not said that women can 'escape oppression by the simple device' of avoiding marriage because the opposite is the case. Why, if I thought that, would I say that the exploitation of domestic work is the basis of *all women's* economic exploitation? If Barrett and McIntosh cannot see how marriage oppresses them even though they are not married, they have a problem! To mention only one of the ways in which marriage affects the situation of all women, it is obvious that the situation of women – therefore of Barrett and McIntosh, and myself – on the labour market, the super-exploitation of *all* women in wage-work, is determined by the domestic situation of *most* women (see Veronica Beechey 1977) and, more precisely constitutes an economic pressure towards marriage (see p. 97). I won't even mention the other penalties attached to spinsterhood, except to say that, to my mind, the punishment of spinsterhood must have something to do with marriage.

They oppose 'mothers' to 'wives' and 'childcare' to 'marriage'. This opposition is interesting; but it certainly is not mine. And their choice in favour of 'mothers' and 'childcare' is equally interesting. For 'wives' refers, even in the dominant ideology, to a *relationship*, whereas 'mothers' connotes a *natural fact*. Marriage is an *institution* whereas childcare is a *task* which can be performed in any relations of production and which therefore does not say anything about its own conditions of execution if they are not specified. The choice of these terms indicates the choice of an ahistorical, technical, asocial approach which is wholly confirmed by the sentence:

an analysis of childcare and women's position with regard to the reproduction of *the species* would lead to an analysis of the role of women in reproducing labour power and the forces and relations of capitalist production generally (my emphasis).

Here we have their theory and all its compounded fallacies in a nutshell.

As regards the confusion between 1 biological reproduction; 2 reproduction of labour power; and 3 social reproduction in general (a confusion which incidentally is *not* 'feminist' but has been put forward by the male French anthropologist Claude Méillassoux), see the excellent critique of Felicity Edholm, Olivia Harris and Kate Young (1977). But the very basis of that confusion is the naturalistic approach. We are confronted here with biologism of an amazing crudeness. But it is not so amazing if one realizes that it is the hidden premise of the whole domestic labour debate – a basis which is revealed in a rather candid, and to that extent endearing way by Janet Bujra, writing as late as 1978:

It is women rather than men who are anchored in domestic labour *simply* [sic] because of their innate link with biological reproduction.
   (Bujra 1978. My emphasis).

One could not be more frank about it. We are dealing with the oldest 'theory' of the social division of labour. It is 'marxist' if by 'marxist' one understands whatever is adopted by 'marxists'. If by marxist one understands materialist, then it is not marxist. How Barrett and

McIntosh can reconcile this naturalistic approach with an analysis in terms of exploitation is a mystery. In their perspective women are exploited because the natural handicap of childbirth, plus the handicap of childcare which is 'naturally' derived from the first, puts them in a vulnerable position.

It is understandable under these conditions that they misread my work and that they do not see that the answers to their questions are contained within it. The term 'mothers' is unproblematic to them. We do not know whether they mean by it 'reproducers' or 'rearers' of children. They do not make the distinction because to them the term connotes both at one and the same time, and it does so because to them one is derived from the other: women bring up children *because* they have given birth to them. They think that I rally to their position by conceding that 'analytically the responsibility for childcare may precede marriage', whereas I say exactly the opposite. I do not say that women who have children are 'mothers' and therefore liable to be exploited. I say rather that because their work is appropriated women must raise children for nothing. I do not say that 'motherhood' explains the appropriation of women's labour, but on the contrary that the appropriation of their labour, which is effected through unpaid childcare among other things, constitutes women as mothers. Thus motherhood, far from being a natural fact giving birth to exploitation, is I believe, a social construct created by exploitation.

The explanation of women's economic exploitation given by Barrett and McIntosh is that a sexual division of labour based on physiology is exploited by capitalism. This argument uses two contradictory conceptual frameworks, one naturalistic and the other social. The reason for this extraordinary marriage can be found only in its political implications. If capitalism, that is society, is seen as taking over from nature, this means that men continue to be exempt from having any interest whatsoever in the economic exploitation of women. As this preoccupation is the only reason to be found for such an eclectic approach, it is easy to understand the anger evoked in Barrett and McIntosh by the study of relations of production inside the home. Such a study can only show that the interests of men and women are not only dissimilar but divergent.

The ideological nature of women's oppression

Their second line of argument is not concerned with the realm of economic analysis, but tries to undermine the very legitimacy of such a concern. This rejection takes place under the guise of the rehabilitation of the study of ideology, a rehabilitation which is hardly necessary as nobody, least of all me, has ever cast any doubt on its importance. This is however how they construe my work. Taken at their face value their accusations are astounding. I have, of course, never said, written, or even implied that I consider the study of ideology unimportant or the role of ideology minor, let alone that I think ideology does not exist at all. Moreover, I have not been content with *mentioning* its existence, I have actually studied it. But it is probably the *way* I study it rather than any total neglect of it which is distasteful to my critics, though what it is in my approach which displeases them so much is not clear. I have sought to do precisely what they require: to produce an analysis 'which relates the ideological to the economic'.

Barrett and McIntosh themselves, however, throughout most of their article, seem actually to oppose the economic and the ideological, since to them merely to study one of these two levels of society constitutes in itself proof of a denial of the other level(s). They seem to imply that the ideological can exist without the economic, or the economic without the ideological, and moreover that where one exists the other cannot be. Further, simply to talk about the economy is construed by them as denying any existence whatsoever to ideology. The conclusion of this is that recognizing the existence of ideology is incompatible with recognizing the existence of other levels of reality, and in particular of the economic. To pose ideology as important is one thing – nobody would take issue with that. But it is quite another thing to assert that recognizing the importance of other levels is tantamount to negating the importance of ideology, because *that* is tantamount to putting a total ban on the study of anything *but* ideology.

This ban contradicts their request that 'the ideological be related to the economic', and most people's very definition of ideology. Barrett and McIntosh offer no definition of this word, other than referring to Althusser's: 'a material, lived relation, which has its own determining powers'. I have no quarrel with that definition, also called the materiality of ideology. But in fact it is clear that they identify ideology in great part with subjectivity – with what can be called psychology – and with reason, moreover, because it is through its internalization by individuals that ideology is most effective, and because only at this level can we reveal ideology in its pure form, i.e. in the specific form of *ideas*. But it is equally clear that their understanding of psychology/ideology differs totally from mine.

They identify the ideological with the psychological, which is not false provided ideology is not *restricted* to the latter; but in addition they totally identify psychology with *one* of its interpretations: psycho-analysis. I criticize this latter attitude in 'For a materialist feminism' below (p. 216), arguing that the blocks which all the many attempts to reconcile marxism and psychoanalysis have encountered came from the fact that their premises are incompatible. These attempts accept the extravagant claim of psychoanalysis to be, not a system of interpretation of subjectivity, but subjectivity itself. All the evidence suggests that Barrett and McIntosh themselves accept the elision of subjectivity and psychoanalysis. But they have read my article and they know that not only do I not accept this equation, but I think it scandalous. They none the less attribute it to me. They equate my criticism of psychoanalysis with a lack of interest in subjectivity, even though when I criticize psychoanalysis it is precisely because with its idealist and naturalist presuppositions it stands in the way of a *truly materialist psychology*. Why do they not discuss *this?*

As to the importance of ideology, I have said of it, against the prevailing ideology for which 'what goes on in the head is not objective, but rather is defined in opposition to what is objective', for which 'when something happens inside the head, nothing has happened'; 'that "sexism", the ideological expression of institutionalized oppression, the surface aspects of patriarchy . . . is as concrete and objective and as external to individual action as the institutional structure' (see p. 114).

It is curious therefore that they should set me against the materiality of ideology as if I trifled with it. It is after all one of the main themes of 'Our friends and ourselves' (p. 106). But perhaps it is because for me the materiality of ideology does not mean its *solitude*. I do not separate it from other material factors, as they do when they plead, for example, for an account of the construction of 'gender identity' as if such an analysis could give the key to sexual divisions and the oppression of women. For me, the study of the way in which gender identity is acquired cannot take the place of the study of the social construction of sexual divisions, albeit it is essential for understanding how these sexual divisions function. The acquisition of gender identity cannot, obviously, explain the very existence of gender, because this must actually exist before being acquired.

Barrett and McIntosh seem not to want to engage in discussion on this field. They find it very uncomfortable to see that for me the materiality of ideology does not invalidate, but on the contrary is complementary to an analysis in institutional and economic terms. For them, declaring ideological processes material gives them a determinant, unique place; it gives them the status of a, or even the, material base, and so removes the other material bases.

However, to say that ideology acts on reality is one thing: but the fact that ideology is material (i.e. can be a cause of certain effects) does not imply that it can be an *ultimate* cause, for this in turn implies that ideology is *its own cause*. To accept this is to fall back into a theory of culture as totally arbitrary, which is but one expression of idealism. Idealism is the theory – in fact little theorized because it is precisely the dominant ideology – according to which the social structure is produced by ideas, which are themselves produced by nothing. We find both these elements in Barrett and McIntosh; the notion that ideology is the determining factor, and the notion that it is a thing apart, of itself. At this point we can no longer talk of ideology but only of ideas. 'Ideology', although made up of 'ideas', is not the same concept as 'ideas'. The concept of 'ideology' says precisely that ideas are the product of the social structure. The notion of the existence of a material base and of its determining role is inherent in the concept of ideology.

It is easy to demonstrate – and it still appears (amazingly) necessary to do so – that an idealist approach is not tenable. If we have both a material exploitation and a devaluing ideology pertaining to the exploited, the relation between the two can go only in one direction. Whereas the existence of sexist, or racist, or classist ideology cannot be explained without exploitation, the existence of exploitation *requires* the constitution of an exploited population, which in turn requires the creation of a sexist or racist or classist ideology. Thus when we find both a material exploitation and a devaluing ideology pertaining to the same group co-existing, the logical primacy of the first is the inevitable conclusion.

Barrett and McIntosh would not take this conclusion to task as regards capitalism, or indeed society as a whole. The real underlying logic of their plea for ideology is not that they do not believe in the primacy and determinancy of the material; but, on the contrary, that they believe in it so much that they want to reserve this privileged seat *for capitalism*. This goal explains their otherwise mysterious juxtaposition of an economic argument about domestic labour and then their total rejection of an economic approach later on.

The motivation for the attack on materialist feminism: the best means of defending men

It is really interesting to observe the path the left (for it is the left in general and not only 'marxist feminists' that we are dealing with) has followed on the question of women's oppression. For a long time they refused any legitimacy to the women's struggle in the name of the supreme and absolute pre-eminence of the economic over the super-structural, it being taken for granted that the oppression of women belonged in the latter sphere and in no way to the first, which was privately owned by the 'working class'. It seems that they have radically changed their battleground. Because women have invaded the economic sphere, not in the traditional Leninist fashion by becoming employed more in the waged sector or by stressing their super-exploitation as 'workers', but, on the contrary, by refusing any longer to accept that certain kinds of labour and certain production – by a strange coincidence, theirs – are neither labour nor productive. They have redefined the economic in such a way as to include their exploitation. They say in the same breath that they work and that their work is exploited. The 'discovery' of housework cannot be dissociated from the denunciation of its being unpaid. It could not be discovered first as work and then as unpaid work. It had to be seen simultaneously as work and unpaid work, i.e. as exploitation.

The women's movement has forced the political as well as the intellectual world to recognize that housework is work, and exploited work at that. Leftists can no longer pretend to restrict women's oppression to the superstructural, to 'backward thinking'. As soon as the threat became inescapable, they resolved to invade the discussion of domestic labour in a last attempt to preserve it from feminism. Not being allowed to say any longer that domestic labour was 'superstructural' or 'non-existent', they tried to 'prove' that it benefited capitalism. The attempt aborted. Having bored everyone to tears whilst convincing no one, the left withdrew, and the more honest adherents (like Jean Gardiner at a seminar held in the University of Bradford, 1979 – on tape) have now admitted that their thesis did not make sense and that is why they had to abandon it altogether. Barrett and McIntosh nevertheless make a half-hearted attempt at pushing this line (as well as the contradictory 'no economy' line) probably from the viewpoint that 'why not try, we've got nothing to lose. If the "ideology-as-material" line doesn't work, maybe the "domestic-labour-as-saving-for-capital" will still go down with some'.

It is from this perspective that we can understand the blossoming of accusations of 'economism'. For where do they come from? From the left groups and parties. Economism is a very precise concept which refers to a very precise position in the analysis of *capitalism*. Originally this accusation was levelled at the rigidity of Leninist orthodoxy, against its conception of the pre-eminence of the economic pushed to the limit of ignoring all other factors. Today, however, the left retains only the derogatory connotations of this accusation and transports it into the feminist domain. But in the process they have managed to change the meaning of the word and they now use it to denote any mention of the economy itself. However, these two words are in no way identical or interchangeable: economism is to economy what biologism is to biology, psychologism to psychology, etc. It is a *reduction*. To reject reductionism, be it biologism, psychologism or whatever, in no way implies or requires the negation of biology, psychology or economics. However, the left is now shouting 'Economism!' each time it sees the word economic. Whence comes this change, if it is a change?

In fact it is just a new way of pursuing old aims, for they use the accusation of economism only as it concerns feminism. We are currently witnessing a determined attempt to ban the study or even the mention of the economic conditions of women, coming not only from *Feminist Review*, but also from *Red Rag* (Diana Adlam) and *m/f* (where the male feminist Mark Cousins goes so far as to pretend that the word economy simply cannot be used in conjunction with the word women). By calling any and every analysis that takes into account the economic aspect 'economistic', not only do they try to invalidate this approach, but they try to negate the very existence of an economic aspect to the oppression of women. In the guise of rehabilitating other factors which hardly need rehabilitating, they get rid of the economic. For the economic is not simply a thing which can be explained indifferently by an economic or by a non-economic approach and still stay the same thing.

A simple example can show this. To approach the role of women from an economic angle is to see housework as work, and, conversely, to see housework as work is to take an economic angle. When approached from another angle, for example that of role-playing, housework is no longer work, nor was it before the women's movement; it is a hobby, a vocation, a proof of love, a character trait, in brief anything and everything except work.

The problem is that we cannot at the same time reject the economic *approach* and keep the economic *fact*, for there are no such things as facts in themselves. We know it well, since the same actual event – a woman doing the washing-up – is not the same fact for that woman and for her husband, nor for a feminist woman and for a non-feminist woman. And it is because 'facts' do not exist but only mental constructs, that ideology itself does not exist *as ideology*. Barrett and McIntosh never defined ideology, with the result that the concept about which they talk so much always remains abstract. This is understandable but unfortunate since they talk of it as if it were something which exists, which is *there* for us to take and discuss and fight.

But this is false: ideology does not exist before the fight. What exist are ideas. Ideology obviously does not present itself as ideology: it appears as an exact reflection, as the *only possible* reflection of the world; as the world, in short, like *all* representations. Ideology is only all those representations which we denounce as false; it *is not there before our denunciation*. And the denunciation must itself be based on *another* representation, on another interpretation of the world. To construct this we must actually study reality. This is why it is doubly absurd to oppose the study of things to the study of ideology. Not only do the two go hand in hand, but it is the study of reality which in a sense *makes up* the ideology we are then going to work on: to transform so as to make accepted interpretations of facts appear as ideology. It is easy to say now that the opinion that women who are at home all day 'do nothing' is 'ideological', but who knew it ten years ago? Without those who showed that housework was work, where would those who now talk of the 'ideology of domestic work' be?

The left does not dream for one minute of invalidating the economic perspective as regards the classic social classes. It would cost them dearly so to do, since it is this perspective precisely which constructs classes as classes. Classes are classes only for the revolutionary: only for those who think that some people exploit others. To the capitalist, in whose eyes exploitation does not exist, classes in the marxist sense do not exist either.

What bothers the left is when *women* apply *to their own situation* a materialist analysis; when they reject the ideology which says that they are naturally inferior or the victims of a culture which happens, unhappily but mysteriously (i.e. without any material benefits for anyone), to be sexist. But women are now saying 'there is no mystery: we are oppressed because we are exploited. What we go through makes life easier for others'. And the left is afraid that women will call a spade a spade, the economic economic, and their own sufferings exploitation.

The strategy is therefore still the same: women and their oppression are sent back to the superstructural and attributed to patriarchal 'ideology', while proletarians are the sole occupants of the economic realm. The left now says that the economy is no longer – 'Bah, rubbish' – the determining instance, and yet at the same time they fiercely oppose the entry of women into it (their theoretical entry, that is, for concretely women have never left the economy). The economy remains the mainspring of the class struggle, and the class struggle remains for the left *the* struggle. Dismissing women to the superstructural therefore means the same old thing as ever: that the women's struggle is secondary.

But there is a contradiction in this approach, for if the left maintains that women are oppressed in the last resort by capital, why is the idea that women are exploited so threatening to them? If women as housewives are exploited by capital, just like other workers (and some marxists do maintain this), all the better. Women as housewives have just as much at stake as proletarians in the overthrow of capital. Three cheers, there is another revolutionary mass to mobilize. Why then is the left in fact so scared of women exploring their economic exploitation? Why do they do everything in their power to make it appear that women's oppression is restricted to the superstructural, to 'ideological factors'? What is the logic underlying the way in which Barrett and McIntosh slide from one line of argument to another? Why tolerate this contradiction between the analysis of domestic labour as a benefit for employers and the denial of the importance of this very economic exploitation?

It is because, for the left, in both cases the oppression of women is linked to capitalism. The contradiction between the arguments invoked does not matter because they have the same end, and this end explains the permanent oscillation of the left between different theses on domestic exploitation. It is always trying to deny the exploitation because recognizing it requires overcoming the hurdle of explaining how it is due only to capital and in no way benefits its immediate beneficiaries (who are only 'apparent' beneficiaries). We have seen that the attempt to jump this obstacle – the domestic labour debate – has largely fallen down, the victim of 'appearances'. This hold-up explains why there is now a return to the *ideological* thesis, this time revamped with a theory of the total autonomy of ideology which is scarcely marxist – but, no matter, the other wasn't either.

To treat ideology as totally autonomous in the face of a material exploitation one must either purely and simply deny this material level, or adopt an idealist approach; and this is what has happened. If the oppression of women is caused by capitalism, it is by the subterfuge of the 'sexist' ideology which capital produces (why?), and economic exploitation is thus once again explained by ideology. Now this is a difficult position for 'marxists' to hold, which is why they always try – as Barrett and McIntosh do – to minimize the economic exploitation so as not to make the inevitable idealism of their position too visible. However, it is equally difficult (read impossible) nowadays to deny the existence of the economic exploitation of women: domestic work is here to stay. So the left finds itself in the uncomfortable position of presenting in relation to women (and only in relation to women obviously, since it is contrary to the very principles which constitute it) an idealist analysis. This divides its political approach to the point of schizophrenia; 'generally' materialist (i.e. as regards capitalist exploit-ation) it finds itself on the intellectual terrain of the right as regards patriarchal exploitation. How is this possible and how is it to be explained?

In my opinion very simply: if the left refuses a materialist analysis it is because this risks leading to the conclusion that it is men who benefit from patriarchal exploitation, and not capital. What better confirmation of this could there be than their resistance – so theoretically inexplicable – to materialist analysis, their insistence on abandoning what is held to be their specific theory, when it comes to women? Does this not show that they *know* what would be the outcome of a materialist analysis? I suggest it is for this reason that they have set up a barrage in front of this question for the last ten years.

The first question a feminist must ask of Marxism, and we should refuse to discuss any other issue until we get an adequate answer, is, what are women's relations to the means of production?

(Silveira 1975).

This purpose – *the exemption of men from all responsibility for the oppression of women* – is the real message, however hidden, of the article by Barrett and McIntosh. The only reason for the anger which pushes them to consecrate an entire article to the demolition of my work is that the latter affirms that men are the class which oppresses and exploits women. While the refusal to accept this thesis is comprehensible on the part of men, hence of the left (which, in so far as it resembles other political formations and all the institutions of our societies, is dominated – it is too feeble a word – by men), this refusal requires some explanation when it comes from women.

For a long time the socialist feminist current has represented within the women's liberation movement an expression of a tendency to protect our enemies. This is, however, a tendency which is not restricted to socialist feminism, and which is also not true of the whole of this current. In France women in the Communist Party, for example, now affirm:

the existence of patriarchy as power of men over women . . . (as) power structured ideologically and economically . . . (which) determines an oppression (having as its) end the maintenance of the appropriation of women by men. It is supported by an economic *exploitation* based on the *unpaid domestic work* of women/wives.

(*Elles Voient Rouges*, May 1979).

And in Britain, the USA and everywhere else there are many socialist feminists who have refused for a long time to accept the crazy idea that: 'patriarchy is the ideological expression of the exploitation of male workers'. Fortunately, more and more feminists are becoming convinced of the obvious; that patriarchal ideology is connected to patriarchal exploitation, and that there are (at least) two systems of oppression, each with its own material base.

Why should it be otherwise? Why has it been otherwise? The line put forward by Barrett and McIntosh as 'marxist feminist' is neither marxist nor feminist, and if it handicaps the anti-patriarchal struggle, it does not serve the anti-capital fight for all that. The refusal to incriminate men is not however peculiar to the socialist feminist tendency. This refusal can take other forms within the movement (and outside it takes the obvious form of *rejecting* the whole movement). It has simply found, in the socialist feminist tendency, an expression which is more elaborate and hence more satisfying in so far as it does not rest on simple negation; or rather it masks this negation by presenting a replacement enemy: capitalism.

But this refusal is also expressed in currents such as that of neo-feminity, for to base the domination of men on their physiology has as its political implication – since this physiology is unchangeable by definition – a refusal to, or rather a sense of the impossibility, the uselessness, of politically confronting men as a class. We could stop here. A refusal to confront the oppressor group, a search for ways out before we come eyeball to eyeball, when the outcome is uncertain and when enormous collective and personal costs and sacrifice are involved here and now, is understandable enough not to need an ulterior explanation.

However, it would be a pity to stop our search for the reasons for not incriminating men here. In 'Our friends and ourselves' (p. 132), I analyse how the explanation of the oppression of women in terms of its being necessary to capitalism implies a double mediation of the oppression of women by that of men, and how it thus reveals a double feeling of unworthiness on the part of women. We feel that we ourselves are unworthy of being directly oppressed, of being oppressed in some way *for ourselves*. We feel that it is – it *must* be – men who are oppressed through us. But there is even more to the theories which make the oppression of women the secondary consequence of antagonisms *between men* than this.

There is also the incapacity to conceive of social antagonisms as existing other than between men. This is the corollary of, but not the same as, the incapacity to see women as a group as protagonists in a fight – hence as equals in a sense to their adversaries. Finally, there is the incapacity to see women as social beings, and in the last resort as human beings.

The refusal to consider women as a class and to consider men as the antagonistic class relates back in the end to its 'unthinkability'. If we dig a bit at these unthinkables we will notice that they themselves relate back to the set of confused representations which turn around the belief that there must necessarily be close and permanent relations between most females and most males at all times. This makes a structural conflict 'dysfunctional', hence unthinkable. But it might be said that this is a question of reality, not of a 'belief'. But this 'reality', or this 'belief' – the belief that such is reality – is not only ideological, it is the very heart of the ideology (i.e. of the representation of the world which supports the patriarchal system).[1] There obviously also, there *above all*, the ideology does not appear as ideology but as *the* reasonable presentation of reality, as reality itself.

The study of the cosmology which informs both patriarchal ideology and the refusal to consider the antagonism of the sexes as a social product – the representation of the world which includes much more than the representation of the present-day relations between the sexes – will be exciting. It is the dominant ideology, of course, but precisely for that reason it has still *to be discovered*. Because it has never been contested, because it has always been, and remains, just the way we see things, of the order of *obvious*, it has always been exempted, as are all obvious things, from declaring itself, from making itself explicit, from justifying itself.

But this is for another article; and since the struggle against ideology which oppresses us all is and *must* be a struggle undertaken in solidarity, rather than impute replies to Barrett and McIntosh I would prefer to open the debate by asking them, now that we have done a tour of the marxist pretexts, to put forward the view of the world (in particular of the relation between the existence of the sexes, the genders, society and the species) which informs their refusal to consider men as a class as oppressors.

Notes and references

1 I think that this will be the next great debate in the movement and that it will be found that the last ideological bulwarks which impede us, and which thus constitute the stronghold of patriarchal ideology, are also the bases of heterosexual ideology. This debate will therefore be of the very greatest importance because it will signify both the breaking of the last ideological barrier *and* the way out of the tunnel on the question of the relationship between lesbianism and feminism.

10. Protofeminism and antifeminism*

In 1974 a book appeared in France which would never have been published but for the emergence of the women's liberation movement. The book, *Parole de femme*, never once mentions its existence. Its problematic (i.e. its way of posing problems) is situated in the very first moments of individual revolt, in what one could call protofeminism, prior to collective action. Each sentence is a reply to the implicit question: 'Am I inferior?'. This question is certainly the start of feminist revolt, but it is also its end if it is not transcended, or rather transformed. And this question – indeed this whole book – is addressed to men. This becomes more and more clear in the course of its pages. In the end the author, Annie Leclerc, challenges men directly: 'You must realise that . . .'. She never addresses women except to rebuke them, to lecture to them, or to hold them responsible for their own oppression.

Nothing could gladden the oppressor more than such a defensive position. Leclerc is both defence and prosecutor, asking men for legitimation ('Please recognise that my fight against you is just'). But it would be too easy to discredit the book simply because its author continues to want to separate herself from other women (i.e. to see herself in competition and not in solidarity with them) and because it has been – hardly surprisingly – applauded by men.[1] What matters is *why* it has been applauded by them; and this is not only because it is defensive but also because it will not advance the liberation of women one jot. On the contrary, it will ease the present system.

However alone Leclerc may feel, and however isolated she may be in reality, her book is in fact a manifestation of a much wider current of ideas. This current is even established in certain groups which declare

---

* First published in *Les Temps Modernes*, no. 346 (May 1976), pp. 1469–1500. An English translation was included in the WRRC pamphlet, *The Main Enemy*, 1977.

they are 'part of the women's movement';[2] but it is a tendency only in so far as it is a more general *temptation*. This is why it is established in various places, and it is also why, because this book offers the only written account of it to date,[3] it must concern us.

The reasons why Leclerc's book and the current of thought it represents pass from protofeminism into antifeminism are basically simple. Leclerc stays on men's terrain, on the terrain of ideology, both in her 'explanation' of the oppression of women and in her 'accusations' against men. Her whole system of thought rests on idealism and its variants, naturalism and biologism. All her arguments take the basic premise of, and are tied to, the dominant ideology.

First, men and women as they are today, and their respective 'situations in life', are given, if not natural, entities. Hierarchy came *after* and independently of these divisions, and of their content.

The division between women's tasks and men's tasks was made according to *other criteria* than those of social oppression; but once the division had been established and recognised, man did everything to ensure that it be seen as a separation between a good and a bad part. [However] the division and distribution of tasks and roles (was) made originally in a judicious and rational fashion.

Second, ideas steer the world: it is values which determine social organization, and not vice versa.

(I have looked to see) in what name (men) exact, despise, and are able to . . . glorify themselves, (and I have found) their *values* inscribed on the firmament of human grandeur and dignity.

Since Leclerc takes the pretext (the thing *in the name of which* men oppress women, the reasons *they* give) for the cause of (the real reason for) the oppression of women; and since she does not question the division of labour (which is logical if it is all a question of moral values), the ground is ready for the conclusion she indeed draws:

The devaluation of woman and her inferior status (are connected in) the depreciation, the contempt and the disgust which she is accorded, *whether it be traditional or natural* (author's emphasis).

One must admire how she puts natural and traditional (i.e. social) divisions of labour on a par with a simple 'whether . . . or . . .'. The confusion she makes, or rather maintains, between two heterogeneous orders of phenomena parallels our society's general confusion of biological males and females and the social categories of men and women. It is the stumbling block of all her reasoning, and it so happens that it is also the basis of sexist ideology. Her biologism leads inevitably to idealism.

Idealist explanations of women's oppression: women's devaluation and men's need for respect

As soon as the cultural division of social activities is *equated with* and *treated as* the differentiation of biological functions of reproduction, the problematic of 'valuation' asserts itself. It may appear *a priori* that because reproductive functions are *given*, oppression can only occur secondarily; but if we then treat the social functions of men and women as *equally given*, the only question which remains is how they are subjectively evaluated. We see here a concrete instance of how biologism sustains idealism.

From the point of view of Leclerc and those who think like her, however, the conjunction of biologism and idealism is unfortunate since it leads them to a tautology. Given their premises, the sentence quoted above could be re-written as: 'If one considers the division of social functions as given, the devaluation of women derives from the depreciation of their work'. But the second half of the sentence involves an elaboration which is really superfluous, because if social functions = natural functions, to do certain work is simply to do woman's work. And what is the difference between being a woman and having a woman's activity? The sentence can thus be re-phrased as 'The devaluation of being a woman derives from the devaluation of being a woman.'

Later on Leclerc augments this equation with a new term:

The claimed inferiority of women could never give rise to solid *exploitation*. This inferiority could never be conceived of if the domestic tasks *which accrue to it* were not considered as worthless, dirty and demeaning by men (my emphasis).

Here there are three stages of causal reversal. 'Inferiority' (an ideological factor) *causes* exploitation; and this 'inferiority' itself is caused by another ideological factor – the 'devaluation' of 'woman's lot'. If the first equation leads to a tautology, this second one is crammed full of paradoxes. Domestic work is not thankless in itself but is *decreed as such*, and this is the cause of the claimed inferiority of women, itself the cause of their exploitation. But how can men be in a position to impose their negative evaluation of domestic work without first being in a position to impose *full stop* (i.e. to dominate)?

If domestic work is 'natural' for women, why be surprised if men judge it unworthy of them? Indeed how can it be judged 'unworthy of them' since from this perspective it is quite simply impossible for them, because it is impossible for them to be women?

Pressing on bravely up a cul-de-sac, Leclerc says:

One would not know how to set about destroying the idea of the woman's inferiority or the fact of her exploitation if one did not also, and *particularly*, tackle the scorn, contempt or pity for the condition of women, whether it be biological (e.g. periods, childbirth) or traditional (e.g. domestic duties) (my emphasis).

Where we ask ourselves, does exploitation come in? If domestic duties are the 'lot' of (what Leclerc always calls) 'the woman', and if the problem is that domestic duties are supposedly unpleasant, is the problem simply that this reputation is unjust and thus false (i.e. that women's situation is *not* unpleasant)? How can Leclerc rebel simultaneously against *the 'miserable lot* of the woman' and against the fact that it is *unfairly considered* miserable? Does our exploitation consist only of the 'unfairness' of the devaluation of our lot as women? Or does this devaluation itself allow the exploitation of a lot which is in itself neither thankless nor miserable? If so, what *is* the exploitation we suffer? Idealism has led Leclerc into an analytical blind alley: into taking the effect (the devaluation) for the cause (exploitation); and into a political blind alley: the analysis implies that we must change *not the reality of women's lives but the subjective evaluation of this reality.* She neither describes nor discusses the real – material – exploitation of women. She mentions it only in order to postulate that it is

1 less important than low evaluation,
2 the (ultimately fortuitous) consequence of this devaluation.

This theme is taken up again in her chapter on the advantages which men derive from the oppression of women:

Woman is not first and foremost exploited . . . (she) is well and truly oppressed, but in quite another way. . . . He (the man) expects from her quite different things than those he appropriates from the slave, the negro and the wog. What he wants from her is respect.

The distinction which Leclerc draws between women's oppression, which is *primarily psychological*, and the oppression of all other human beings, which is primarily material, is as arbitrary as it is radical. All oppression produces a psychological advantage – respect – among other benefits. It shows a singular lack of political sense, and quite simply a lack of knowledge of *contemporary* political movements, to ignore this. You do not need to look far. Militant American Blacks (what am I saying, even liberal American sociologists!) have written on this subject with regard to Black-white relations in the south. And if you hate translations, for those readers who like to have things in good French, see Aimé Césaire and Franz Fanon. The self-sacrifice and admiration of slaves and servants are the themes of a whole, touching literature. Flaubert and Jack London, to name but two, have devoted immortal and universally known short stories to it.

'Respect' is however but *one* benefit among others – albeit it is also a *means* to get the others. It allows:

1   The extortionate nature of the services rendered by the oppressed to be veiled, making them appear freely given.
2   The mechanisms of the extortion also to be veiled. Thus the serf does not give (i.e. is not seen to give) his work to the lord gratuitously (i.e. because the latter has appropriated the means of production, the land). He is seen as giving it in recognition of the protection he receives from his lord (against the other lords, i.e. against the likes of himself).
3   Above all it allows extortion to take *diverse forms*. This is not something which distinguishes the oppression of women from other oppressions. Rather it is something which distinguishes oppressions of allegiance, of *personal dependence* (slavery, serfdom, marriage) from oppressions of *impersonal* dependence (capitalist exploitation). Personal dependents (wives of husbands, serfs of lords, slaves of owners) do not owe a precise gift of a particular kind or an amount of time to their masters, but rather their entire capacity to work, which the master can use as he thinks fit.

Respect, admiration and love are, however, also satisfactions, rewards, in and of themselves.

Because 'the man' (to follow Leclerc's use of essences) may sometimes dispense with a particular piece of work from his wife, Leclerc deduces that he can *always* do without her *labour power*. Because respect is one of the benefits of oppression, she concludes that it is the most important one in relations between men and women. Because she has decreed it to be the most important one, she leaps to the conclusion that it is the determining benefit: that material benefits are but *by-products* and, further, that they are *contingent* – not necessary – by-products.

Idealism and its incarnation, psychologism, are clearly at work here. Leclerc takes the manner in which oppression is justified and continued for its real cause; and she concludes from this:

That he (The man) sometimes makes her (the woman) sweat blood and kill herself with work is only a particular consequence of their type of relationship and is not at all determining.

'A particular consequence of their type of relationship' – how nicely put! And what a nice nothing, because what, between two people or two groups, is *not* a 'particular consequence of their type of relationship'?

When we have finished admiring, we can clearly recognize a variant of the ideological account which says that women do the housework, not because this is how they *earn their living*, but for love and 'freely'. An account which says that it is but a statistical accident, a fortuitous coincidence, that all women have chosen to prove their love in the same way and at the same time.

Once respect has been set up as *the* prime mover and *the* benefit men derive from the oppression of women, any material oppression is automatically excluded as a motive and benefit. Women's being killed by work stays as a *fact*, and an embarrassing fact; but the theory of respect goes on to show us that it is necessary only from a psychological point of view.

It is necessary that domestic work should be seen as lowly, humble . . . it is even necessary for the woman to suffer so as to bear witness of her respect.

The loop is looped. What women suffer is not due to their exploitation; on the contrary, their exploitation derives from their suffering. It is but a means to make them suffer. And to make them suffer is not even the objective: suffering itself is but a means to prove devotion. It is no one's fault (?) if devotion can only be proved by suffering, and it is pure chance if in the course of suffering women perform certain work from which men profit, again by chance. They would be equally happy if women could suffer while doing nothing.

This is an interesting theory in that it shows how, not content with learning the lessons of the ideologies of various epoques, Leclerc has sought to integrate them. We find the popular nineteenth-century doctrine according to which the wealth of the rich was but a demonstration of their moral superiority, and the poverty of the poor the result of (the punishment for?) their immorality; set alongside the more 'scientific' doctrine which in the same period made surplus-value the 'recompense' for the frugality of the capitalist. To these she has added the triumphant psychologism of the twentieth century – psychoanalysis – which (as seen in its most edifying expression in *The Night Porter*) explains concentration camps by the 'masochism' of the Jews, and the oppression of women by the 'sadism' of men.

Leclerc thus unites psychologism and biologism (the other incarnation of idealism) – which is not surprising since psychologism, biologism and idealism are the three udders of sexist ideology. The reversal of causality – the belief that the ideological superstructure (the devaluation of women) is the cause and not the effect of the social structure – is not one idealist interpretation among others: it is the dominant ideology itself. Naturalism – the popular version of biologism – is both the expression and the prop of idealism. Because the 'theory' previously mentioned stresses that the division of tasks between women and men should be seen as derived from (and of the same order as) sexual division in procreation, it is an *indispensable* condition of this indispensable division that the problematic of valuation be situated at the level of moral values, and *only* at this level – that it be abstracted from the material base of the evaluation.

Idealism needs biologism further, since it asserts that ideas – values – steer the world and, more precisely, determine social organization. The origin of these values must therefore be sought *outside* society. Whether this origin be in the natural order (immanent) or in the universe of ideals (transcendent) makes no difference. One can in any case pass easily from one to the other: values can be attributed to nature. In both cases the values are extra-social and extra-human. Immanence and transcendence are two interchangeable forms in which society can project its creations outside itself. It is then possible for 'man' (in the person of Annie Leclerc) 'to be paid in the counterfeit of his dreams'.

Biologism is thus but one way of attempting to find extra-social explanations for facts. But it is a form of explanation one can be sure of coming across at some stage or another in most authors. What is astounding in Leclerc is that her search for the immanent production of transcendent values leads her to the aberration that the origin of the values of oppression – or as she puts it 'masculine' values – resides in . . . *men's mode of ejaculation*. You read aright.

Countering sexist ideology, or revamping it?

To use men's way of thinking (and that of other oppresssors, since I don't think that ideology is secreted like a hormone, i.e. by a type of biological person) cannot, by definition, either explain or clarify the oppression of women: and Leclerc proves it *a contrario*. Ideology cannot be used against itself, and in this sense the term 'counter-ideology' is false, because a true counter-ideology would be an analysis which unmasked ideology for what it is: ideology. To invert the conclusion while using the same method does not destroy ideology, nor does it produce a counter-ideology. It merely produces another ideology, or rather another version of the same ideology. This is precisely what Leclerc does.

To struggle over ideology is, of course, useful in at least two ways (i.e. it has two meanings or two principal functions).

1 It is useful in analysing the dominant ideology *as* ideology, i.e. in showing that it is a *rationalization* for the actual oppression of women. To prove it is a rationalization we must prove it is, first, false, and second, useful to the system. This implies, or rather requires, that we produce a non-ideological – non-idealist – explanation of the oppression of women.
2 It is useful in helping us to acquire another image of ourselves. This requires the destruction of the negative image of women given by the ideology. To do this it is not enough to show that the content of the ideology – the negative image – is false. Once again it must be shown to be ideological. That is to say, the false content must be related to *what produces it* and *what it justifies*: the social, and more precisely the oppressive, structures of society.

Leclerc's book however fails to reach the first objective (to explain the oppression of women) for the same reasons as it fails to reach the second (to give women a new understanding of themselves).

If we look closely we can see that Leclerc's reasoning is the exact mirror image of sexist ideology. It is inverted but identical. Like sexist ideology, she bases the antagonism of the sexes on an antagonism of *values*. Just as men 'prove' women's 'inferiority', so she 'proves' our 'superiority'. In order to do this she resorts to using a *natural order of values* – as does sexist ideology.

Leclerc concludes, not that 'the natural order of values' is an ideological construct, but that we have read it wrongly – or perhaps even that it has been wrongly constructed. We have replaced the *true order* – which exists – with a forgery. Her whole account is aimed at showing this. But first – like all ideologies – she has to assert a *supreme value*, a value unto itself, a value which can be evaluated only in terms of itself and which is thus the source and the measure of all other values. The value is *Life*. Just as other standard measures in France are deposited at the Pavillon de Sèvres, so Leclerc deposits the life-measure in the firmament of Platonic ideals, which she calls 'the Universe of Values'. Life is to replace the (false) 'masculine' values which have usurped it.

Having done this, it only remains for her to 'show' that 'masculine' values are stripped of value when measured against this Value. They cannot fail so to be, since she calls them 'death values'. To show this she either cleverly (i.e. arbitrarily) chooses a few texts by phallocrats or notorious sots, like Malraux – which is foul play; or she cleverly (i.e. arbitrarily) interprets garbled quotations from less notorious phallo-crats, like Sartre. Finally, equally cleverly (i.e. by an abusive general-ization) she implies that her findings apply to the generality of men, i.e. to a biological category.

I would not deny that this affords great satisfaction to certain women and certain satisfaction to a great many women. It is always amusing to show an enemy that you can turn his way of seeing things back on him. But there is a big difference between amusing yourself and thinking you have got hold of the ultimate weapon; and it is dangerous to confuse the two. For just as you turn the weapon on him, so the enemy can turn it back again, etc.

What is surprising is not that Leclerc has played this little game, but that she really believes in it. The inversion of the masculine account which she produces should have demystified not only the conclusions but the very procedure for her. If a supreme value, a standard value, really existed it would be external to all authors, and thus the same for everyone. But whereas Leclerc sees the supreme values as Life, and the capacity to give life, St Augustine saw things differently. (I'll spare you the details . . .). Both of them, and I am sure fifteen or sixteen thousand others, chose their measure according to the conclusion they want to reach, and they establish it in advance.

Against her own advice, Leclerc uses throughout what she calls 'man's speech', i.e. the system of thought and the methods of oppression. Her *whole book* is an exercise in 'masculine' rhetoric: in ideology. We find in it all the procedures of this rhetoric: simplification, reduction, confusion of the part and the whole, and *substitution of analogy for analysis*. These procedures are particularly flagrant in a bravura section on the 'mode of ejaculation'. To be able to *deduce* the existential manner of functioning of a whole category of individuals from the functioning (or rather the interpretation of the functioning) of one of their physical organs, involves an unscrupulous indulgence in a few sophisms which derive directly from magical thinking. It is:

1 to move directly from the fact of physical sexual differentiation to the hypothesis (treated as a given, even though to this day it has not a trace of a foundation even as a hypothesis) that psychological differences exist between the sexes;
2 to assume also something which is not only difficult to imagine, but which is quite impossible: the replication of physiological mechanisms at the psychological level;
3 to assume that the functioning of the whole person is *a* aptly *b* sufficiently i described ii explained by the functioning of certain of his or her cells;
4 completely to discredit the intervention of consciousness, which is not only what distinguishes the psychological level from other levels, but also what establishes it as a distinct level;
5 in return (as one might say) for this removal of consciousness from the psyche, to describe physiological processes by terms which apply only to the phenomena of consciousness (activity, passivity, etc.) – in short, to inject into physiology the very consciousness refused to the psyche.

We can recognize here the same reasoning as enabled St Paul, Freud, Suzanne Lilar, St Augustine, Menie Gregoire, and others we'll let pass, to create their various theories of 'femininity'. We can further recognize the reasoning which allows the 'scientific' inference of the 'passivity' of women (creatures fully endowed with consciousness) from the passivity imputed to . . . the ovum, and the 'activity' of men (creatures fully endowed etc.) from the activity attributed to a spermatozoid. Leclerc purely and simply inverts the conclusions while starting with the same premises. To attribute as she does a 'death value' to ejaculation is to return the ideology of 'A woman is determined by her uterus' to its sender: 'A man is determined by his ejaculation'.

This inversion is again demonstrated in her conclusion to the fable of origins, which she no more spares us than have Freud, Engels, etc. She does not even have the merit of originality in making such an inversion, since Mead, Bettleheim and Hayes, among others, long ago found parallels for 'penis envy'. Fear of castration (according to Hayes) or jealousy of the ability to bear children (according to Mead and Bettleheim) become (according to Leclerc) '[the man's] resentment of his mother'. It is not a new temptation to want to explain the social by the psychological. On the contrary it is as old as the hills.

Nothing in *Parole de femme* gives even the beginnings of the shadow of a key with which to approach the problem of the oppression of women, let alone an explanation of it. Whether discussing the present situation, or its origins, Leclerc, like others, always ends in the same impasse because the same approach is to be found everywhere: because idealism rages everywhere. Leclerc has made a catalogue of motives for men's oppression of women; but just as a mass of bad reasons do not make one good reason, so a pile of motives does not give an analysis. The initial question remains. Why and how do men do it? It may be that men want and need respect. (And are they alone in this?) But what is it that gives them the *means* to obtain it? To suggest that their biology condemns them to disparage life-values does not explain what enables them to impose their 'counter-values'. They (and indeed she) are free to experience 'resentment' of their mother, and indeed even worse things. But between even the most intense hatred and *vengeance*, between the thought and the act, is a big step: that of *instrumental possibility*. And this is the thing which interests us, and it is this which, by chance, everyone passes over. We are given instead 'reasons' for men's domination *which presuppose it*: the existing 'predominance of their values' and their need for respect.

Leclerc's account is invalid, however, not because she has chosen to situate her account at the level of values. By itself this would at most have meant risking reducing the interest of her book because it has already (indeed often) been done before. More than one author (female or male) has shown, convincingly, that the devaluation of women is not only unjust but also in contradiction with the avowed values of our culture. The contrast between the shabby pursuits of men and their pretensions has rarely escaped women's attention, and when they bring it to light they are always sure to score a bull's-eye. This can provide emotional outlets, and we should never spurn the opportunity for a good laugh, but Leclerc knows (for she says it) that if ridicule could kill, the male of the species would be on the verge of extinction. What then can she hope to gain from the 'cut of ridicule'?

Her approach is also not invalid because she tries to attack the myths which make the biology of women itself into a handicap. Quite the opposite. This ideological struggle is welcome, good, useful and necessary; and this is doubtless why the book, while on the whole reactionary, has been of interest even to radical feminists.

Her fault, indeed her sin – what makes her work invalid – is that she never relates these values to the material and social structure. This would be a simple omission if she had chosen to talk of values at a *purely descriptive level*, as many others have done. But she does not limit herself to this. She attributes them a causal role in oppression on the one hand, and, what is more, she explains these values by other values. It is thus no longer a question of the choice of a level of description, but the choice of an explanatory theory. This stance voids the two objectives of her book: namely, the recovery by women of a positive image of their biological selves; and the production of a theory of oppression.

Leclerc's treatment of the devaluation of the biological 'condition' of women is distorted and felled by her idealism, mainly because we cannot recover a positive image of ourselves solely or principally by recovering a positive image of our 'procreative' functions. We must also and above all develop a capacity to define ourselves other than by these functions. We must recover as specifically part of women (i.e. as an equally integral and defining part of ourselves) our *non-procreative* organs and functions. It is a real indictment of the present view of women that this should be necessary.

While Leclerc's book strives to revalue women's procreative functions, it also strives to imprison us in them: to reduce our being, our pleasures, our value (and even our whole value, 'The undeniable, original value of woman', the quality of life-possessing, etc.) to them. In short, she continues to define women in the same way as men (and the general ideology) do: by their relationship to men, and more particularly by their usefulness to men. Our use lies in our ability to bring into the world the only thing men cannot make.

Revaluing women's bodies

We do nevertheless certainly need to revalue our bodies, our physical way of being in the world, even though this will only make sense as part of a broader attack. Leclerc however both dissociates this objective from a collective political struggle (which she does not envisage) and, even at the level of women's physicality where she places herself, she allows a major ambiguity to reign: just how in fact the revaluation is to occur. This is because she totally isolates the ideological level. She considers it the most important level; she considers it independent of other levels; and she considers it the *only* field of battle.

When trying to 'revalue' our bodies she uses only words which denote very physical things and acts: vagina, childbirth, menstruation etc. However, while there is certainly a physical, non-social element in our bodies and actions, there is also a social component. It is essential to recognize that the meaning of periods for instance, is not *given* with and by the flow of blood, but, like all *meaning*, by consciousness, and thus by society.

A particular culture not only imposes a meaning on an event which, being physical, is in and of itself bereft of meanings. Society (culture) also imposes a material form through which the event is lived, or rather is moulded in a constraining way. A 'pure' childbirth does not exist, but rather childbirth in Europe, Africa, Polynesia, etc. You do not have 'a' period, the same in all situations and all countries. You have *your* period, different in each culture and subculture. In the west we have unpleasant periods because the culture devalues the flow of blood. It is an objectively disagreeable material event, made so by the society. It is not just a question of *my attitude* to my periods. The attitudes of others, their requests, their expectations, their demands are for me as concrete, as tangible, as a chair. The social period is a material framework of conduct for the individual.

In France, we have to hide our periods. This is not my idea, not my own invention; it is a constraint imposed on me which is quite outside (and material for) me. As Leclerc herself says, people compel me to behave 'as on other days'. But this is materially difficult, whatever my 'values' may be. Whatever my interpretation of the flow of blood may be, I cannot experience this obligation to pretend as other than something disagreeable. Not only am I not able to talk about it, it is also not an acceptable excuse for absence. (When I was young, whenever I had a pain during my period I used to talk of attacks of appendicitis.)

I do not have the right to have my periods. This is shown very simply and effectively by the fact that, in addition to the taboo on my talking about them, I also do not have the means to have them. The society is materially understood and made for a population without periods. To have a period away from home is always to be in a situation which is, if not dramatic, at least extremely embarrassing. There are neither sanitary towels nor tampons in French public toilets (nor in many in England); there is nowhere to change and nowhere to throw tampons or towels – in doing so one risks blocking the WC. Leclerc is clear about this constraining character. Why, she asks, should I have to be as on other days? I am *not* as on other days. But she seems to ignore the essential question: how can women change their *attitude* while having a period remains the same *concrete experience?*

Society does much to make us think that the material conditions of periods or motherhood derive from the physical event: that their *socially constructed* conditions are *natural* conditions. And we have believed it for a long time. Many see no possibility of getting rid of the disagreeableness of a period or of being a mother, except by getting rid of the physical event itself. Leclerc follows the same reasoning, even though she inverts the conclusion: for her, too, periods or motherhood are entirely natural – but naturally 'good'. She ignores with good intent what the society ignores with ill intent: that culture has transformed these events, in themselves neutral, into actual *handicaps*.

There are thus not one but *two* cultural interventions:

1 the devaluation of women's bodies and physiology;
2 the material handicap created by the social conditions.

The two are obviously linked. It is even easier for society to devalue the flow of blood – the fact of being female – if all women can verify that it really is a handicap to have a period. Conversely, it is even easier for society to impose these conditions as inevitable once women are convinced that periods – the fact of being female – is a natural misfortune. It is in the interests of society to hide the fact that periods are not a natural phenomenon but a constructed phenomenon. In this situation, ideology – the interpretation of the phenomenon – plays an important part. It is internalized and reappears among those involved under the guise of *strongly felt shame*. But this ideological aspect is absolutely inseparable from the material part. The two are continually and necessarily part of one another. To hide one's sanitary towels is at first an external constraint; it gives rise to subjective shame; and finally, in a third phase, the hiding appears to be the *expression* of the shame which in fact caused it.

Women in devaluing their periods are not only obeying their brain-washing; not only 'adopting masculine values'. We are also reacting, and in a healthy (non-masochistic) way, to a real handicap. However, when we devalue our periods as such – as a physical phenomenon – in addition to depreciating ourselves, we accept the ideological version: that the handicap is natural and not social. The struggle thus consists in separating and distinguishing elements which are distinct but which the society confounds.

But if we do not analyse what is social, what is *constraining*, in the phenomenon currently experienced by all women under the name of 'periods', we are playing society's game. Because (if one does not make allowance for the social) it is impossible to feel proud of something which is *actually* unpleasant; to value periods. In addition, if it *were* possible, it would lead, in so far as conditions were unchanged, to our 'accepting' the handicap – as society asks us to; and all arguments which lead us better to accept social constraints are dangerous, and can never ever be styled 'liberating'.

This is why the 'revaluation of women's bodies', without further specification, is an extremely ambiguous project. On the one hand it can mean a struggle against the actual handicap – which is the necessary condition for the revaluation of the natural function. It is only once it is materially revalued that it can become subjectively experienced as positive. And the fight to change attitudes is itself only positive on the condition that it changes something concrete in women's lives: that it leads into a struggle against the constraints imposed on our bodies.

On the other hand, 'revaluation' can mean the *abandonment* of this struggle. It can go in the same direction as the ideology. The latter says that all the dissatisfactions women experience are due to a refusal of themselves, of their bodies. The 'revaluation' undertaken by psycho-analysis, by the feminine press in France, and by Margaret Mead (among others) is destined to make us swallow the social handicap in the same mouthful as the physical phenomenon. That mouthful verges on masochism. It leads to women being made to accept that to love themselves is to love suffering.

'Self-acceptance' as a value is not neutral. It addresses itself only to female individuals, and it is of recent origin. It appeared at precisely the time when feminism was born, as a new ideological weapon to make women accept their submission. Thus 'valuation' or 'revaluation' of womanhood should be very closely examined. It can go in two directly opposite directions. A new version of the dominant ideology can be camouflaged under the guise of 'liberation'. The term 'self-acceptance' is also suspect because of the problem of what it is 'to accept oneself'. What is the 'self' one accepts? In so far as the 'self' is taken without question, is equated with the historical person (albeit the historical aspect is not mentioned and is thus implicitly denied – the historical individual being considered as a natural person), this is an ahistoric and reactionary notion. It seems that Leclerc's procedure (whatever its intentions), by its omissions and its implications, objectively goes in the same direction as the dominant ideology, and thus furthers the repression of women.

Domestic work or women's material oppression

Leclerc notes that *everything* women do is lowly valued – and that this includes women's work and housework. She none the less comes back time and again to the question of the *intrinsic nature*, the *intrinsic interest*, the *intrinsic value* of housework. Clearly, however, it is not what is intrinsic to housework that is in question, because everything which women do has little value. So, how does she deal with this?

She replies that men 'are mistaken'. That women's work, *including* housework, is valuable. She argues on the same grounds as those which allow men to assert, equally peremptorily, that it is not. She ought rather to have replied to her own question: 'What does "the interest" or "the value" of a task mean?' She would then have realized that the interest and the value of a task is unrelated to its nature and is determined by *other criteria*. It is the relations of production within which a task is done which explain, simultaneously, its subjective interest and its objective (i.e. its social) value.

So what does 'the interest of a task' mean? And, more precisely, what does 'task' mean in this phrase?

The word task is mystifying as used here in that it is employed as equivalent to, as synonymous with a trade or a job. To reduce a trade or a job to a technical task allows a false question to be put: namely, what is more interesting about the *tasks* of a company director than the *tasks* of a schoolteacher; the *tasks* of schoolteacher than the *tasks* of a road sweeper? The sophism of the question lies in the fact that in this problematic the definition of a road sweeper is: 'a man who pushes a broom'. Nothing could be further from the truth. A road sweeper is a man who pushes a broom *on the instructions of someone else* and in exchange for a *derisory wage*.

We can thus see that the very fact of posing the question of 'the intrinsic interest of household tasks' rests on confusion between the technical task and the job. The latter comprises not only the technical task but also its *conditions of performance and remuneration* (in money and prestige), the social status of those who do it, etc. The question as put totally obscures all these factors and is thus ideological. It must be renounced. We shall see later how *not* giving it up leads Leclerc into other blind alleys.

Leclerc questions the reasons which have been put forward for deeming domestic work uninteresting. She is right. As a *task*, housework is neither more nor less interesting or stupefying than other tasks. This is proven by the fact that one can maintain (equally convincingly each time) that domestic work is particularly expressive or creative, or on the contrary that it is particularly repetitive and alienating. To doubt the validity of the judgement should logically have led Leclerc to glimpse, fleetingly at least, that the reason for the low value set on domestic work cannot reside in its 'interest': that the *criteria* employed are not good ones.

But no, she sticks to them. She does not question the criteria themselves, but simply the way they have been used. She takes sides in the sterile argument about housework being 'creative/repetitive'. She does not challenge the question but the answer, without seeing that the question is badly posed – and not by chance. If she could see that it is not women's *tasks* which are devalued, since we do all sorts of tasks, but our *jobs*, she would be all set to pose the right question: namely, for whom do women do this work; in what relations of production is it done? But she persists in thinking that domestic work has been devalued because it is 'judged uninteresting' (note that she totally identifies social utility and subjective *interest*). She persists in her search for the criteria of interest (or usefulness) which are supposedly extra-social and based on an experience both subjective (the subject's) and independent of social relations.

In this she follows de Beauvoir who sees (saw?) the oppression of women as due to the 'immanence' (!) of their tasks. The 'immanence' and the 'subjective interest' of a task are of the same order: they are mystifying concepts in that they suppose and suggest that social relations are based, in the final analysis, on relationships with things, with the natural world. But not only do relationships with the natural world not exist, but to *disguise relationships between people* as relations between or to things, is (or should be) a well-known characteristic of bourgeois ideology. (I refuse to give page references to the great ancestor who first taught us this.)

The tale of Leclerc is a good example of that standing of history on its head which is typical of ideological thought. She describes a hypothetical society where women would be the superiors because they 'give life'. She thus postulates a 'natural value'. But this phrase is quite simply a contradiction in terms. Nature does not know and cannot produce values. Values are produced by societies, human societies, as are all phenomena which imply *consciousness*. The idea that a society's values could originate *outside it* is simply a return to Platonic universals.

Throughout her account it is clear that for Leclerc the social hierarchy is a hierarchy of *values*, and that these values not only pre-exist the social order, but come from Nature. It is a reversal, a negation of materialist, or quite simply political thought, according to which if values have a function in the hierarchy, it is in so far as they reflect and justify it, as means created by and for it, and not as causes.

The source of the present hierarchy of the sexes

Leclerc follows all too many authors into the trap of seeking the explanation for the *present* hierarchy in the 'original conditions of humanity'. Since the conditions within which humanity evolved, and the form of the earliest social structures, have been (and will remain) unknown, it means that she can obviously only be using a pretext for projecting (or perhaps it would be fairer to say injecting) present conditions into pre-pre-history. At the end of this projection she (like others) makes the present situation re-emerge, with a history. Of course, it is not history proper which is being set up (historians can at least defend what did and did not happen in historical times, albeit feebly). She is setting up an 'origin' which can only be 'reconstructed': in truth, invented. This mythical reconstruction is a negation of the spirit if not the letter of historicism.

Leclerc thus goes ahead with her projection of what poor old 'primitive humanity' must have been like; and although she does not cite her sources here, they are recognizable. She uses Engels' theory, which is decidedly well worn. According to him (1884), the first division of labour was 'the natural division of labour between men and women'. This was the first – meaning the greatest – of Engels' mistakes. Having shown that all divisions of labour are the consequence and the means of hierarchy and oppression, Engels none the less found the division of labour between the sexes to be 'natural'; and he said that in this case, and in this case *only*, hierarchy *followed* and did not *precede* the division. He thereby disavowed his own method and so threw a cloud not only on this analysis, but on all his others. For if one can turn the marxist causal order upside down for women, why not in other cases? The worm was in the bud of marxist method. However, a hundred years have elapsed since Engels wrote and many studies have shown that the *content* of the division between men and women is *variable, and hence not natural*.

But let us leave Engels and follow Leclerc, who, again following many others, looks for the cause of hierarchy and differential evaluation of jobs not only in their origins, but also in the different utility of the jobs themselves. It is interesting here to compare her account with that of Elizabeth Gould Davis (1973). Davis holds that the 'original' women did not do 'what is commonly believed', but rather 'useful' things – agriculture, etc. – and that *consequently* (it is the 'consequently' which is interesting) they *must* have been at the top of the hierarchy. Leclerc however maintains that the 'original' women did indeed do 'what is commonly believed', but she then argues that these things were (are) as 'useful' as other things which men did/do). She and Davis thus disagree on whether the issue is to show that women did things which were judged useful by our culture (i.e. that *we have been mistaken about the nature of their past tasks*); or to show that women did things which were judged useless, but which are 'in reality' useful (i.e. that we have been mistaken as to what is useful). Both rely on the naïve idea that the *social value* of jobs is determined by their *social utility*. Someone a hundred years ago showed that if any group was 'useful' it was the workers. So is it just a question of the ruling class having been 'mistaken' – of their obviously not having *noticed* the usefulness of the proletariat?

Leclerc thus makes the same mistake historically as she makes in analysing contemporary society. We know that the sexual division of labour varies, but that in cultures where men do what women do in our culture, their work is not lowly, but on the contrary highly valued. We would have to be blind not to see that it is not the intrinsic utility of a task which determines the authority which is commanded (and the prestige which is received) by its performer. On the contrary, it is the authority which the performer commands which determines the society's appreciation of the 'utility' of the task.

One thing is common to all the jobs done by women, and this is not their contents. It is their relations of production. This answers Leclerc's questions: 'Why has woman's lot always been judged inferior, lowly, etc.?' There is, therefore, no longer any need to resort to looking at the content of our lot. Indeed it is *impossible* to resort to this, since the details of women's situation vary.

What is the difference between planting millet and planting sweet potatoes? In one African society, however, one is 'glorious' — high status, the other 'humiliating' — low status. Women plant millet which is appropriated by the men; and the men plant sweet potatoes which they appropriate for themselves. High and low status thus express in the realm of moral values the reality of the relations of distribution of material values between men and women. But they do more: they justify these positions. In a reversal typical of idealist thought processes (which are here clearly demonstrated to be coterminous with the ideology) the inferior value of women's work (which is the expression and therefore the consequence of women's inferior status) is advanced as its cause. Women's dispossession of their produce is 'explained' (justified) by the 'inferiority' of their work, by their doing less important things. In the same way women and reproduction are devalued in our own culture not because men happen to be dominant and because they 'happen' not to value life, but because women have children *for men*.

We can now pose another question which Leclerc does not ask (and with reason). If all work done in certain conditions is devalued – those conditions being that the product of the work is appropriated by some- one other than the producer – what then is the purpose of a division of labour?

If one looks closely at the sexual division of labour, and if this is defined as a differential and rigid attribution of tasks according to sex (i.e. as a *technical* division of labour by sex), we see that it does not really exist. For instance, women keep accounts for their husbands, i.e. they do the same work as highly paid (and respected, i.e. valued) accountants. They act diplomatically for their husbands, i.e. they do the same operations as highly paid (and respected, etc.) diplomats. . . . When we stop confusing the *task* – the technical operation – with *the whole job* – we see that the technical division of labour tends to vanish, to disappear as an empirical fact, under the observer's very eyes. The differential valuation of jobs does not spring from the technical aspect of the division of labour. We then see that the question put by Leclerc is remarkably circular. .She asks why a given job (e.g. a wife doing the accounts for her husband) is not prestigious; but the non-prestige is already an integral part of this job: doing a task *unpaid for someone else*.

In so far as a certain division of labour by sex does exist, it is not a question of tasks done, but of the status of the work as a whole. The task is only part of this. Thus it is said that domestic work is women's work; but this is only true if what is meant is the status, the conditions of doing it, the relations of production of this work. It is not true of the technical operations which comprise domestic work at the instrumental level: washing, ironing, cooking, etc. Launderers, washers-up and chefs do the same *technical* operations. What makes housework housework is not each particular operation, nor even their sum total; it is their particular organization, which is itself due to the relations of production in which the person doing them finds herself. The place where they are performed, for example, appears as a 'technical' feature, but it is directly derived from the relations of production. The fact that housework is done 'at home' flows from its being done 'for the husband without payment'.

Like everybody else, Leclerc thinks she can justify her faulty analysis of the present by finding it a base in the past. She thus projects what she thinks is the reason (in the sense of 'good reason' – i.e. good grounds) for the division of labour by sex back to an origin – .and she gives us a well-known reconstruction. She treats us to the hackneyed (but always sickening) scene of a pseudo 'primitive horde', where all the women are pregnant and breastfeeding (all at once, and constantly) and where all the men are hunting (all at the same time, etc.) – even though she earlier denounced as a myth the idea that motherhood engenders incapacity.

Why did it have to be a man – Theodore Sturgeon (1960) – who first ridiculed these 'historical reconstructions' and their authors? Who asked why the strongest women were not hunting with the strongest men, while the weakest women stayed in the camp with the weakest men? It is an indication of the prevailing level of idiocy that we have to admit that, in the present state of things, his piece of science fiction is a daring effort of the imagination. Not that it goes far enough, for we must question not only the assumptions: 1 that strength was more important then than it is nowadays; and 2 that individuals were classified according to their strength; we must also question 3 why they were classified into only *two* classes. As soon as the 'primordial encampment' is evoked, any and every fantasy becomes permissible.

But in fact the fantasies of primitive societies are strangely well ordered. They are collective fantasies. They all follow the same lines.

1 All the women are pregnant or nursing at the same time, and, furthermore, all the women are *always* pregnant or nursing.
2 Pregnancy or breastfeeding makes women totally incapable of meeting their own needs.
3 To imagine women would be perpetually pregnant if this made them incapable implies that they had no control of their fecundity. (If they had had control they would certainly not have allowed themselves to be so disabled.)
4 This implies (and the more one sees pregnant women in the primordial camp the more necessary is the implication) that women must have *already been dominated*.

There is thus, again, a circular argument. Domination is again supposedly being explained by a situation which already presupposes it.

(For *actual facts* about the existing economies which most nearly approach what could have been the first economies, i.e. those of hunters and gatherers, see Sahlins (1974), especially his chapter on 'The original affluent society'. Briefly, such economies are exactly the opposite of western myths. Gathering provides ample food, and is neither arduous nor time-consuming. In a few hours women, including pregnant women, can collect an abundant supply to feed themselves. They do it every day and still find time (as moreover do the men) to take plenty of little naps, thank you very much.)

These collective myths of origin are, furthermore, self-contradictory. Even if we accept, for the purposes of argument, that pregnancy and breastfeeding occasion, not total incapacity (that goes beyond the limits of good sense), but at least reduced mobility, how can we explain the move from the partial and temporary incapacity of a few women to the permanent exclusion of all women from entire categories of activity or, more accurately, social positions? The latter (a rigid sexual division of activities and status) is however presented as a *natural* consequence of the former. It is very clear that it is not a question of a *natural* consequence, nor a concern with the 'rationalization' of work. It is rather a case of shutting one's eyes to the fact that, in this move, 'nature' not only does not play, but cannot play, any role whatsoever, and that the social must necessarily intervene.

An attempt is made to veil this intervention by presenting the passage from situation A to situation B as being a very 'gradual', 'unconscious', etc. *evolution*. But whatever the time over which this transition may have been spread, it is not a question of a gradation, but of an abrupt change. It is a question of a passage from the natural to the social. The date or the duration is irrelevant. The inventors of this 'transition' cannot avoid the fact that the assumed slowness of the process cannot warrant a non-existent continuity between the natural and the social. Since this is in fact what they are claiming, they are making a horrendous epistemological (or simply logical) leap.

It is not a question of our needing another, different, reconstruction; of adding another stone to the edifice when it is its very foundations which are tottering. It is rather a matter of not going back into an unacceptable problematic. For in fact, under cover of putting an historical question, an ahistorical one has actually been posed: 'What are the *natural* reasons for male supremacy?' It is being suggested that the 'original society' was, must have been, less 'social' than the societies which succeeded it.

It is also a question of it being thought, without it being said, that if it could be 'proved' that the oppression of women is due in the final instance to our 'weakness', this would equally establish that this oppression is legitimate. In this case, and *only in this case*, it is held that the fact that domination is materially *possible* makes it morally *just*. There is thus an implicit interpretation of the facts that are held to be established; and this interpretation (once again intended only for the case of women) ties together *inevitability* and *legitimacy*. This is moreover the *only* reason why an attempt to prove that the oppression of women was 'inevitable' is made. The premises of this 'question' thus already include a moral assumption, a political judgement, and an unacceptable 'scientific' assumption. Present *social* structures and rationalizations – in particular the transformation of women's biology into a handicap by oppression

– are injected into the 'nature' (deemed more 'constraining') of this mythical and barely social society. In other words, the culture of our own society is attributed to the 'nature' of a hypothetical society.

It is thus, to repeat, not the answers to the question of origins which are in question. It is the question itself. We must quite simply abandon the problematics with which it is in practice associated and from which it is logically inseparable – namely, the psychologistic and idealist problematic of domination as a consequence of 'intolerance of difference';[4] and its premises: the 'natural' division of lots, the 'natural' opposition of social categories (identification of males with men, females with women), etc. So too must the other false questions we have encountered (the discussion of the 'intrinsic' interest or usefulness of tasks). The political problematics which flow from all of these, or are at least associated with them – 'revaluation' of the 'situations' of men and women; the revindication of 'difference' between the sexes, etc. – must consequently also go. They are invalid because they come from idealist problematics and because they themselves, inevitably, are idealist and hence reactionary. They transform the *concrete* struggle of *concrete* individuals against a *concrete* oppression into a quarrel over 'values' or a conflict of 'essences' (when it is not one of 'principles').

We have thus arrived at the following conclusion: if a rigid division of technical work between the sexes *were* to be established anywhere, it would be a fact of culture not of nature. In our own society, however, it is not a case of certain tasks being forbidden to women, but of our being allowed to do them only in certain conditions. It is not that women may not act diplomatically, but that we may not be diplomats; it is not that women may not drive a tractor, but that we may not get on to one as the boss, nor even as a *paid* worker, etc.

A technical division of labour is thus not necessary to the sexual hierarchy. Does one therefore exist? And if it does, where and why? *This* would be a valuable topic for research. The only hypothesis we can make (in our present state of non-information) is that where it does exist – where *tasks* and not *jobs* are forbidden to women – it is because for some reason these tasks have but one mode of performance. In other words, in cases where the task is indissociable from its mode of performance, *tasks which cannot be done in a subordinate mode must be forbidden to women.*

It appears in sum, that:

1   The sexual division of labour is not a division of tasks but a division of jobs.

2   Jobs comprise as an integral part of their definition relations of production: the relationship of producer to product.

3   The division of specific tasks by sex, where it exists, is a by-product of the hierarchy of statuses (whose basis is obviously the relations of production). For example, in Africa the different relations of production also, and rigidly, correspond to different material products. This animal or vegetable product is *always* produced in a given mode of production, that other product in another mode.

Protofeminism or antifeminism?

When Annie Leclerc says, 'I don't ask why this lot has been given to women, but why this lot has been judged inferior', she is way off course. She cannot reply to the second question without asking the first; and if she doesn't ask the first question it is because, like many others, she wonders why the job is devalued, but considers only the task. She evades the crucial intermediary variable: the fact that the job is defined not only by the task, but also and above all by the relations of production. It is work done in a subordinate relationship, and not the task, which is devalued, and for one very simple reason – namely, that it is relations of production which devalue (or give value): it is the relationship of the producer to the *value* produced.

Consequently, as soon as *a* 'lot' is attributed to women, Blacks or proletarians (the 'lot' consisting not of tasks but of jobs and thus relations of production) *the hierarchy (the 'valuation' in Leclerc's terms)* is set up. It is not established after, nor independently, but in and by the very process of attributing 'lots': by the social, not technical division of labour.

The question of subjective interest and moral evaluation of a task is resolved: these reflect a particular reality. The objective valuelessness (its unpaidness and the obligation to do it – the two are bound together) of domestic work is reflected in its lack of interest and low evaluation. Leclerc's claim that this work should be 'revalued' (i.e. given a higher place in the disincarnate universe of values) is therefore absurd, and also criminal. For once we know the origin of the objective value of housework, which has nothing to do with its social utility, to try to enrich its subjective value is purely and simply to reinforce the brainwashing which helps prevent women from rebelling against their enslavement.

This attempt is not new: a whole generation of American ideologues, including Margaret Mead (1958) and Ashley Montague (1952), not to bother to name the psychoanalysts, have been employed on it. They have done nothing more than improve the every day glorification of the role of wife and mother by presenting it under a pseudo-scientific – and worse, *pseudo-feminist* – disguise. Leclerc's conclusion is completely in line with this school, which Caroline Bird (1968) calls 'neo-masculinist': an antifeminism disguised as pseudo-feminism.

The ideas of this school are simple. The domination of women by men is bad and should cease. But there is no question of trivial things like women's economic dependence or their material oppression ceasing. No. It is all a question of Values. What is deplored is the lack of respect which women suffer. Similarly, women don't *do a job*, they *carry* values – moral values of course, the values of the 'female principle': gentleness, respect for life, etc. Women's 'secondary status' (oppression is a dirty word, or should be kept for those who really deserve it) comes from these values not being given their rightful status.

These values – not the women – have, however, a contribution to make to a world which, as everybody can see, is going awry. Fortunately – what luck! – feminine values, the above-mentioned gentleness, understanding, concern for others, innate aptitude for washing nappies, and other Platonic ideals, will counterbalance, if they are needed, the violence (dynamic) and closeness to death (promethean nature) of masculine values. Masculine values are good in themselves – indeed they are the fountainhead of the culture – but they should not be carried to extremes. And they have been, witness all the wars – and now pollution – caused by *values* (!) Could we but recognize and use the antidote which grows just beside the poison – how well-made the world is! – we could kill two birds with one stone. We could use feminine values to balance the world (to restore it to its natural equilibrium) and also keep women happy. Such an ideology is not only *based* on the idea of a total and equal partitioning of the world, it *extends and perfects* the idea: it even divides out universal values.

This school also, especially when applied to women, stresses the notion of *participation* so beloved of de Gaulle. Just as capital and labour must recognize that they are mutually necessary and must value each other to this extent, so must men and women. Now, mutually necessary men and women may be, but in what way? The proposition that 'without game there is no hunter' does not have the same meaning for the hunter as the proposition that 'without the hunter, there would be no game' has for the game. The 'complementarity' so vaunted by Leclerc, whether it be between capitalists and proletarians or between (social) men and (social) women, *has no other meaning*.

Postscript

Let me repeat, I have analysed *Parole de femme* not because it is unique but, on the contrary, because it speaks for a much wider current of thought. This current is important not because of the ideas it defends – which far from being original are on all points those of the dominant ideology – but because of its political position.

The women's movement has in fact released a general counter-offensive and backlash (as one could have expected). This is coming from all sides – from the university and the government, the right and the left – and is taking all sorts of forms – from obscene attacks (the most frank) to skilful recuperation of losses (the most dishonest and thus the most effective). Undoubtedly the extreme, and thus the most danger-ous, form of this recovery is the one which is most 'internal' to the movement on both the institutional and the political planes. The two characteristics of the trend which Leclerc's book demonstrates are 1   that it is expressed through a woman's voice, and 2   that it presents itself as aimed at the *liberation* of women.

Three months after this article was submitted for publication, an article appeared in the *Nouvel Observateur* (Righini 1974) which confirms that we are right not to treat Leclerc's book as an isolated case but as an example of a trend. The author follows Leclerc's procedure and cites her frequently, along with other neo-masculinists of previous generations, such as Lilar[5] and Breton. The English writer Penelope Gillott took exactly the same line in an article in *Cosmopolitan* (1974), as did the collective article on motherhood which appeared in a special issue of *Les Temps Modernes* (*Les chimères* 1974). Finally, it is said that *Parole de femme* bears an astonishing resemblance to a transcript of talks held in the group Psychoanalyse et Politique, and some women from this group have squarely accused Righini of stealing *their* ideas on 'otherness' and 'difference'.

The degrees of involvement of these women in groups within the women's movement are very different: Leclerc has never heard of the movement, Righini has crossed and then overtaken it, Gillott has 'taken part' and left, the motherhood collective and Psycho et Po claim to take part in and to be integral to it. The motives of the individuals and groups also doubtless differ; and there seems no evidence of these being concerted efforts. But they do show a trend in that, despite their lack of consultation, they all display major traits in common:

1   They start with an avowed concern for women's liberation – sincere or insincere (the question of actual individual motivation is irrelevant).
2   They use the ideology's problematics both in their analysis of oppression and in order to work out 'remedies' for it.
3   This leads on logically to a 'revamping' of the dominant ideology, only this time (and this is most important) it is presented as a demand for liberation.

It is as if the best way of escaping from the disturbing implications of the struggle were to pretend to lead them. This allows the same things to be done as before, but this time with a 'good revolutionary conscience', while pretending that 'from now on it's for other reasons'. It is as if the resistance to the challenge of feminism came mostly from the *interior* of its movement – just as for Gribouille the river was the only place where one could be protected from the rain. . . .[6]

The positions of this trend are presented as the results of using, and at the same time of *getting beyond*, feminist questioning. Here, it might be said, the ambiguity is clear. It is easier to think oneself *further along* a road if one has never used it, than if one has traversed it; to think oneself further on when one is not only elsewhere but *staying* elsewhere: when one has not even set off. In this way ante-feminist positions can be presented as positions which are not only feminist but even *post*-feminist (which in itself is suspect; and which, in the way it is always put forward, implies a gross deformation of feminism). A great danger lying in wait for the women's struggle today is that the 'before' of the feminist question can be presented as its 'after' – thus sparing us the trouble of fighting. An ideology which oppresses women – or rather the entire system of which ideology is but a part – may be presented as new *invention* and as a *means* to women's liberation. *Proto*feminism promoted as *post*-feminism and becoming militant is *anti*feminism.

Notes and references

1   See the comments in the newspapers, in particular that in the

Quotidien de Paris: 'This book, while part of the women's liberation movement, radically contests its foundations.' I am quoting from memory so the words are approximate, but there can be no doubt that as far as the writer was concerned it was intended as a compliment.

2 In the tendency called 'Psychoanalyse et Politique' (Psychoanalysis and Politics).

3 There is also a book by Luce Irigaray (1974) which is a psycho-analytic revision and revindication of 'woman' as 'the other'. This represents a different aspect of the establishment of this current of ideas and must be dealt with elsewhere (see Pedinelli-Plaza 1976).

4 This is explicit in Irigaray (1974).

5 Lilar's *Le malentendu de deuxieme sexe* is a book attacking Simone de Beauvoir, which seeks to 'prove' that de Beauvoir was 'wrong' by using reassurances from biologists that men and women *do* have different sex organs!

6 Gribouille is a famous French folk-character, created in the nineteenth century by the Comtesse de Ségur.

11. For a materialist feminism*

Feminism is above all a social movement. Like all revolutionary movements, its very existence implies two fundamental presumptions. First, that the situation of women is cause for revolt. This is a platitude, but this platitude entails a corollary, a second presumption, which is much less frequently admitted. People do not revolt against what is natural, therefore inevitable; or inevitable, therefore natural. Since what is resistible is not inevitable; what is not inevitable could be otherwise – it is arbitrary, therefore social. The logical and necessary implication of women's revolt, like all revolts, is that the situation can be changed. If not, why revolt? Belief in the possibility of change implies belief in the social origins of the situation.

The renewal of feminism coincided with the use of the term 'oppression'. Ideology (that is, common-sense, conventional wisdom) does not speak of 'women's oppression' but of 'the feminine condition'. The latter relates to a naturalistic explanation, to a belief in the existence of a physical constraint. This puts exterior reality out of reach and beyond modification by human action. The term oppression, on the other hand, refers to something arbitrary, to a political explanation and a political situation. Oppression and social oppression are therefore synonyms; or, rather, social oppression is a pleonasm. The notion of a political (that is a social) cause is integral to the concept of oppression.

The term oppression is therefore the base, the point of departure, of any feminist research, as of any feminist approach. Its use radically modifies the basic principles, not only of sociology, but of all the social sciences. It nullifies any 'scientific' approach which speaks of women in one way or another, at one level or another, but which does not include

* First published in *L'Arc*, 61 (1975). An English translation by Mary Jo Lakeland and Susan Ellis Wolf was published in *Feminist Issues*, 1, no. 2 (Winter 1981).

the concept of oppression. A feminist study is a study whose objective is to explain the situation of women. When this situation is defined as a situation of oppression, theoretical premises which do not include this concept, i.e. which exclude it, can be used only at the risk of incoherence. Having a feminist approach is thus not just a matter of applying the unchanged premises of the established sciences to the study of women, with good political intent. It is useless for feminists to try to develop such studies when their premises are nullified in each particular discipline.

The premises of sociology, for example, deny the oppression of women, and in consequence the discipline 1 cannot account for it – cannot find at the end what it denied at the beginning; and 2 can only mask the oppression, and to that extent contribute to its perpetuation. There are, of course, certain approaches within sociology which are compatible with feminism, with revolt; the notion of the social origin of social phenomena for instance. But this compatibility has remained virtual, because:

1 a theory can be called sociological without so being. Most sociological theories deny not only the oppression of women, but also the social itself. Functionalism, for example, is, in the last analysis, a typical case of psychological reductionism. Structuralism is equally psychologically reductionist, although differently from functionalism. Functionalism rests on Freudianism (on the universality of the emotional structures) while structuralism rests on the universality of cognitive structures. They both explain different social formations, and the phenomenon of the social itself, by human nature.
2 All these theories are expressions of idealism and thus totally incompatible with the revolt of oppressed groups. They affirm *a* that history is the product of an individual – universal – biological functioning; and *b* areas exist which are indifferent to, and independent of, relationships of power between groups.

A feminist – or a proletarian – science aims at explaining oppression. In order to do this, it has to start with oppression. If it is coherent, it inevitably comes up with a theory of history in which history is seen in terms of the domination of some social groups by others. Likewise it cannot at the start consider any area of reality or of knowledge, as outside this fundamental dynamic. A feminist interpretation of history is therefore 'materialist' in the broad sense; that is, its premises lead it to consider intellectual production as the result of social relationships, and the latter as relationships of domination.

The implications of this concern not only precise theories or areas – i.e. their content; they also directly concern the intrinsic character of these areas – the principles which constitute them (i.e. the principles according to which the real is divided into areas of knowledge). All categorization, all separation into areas, actually presupposes an implicit theory of human nature, of the nature of the social, and of history.[1]

The division of knowledge into tight areas is an effect and a tool of ideology, as is also the content of these areas or disciplines. The idea that there are separate areas of experience which are the concern of the different disciplines, each with its own methods, and that these can afterwards be joined so as to juxtapose their findings, is typically anti-materialist. For what is this confrontation, this highly vaunted 'interdisciplinarity'? It is in fact nothing but the result of the disciplinarity that it presupposes. The latter is founded on the postulate that subjectively distinct levels of experience – distinct in the subjectivity of our society – all obey their own 'laws': the psychological obeys the laws of the instincts, the social obeys the laws of interaction, etc.

The reactionary character of this approach can be seen very concretely for example in studies of the family. Here the sexual relationships of husband and wife, their economic relationships, and their social relationships, etc., are studied separately, as if they each obey a distinct and heterogeneous logic. These heterogeneous 'results' are then put together and we end up with an uninteresting mosaic. It is devoid of meaning; but this is precisely in the interest of 'science'. It thereby negates the profound unity of these 'levels', and the way in which they are all locations and means of oppression.

The objective (and the result) of official science and its division into disciplines is thus the rendering unintelligible of human experience. This is true not only of sociology but of all the disciplines which with it comprise the social sciences. Psychoanalysis, for example, claims and asserts sexuality as its domain. Yet neither psychoanalysis nor sociology takes account of the oppression of women. Not taking it into account, they necessarily interpret it in their own terms – they integrate it as a given. They thus study the domains of social life and of subjective experience where and by which women are oppressed, without this oppression appearing as such. They thus have a precise ideological function: to make the oppression of women disappear from the results of their studies. Since everything is circular, this is accomplished only by having denied it at the beginning.

Can we, then, utilize the existing disciplines and their concepts at all to study the oppression of women, given that the body of knowledge they comprise presupposes it? Can we even utilize 'elements' from them? The positive response to this question prevalent today suggests we can dissociate the social philosophy of certain theories from their concepts. However, even these elements are obtained from epistemological premises. Each science constructs its own·object. This means that not only its theoretical content, but also its limits, and the definition of its field of application, its very domain, far from pre-existing the discipline, are its creation; and the premises of all the social sciences, to the extent that they do not posit men/women relationships as relationships of oppression, posit them, by commission or omission, as something else.

These premises are thus in radical opposition to those of women's liberation and women's studies. A field of knowledge which starts from the oppression of women cannot be content with questioning this or that result of this or that discipline. We must challenge the premises themselves, we must start with how the results were obtained; the point of view from which the 'facts' were regarded; the point of view which concerns us, but also the outlook which perceived the object, and the object that it constituted – right down to the most apparently 'technical' and 'neutral' concepts.

It is illusory to pretend to arrive at different interpretations with the same conceptual instruments. These are no more neutral, no less constructed, than the areas they delimit, nor than the theories – the content of the disciplines – they generate.

Rejecting interdisciplinarity does not, however, mean refusing to recognize that subjective experience[2] is aware of different levels. What it does mean is rejecting the current cutting-up of reality into disciplinary domains – into fiefdoms; a cutting up born of, and accrediting, the idea that entire areas of experience are outside of oppression, i.e. of the political.

To the patchwork of interdisciplinarity and disciplinarity a materialist feminist approach opposes a unique dynamic which expresses itself differently at different levels. This approach has yet to be fully defined. It will challenge structuralism, for example, not because structuralism suggests that a subjectively distinct cognitive level exists, but because it imputes to this level a content independent of social relationships. This approach will challenge psychoanalysis not because psychoanalysis suggests the existence of a purely subjective level, but because it imputes to this level a content independent of social relationships.

Obviously the social which is at issue here is not 'the social' of journalists. It is not the exterior as opposed to 'the interior', the super-ficial, surface events as opposed to the inner depths. It is the political as opposed to 'the private'. Nor does the pre-eminence we accord this concept of the social have anything to do with the chauvinism of a specialist. It is, on the contrary, a theoretical position that is opposed to the prevalent concept of 'specialism'. It is a global view of history, hence of the social sciences; it prohibits all recourse to extra-social and extra-historical factors. Such recourse, however limited it may be, is incom-patible with the concept of oppression.

It is a commonplace that there is no neutral knowledge, but from our point of view this has a particular meaning. All knowledge is the product of a historical situation, whether it is acknowledged or not. But whether it is acknowledged or not makes a big difference. If it is not acknowledged, if knowledge pretends to be neutral, it denies the history that it pretends to explain. It is ideology and not knowledge. Thus all knowledge which does not recognize social oppression, which does not take it as its premise, denies it, and as a consequence objectively serves it.

Knowledge that seeks to take the oppression of women as its point of departure constitutes an epistemological revolution, not just a new discipline with woman as its object, and/or an *ad hoc* explanation of a particular oppression. Such knowledge is an expression of materialism, but also a renewal of it. It applies a materialist point of view to some-thing materialism has ignored, i.e. the oppression of women. It is a new perspective and not a new object. This perspective necessarily applies to the whole of human experience, individual and collective.

How then can materialism be 'extended'? Up to now materialism has implied, denoted, a theory of history as the history of the class struggle. But women as a group were excluded from the classes involved. Their oppression was not thought of as a class exploitation. I maintain that it is the absence of women from history, from the representation of history, which has left the field open to the establishment and/or upholding of private 'areas' and to the monopoly of the 'disciplines', i.e. which has led to the dominance of idealist views of entire sectors of experience.

In so far as materialism has been applied to understanding the process of the production of ideas in relation to the exploitation of the proletariat and the class struggle (as traditionally defined), so the areas of life designated as subjective – affective and sexual[3] – have escaped it. This was an obvious but inevitable contradiction. But equally it could not fail to appear insoluble. The whole intellectual history of the first, and perhaps also of the second, half of the twentieth century is marked by attempts – constantly renewed – to unify certain principles of explanation. These attempts have predominantly taken the form of attempts at conciliation and reconciliation between Freudianism and marxism. Needless to say the fact that there have been so many is both because the contradiction is distressing, and because each attempt to resolve it has ended in failure. This failure was inscribed in the very premises of the proceedings, because people have tried to reconcile the results, the findings, of the two approaches, forgetting that their epistemological premises were irreconcilable. The failure of all the attempts is due to their acceptance of the extravagent claims of psychoanalysis to be, not *a system of interpretation* of subjectivity, but subjectivity itself.

I refuse to accept that objecting to the theory of psychoanalysis is synonymous with a lack of interest in its object. Rejecting Freud's ideas does not mean one is indifferent to – or that one negates – the existence of subjectivity, though not only the adherents of psychoanalysis but also the vast majority of people claim it does. Once psychoanalysis's claim is accepted, however, attempts to resolve the contradiction of materialism's failure to come to grips with subjectivity are doomed, because to come to grips with subjectivity, it is held, one must accept the premises of psychoanalysis. And to accept them means to reintroduce idealism on to the scene. Under the cover of introducing materialism into subjectivity, one in fact introduces the enemy in its place: one introduces idealism into history.

But why must attempts to reconcile marxism and Freudianism accept the premises of psychoanalysis, when the latter is only one form of 'psychologism', itself a form of idealism? Especially when the areas monopolized by psychologism were *not* places of confrontation between the only groups materialist theory recognized as classes: proletarians and capitalists? For, so long as only these groups were recognized as classes, and so long as the materialist theory of history was reduced to the history of *their* confrontation, the domains where this confrontation did not exist were necessarily left outside of the problematic of the class struggle, and therefore of materialism. (Wilhelm Reich's attempt at reconciliation is exemplary in this respect. He believed he could re-introduce sexuality under the wing of materialism, while in reality he did nothing but betray materialism by psychologizing the class struggle.)[4]

Sexuality is, however, very much a place of class struggle. It is one of the fields of confrontation of two groups; but the groups are not the proletarians and the capitalists, but social men and social women. Only the women's struggle, and the simultaneous conceptualization of women's condition as oppression, has brought sexuality into the political arena. Feminism, by imprinting the word oppression on the domain of sexuality, has annexed it to materialism. It was the necessary condition for this annexation.

Calls for a materialist psychology are not new. How then do we explain why, despite the recognized necessity of considering 'subject-ivity' as one of the expressions, if not one of the mechanisms, of social organization, the reverse process has made ceaseless progress through-out the time during which these calls have been made? Why have biologism and instinctualism continued to reign over, better to con-stitute, the study of 'the psyche'? Why has psychologism not even limited itself to the study of subjectivity, but has grabbed the study of interaction, of groups, and even of institutions? How do we explain this except by admitting that the political base for such knowledge is missing?

If the women's struggle is the necessary condition for the inclusion of new areas of experience in materialist analysis, equally materialist analysis of all the instances of women's oppression is one of the pro-cesses of this struggle – and an indispensable process.

So long as an area of experience stays outside the class struggle, it remains out of the reach of materialism. To change this it was not sufficient for it to be a site of real antagonisms. It was necessary for these antagonisms to take the form of a consciously political confrontation. This was why the emergence of the WLM was significant. Conceptual-ization followed, because it could not *but* follow a real social movement. The condition of women did not give rise to a struggle because it was 'political'. 'Political' is a concept, not an element of concrete reality. The condition of women became 'political' once it gave rise to a struggle, and when at the same time this condition was thought of as oppression.

Today the conditions are present for the advent of a new stage of knowledge. Women were oppressed before, and oppressed also in and by 'sexuality', but that was not sufficient for sexuality to be envisaged from a materialist point of view.

In the same way, proletarian class consciousness is not the result of Marx's theory of capital. On the contrary, Marx's theory of capital was founded on the necessary premise of the oppression of proletarians. Oppression is one possible way of conceptualizing a given situation; and this particular conceptualization can originate only from one standpoint (that is, from one precise position in this situation): that of the oppressed. It is only from the point of view and life experience of women that their condition can be seen as oppression. This coming consciousness takes place neither before nor after the struggle. In other words, it is a question of two aspects of the same phenomenon, not of two different penomena.

The women's movement is a concrete political fact, which cannot but add a new element to the political domain, and which may overturn it from top to bottom. The same thing could be expressed by saying that women's consciousness of being oppressed changes the definition of oppression itself.

Materialist feminism is therefore an intellectual approach whose coming is crucial both for a social movement, the feminist movement, and for *knowledge*. This approach will not – cannot – be limited to a single population, to the oppression of women alone. It will not leave any aspect of reality, any domain of knowledge, any aspect of the world untouched. As the feminist movement aims at revolution in social reality, the feminist theoretical point of view must also aim at a revolution in knowledge. Each is indispensable to the other.

Notes and references

1 For example, are 'body' and 'mind' divisions of something concrete, or are they entries in western dictionaries? And what is the western dictionary, if not the intellectual product of, the rationalization for, an oppressive social system?

2 i.e. in the subjectivity of this society, hence in its ideology.

3 Which is considered *a thing in and of itself* (like 'the psyche') by both common sense and the 'science' which reproduces these categories; and which is linked to 'the psyche' by that same science which

reproduces the spontaneous theory of common sense, that is, ideology.

4 What have we retained of Reich's theory? That sexual repression *caused* fascism.

Bibliography

Acker, J. (1973), 'Women and social stratification: a case of intellectual sexism', *American Journal of Sociology*, no. 78, pp. 936–45

Adams, R. N. (1971), 'The nature of the family', in J. Goody (ed.), *Kinship*, Harmondsworth: Penguin

Adlam, D. (1979), 'Into the shadows', *Red Rag*, no. 14

Alzon, C. (1973), *La femme potiche et la femme bonniche*, Paris: Maspero

Allauzen, M. (1967), *La paysanne française d'aujord'hui*, Paris: Gonthier

Archer, M. Scotford and Giner, S. (eds.), (1971), *Class, Status and Power*, London: Weidenfeld and Nicolson

Barker, D. Leonard and Allen, S. (eds.) (1976a), *Sexual Divisions and Society*, London: Tavistock

Barker, D. Leonard and Allen, S. (eds.) (1976b), *Dependence and Exploitation in Work and Marriage*, London: Longman

Barrett, M. and McIntosh, M. (1979), 'Christine Delphy: Towards a materialist feminism?', *Feminist Review*, no. 1

Barron, R. and Norris, G. (1976), 'Sexual divisions and the dual labour market', in Barker and Allen (eds.)

Bastide, H. (1969), 'Les rurales', *La Nef*, no. 38

Bastide, G. and Girard, A. (1959), 'Le budget-temps de la femme mariée à la compagne', *Population*

de Beauvoir, S. (1949/1953), *The Second Sex*, London: Jonathan Cape

Becouarn, M.-C. (1972), *Le travail des femmes d'exploitantes dans l'agriculture et l'evolution des techniques*, thèse de 3ᵉ cycle, Tours

Beechey, V. (1977), 'Some notes on female wage labour in capitalist production', *Capital and Class*, no. 3

Beechey, V. (1979), 'On patriarchy', *Feminist Review*, no. 2

Beechey, V. (1980), 'Patriarchy, Feminism and Socialism', paper to the Jornadas de estudio sobre el Patriarcado, Barcelona

Benston, M. (1969), 'The political economy of women's liberation', *Monthly Review*, **21** no. 4. Reprinted in Tanner (ed.) (1970)

Bettleheim, B. (1954), *Symbolic Wounds*, Glencoe: Free Press

Bird, C. (1968), *Born Female*, New York: Pocket Books

Bland, L., Brunsdon, C., Hobson, D. and Winship, J. (1978), 'Women inside and outside the relations of production', in CCCS, *Women Take Issue*, London: Hutchinson

Bloch, M. (1964), *Les caractères originales de l'histoire rurale française*, Paris: Armand Colin

Blood, R. O. and Wolfe, D. M. (1960), *Husbands and Wives: The Dynamics of Married Living*, Glencoe: Free Press

Boigeol A., Commaille, J. and Roussel, L. (1975), 'Enquête sur 1000 divorces', *Population*

Bottomore, T. B. (1965), *Classes in Modern Society*, London: George Allen and Unwin

Bourgeois, F., Brener, J., Chabaud, D., Cot, A., Fougeyrollas, D., Haicault M., and Kartchevsky-Bulport, A. (1978), 'Travail domestique et famille du capitalisme', *Critique de l'Economie Politique*, Série numero 3

Bujra, J. (1978), 'Introductory: Female solidarity and the sexual division of labour', in P. Caplan and J. Bujra (eds.), *Women United: Women Divided*, London: Tavistock

Cazaurang, J.-J. (1968), *Pasteurs et paysans béarnais*, Pau: Marimpouey

Chester, R. (1973), 'Divorce and the Family Life Cycle in Great Britain', paper presented to the 13th Annual Seminar of the Committee on Family Research of the ISA, Paris, mimeo

'Les chimères' (1974), 'Et mon instinct maternel', *Les Temps Modernes*, no. 333–4

Code Civil Français, Librarie Dalloz, Paris (1970, 1974, 1978)

Cousins, M. (1978), 'Material arguments and feminism', *m/f*, no. 2

Dalla Costa, M.-R. and James, S. (1972), *The Power of Women and the Subversion of the Community*, Bristol: Falling Wall Press

Davis, E. Gould (1973), *The First Sex*, London: Dent

Dezalay, Y. (1976), in D. Leonard Barker and S. Allen (eds.), *Sexual Divisions and Society*, London: Tavistock

Douglas, C. A. (1980), interview with Christine Delphy and Monique Wittig, *Off Our Backs*, **10**, no. 1, pp. 6 ff.

Duchen, C. (1983), 'French Feminism Since 1968: a study in politics and culture', (PhD thesis, New York University)

Duchen, C. (1984), 'What's the French for political lesbian?', *Trouble and Strife*, no. 2

Duvall, E. M. (1957), *Family Development*, New York: Lippincott
Edholm, F., Harris, O. and Young, K. (1977), 'Conceptualising. women', *Critique of Anthropology*, no. 9/10
Eisenstein, Z. (ed.) (1979), *Capitalist Patriarchy and the Case for Socialist Feminism*, New York: Monthly Review Press
Engels, F. (1884/1972), *The Origin of the Family, Private Property and the State*, edited and with an introduction by E. B. Leacock, London: Lawrence and Wishart
Féministes Revolutionnaires (1976), 'Patriarchal justice and the fear of rape', mimeoed paper
Ferchiou, S. (1968), 'Différençiation sexuelle de l'alimentation au Djerid (sud tunisien)', *L'homme*, 1er trimestre
Finch, J. (1983), *Married to the Job: Wives' Incorporation in Men's Work*, London: George Allen and Unwin
Firestone, S. (1971), *The Dialectics of Sex*, London: Jonathan Cape
Flaubert, G. (1970), *Three Tales*, Penguin
Girard, A. (1958), 'Budget-temps de la femme mariée dans les agglomerations urbaines', *Population*, no. 4
Girard, A. (1959), 'Budget-temps de la femme mariée à la campagne', *Population*, no. 2
Girard, A. (1961), *La Réussite sociale en France*, Paris: Presses Universitaires de France
Girard, A. (1964), *Le Choix du conjoint*, Paris: Presses Universitaires de France
Galbraith, J. K. (1973), *Economics and the Public Purpose*, London: André Deutsch
Gillott, P. (1974), 'Confessions of an ex-feminist', *Cosmopolitan*
Goode, W. J. (1956), *Women in Divorce*, New York: Free Press
Hanmer, J. (1978), 'Violence and the social control of women', in G. Littlejohn *et al.* (eds.), *Power and the State*, London: Croom Helm
Hartmann, H. (1974), 'Capitalism and Women's Work in the Home, 1900–1930', PhD thesis, University of Yale
Hayes, H. R. (1965), *The Dangerous Sex*, London: Pocket Books
Hennequin, C., de Lesseps, E. and Delphy, C. (Quelques militantes) (1970), 'L'interdiction de l'avortement: exploitation economique', *Partisans*, no. 54–5
Himmelweit, S. and Mohun, S. (1977), 'Domestic labour and capital', *Cambridge Journal of Economics*, 1 no. 1

INSEE (National Institute for Statistics and Economic Studies) (1973), *Principaux résultats de l'enquête permanente de 1971 sur les conditions de vie des ménages*, no. 82

Irigaray, L. (1974), *Speculum de l'Autre Femme*, Paris: Editions de Minuit

Jackson, J. A. (ed.) (1968), *Social Stratification*, Cambridge: Cambridge University Press

Jousselin, B. (1972), 'Les choix de consommation et les budgets des ménages', *Consommation*

Kandel, L. (1980), 'Journaux en movements: la presse féministe aujord'hui' and 'Post-Scriptum: une presse "anti-féministe" aujourd'hui: "Des femmes en movements" ', *Questions féministes*, no. 7

Kooy, G. A. (1959), *Echtscheidingstendenties in 20ste eeuws Nederland inzonderheid ten plattelande*, (Divorce Trends in the rural areas of the Netherlands in the twentieth century), Assen: Van Gorcum

Larguia, I. (1970), 'Contre le travail invisible', *Partisans*, No. 54–5

Larguia, I. and Dumoulin, J. (no date about 1973), *Towards a Science of Women's Liberation*, *Red Rag* pamphlet, no. 1

Leclerc, A. (1974), *Parole de femme*, Paris: Grasset

Lenin, V. I., *Collected Works* (French edition) vol. xxiv, Moscow

Lewis, J. (1981), 'The registration of "MLF" in France', *Spare Rib*, no. 108

Lilar, S. (1969), *Le malentendu de deuxieme sexe*, Paris: PUF

London, J., *Tales From the South Seas*, London

McAffee, K. and Woods, M. (1969), 'Bread and roses', *Leviathan*, no. 3. Reprinted in Tanner (ed.). (1970)

McDonough, R. and Harrison, G. (1978), 'Patriarchy and the relations of production', in A. Kuhn and A.-M. Wolpe (eds.), *Feminism and Materialism*, London: Routledge and Kegan Paul

Mainardi, P. (1970), 'The politics of homework', in Tanner (ed.)

Mandel, E. (1962), *Traite d'Economic Marxist*, Paris: Union gènerale d'Editions

Marceau, J. (1976), 'Marriage, role division and social cohesion: the case of some French middle class families', in Barker and Allen (eds.) (1976b)

Marczewski, J. (1967), *Comptabilité nationale*, Paris: Dalloz

Mead, M. (1950), *Male and Female*, republished by Penguin in 1962

Milhau, J. and Montagne, R. (1968), *Economie rurale*, Paris: PUF (coll. 'Themis')

Mitchell, J. (1974), *Psychoanalysis and Feminism*, London: Allen Lane

Molineux, M. (1979), 'Beyond the domestic labour dispute', *New Left Review*, no. 16

Montague, A. (1952), *The Natural Superiority of Women*, New York: Macmillan

Murdock, G. B. (1949), *Social Structure*, New York: Macmillan

Naville, P. (1971), 'France', in Archer and Giner (eds.)

Nouacer, K. (1969), 'Maroc, la sègrégation', *La Nef*, no. 38

Olah, S. (1970), 'The economic function of the oppression of women', in S. Firestone and A. Koedt (eds.), *Notes From the Second Year*, New York: Notes from the Second Year

Parti Communiste Français (1970), *Les Communistes et la Condition de la Femme*, Paris: Editions Sociales

Perrot, M. (1961), *Le mode de vie des familles bourgeoises*, Paris: Colin

de Pisan, A. and Tristan, A. (1977), *Histoires du M.L.F.*, Paris: Calmann-Levy

Pedinielli-Plaza, M. (1976), 'Difference de sexe et réalité des femmes', mimeo.

Plaza, M. (1977), 'Pouvoir "phallomorphique" et psychologie de "la Femme" ', *Questions Féministes*, no. 1. Translated in *Ideology and Consciousness*, no. 3 (1978).

Righini, M. (1974), 'Être Femme enfin!', *Nouvel Observateur*, 15 March

Rich, A. (1980), 'Compulsory heterosexuality and lesbian existence', *Signs*, 5 no. 4

Rubin, G. (1975), 'The traffic in women: Notes on the "political economy" of sex', in R. R. Reiter (ed.), *Toward an Anthropology of Women*, New York: Monthly Review Press

Sahlins, M. (1974), *Stone Age Economics*, London: Tavistock

Silvera, J. (1975), *The Housewife and Marxist Class Analysis*, Seattle: Wild Goose Pattern

Stoetzel, J. (1948), 'Une étude du budget-temps de la femme dans les agglomérations urbaines', *Population*, no. 1

Sturgeon, T. (1960), *Venus Plus X*, New York: Pyramid Books

Tanner, L. B. (ed.) (1970), *Voices From Women's Liberation*, New York: Signet Books

Terray, E. (1972), *Marxism and 'Primitive' Societies*, New York: Monthly Review Press

Veblen, T. (1899), *Theory of the Leisure Class*, reprinted by Mentor, New York (1953)

Wolfelsperger, A. (1970), *Les biens durables dans le patrimoine du consommateur*, Paris: PUF

Zelditch, M. (1964), 'Family, marriage and kinship', in R. E. L. Faris (ed.), *Handbook of Modern Society*, Chicago: Rand McNally

Zetkin, C. (1934), 'Les notes de mon carnet', *Lénine tel qu'il fut*, Paris: Bureau d'éditions

Index

142–5; distinction from continuum with consumption 40–1, 64, 85–7; family as unit of 63–72, 81–7; GNP, exclusions from 65, 82–5, 87, 90; housework and childcare as production 59–61, 78, 84–5, 87
Programme Commun 77
proletariat, relationship of left intellectuals to 148–50
prostitutes, wives compared to 126–7
proto-feminism 182, 206–9
pseudo-feminism 207
Psychanalyse et Politique 10, 13, 131, 137, 208–10
psychoanalysis 9–10, 142, 161, 172, 188, 196, 207, 210, 213, 215–17
Psychoanalysis and Feminism 142
psychologism 9, 187–8, 192, 216
psychology 171–2; psychological differences between the sexes 191; patriarchy/sexism as psychological traits 113–14, 141; women's oppression as primarily psychological 184–91
public and private spheres 8, 141

Questions Féministes 10, 12, 106

race 23, 128, 206; Black men's attacks on white women 121–2; exploitation of immigrant workers 114–15; intellectuals and anti-racist struggles 107, 186; origins of non-mixed organizations in the USA 110–12; WLM and anti-racist struggles 12
radical feminism 9, 59, 140–5
radical lesbianism 12
rape 21
Red Rag 175
Reich, W. 133, 217, 219
relations of production 29–30, 38–9, 57, 90, 158, 197–9, 206; difference between

men's and women's 59–72, 167, 201–2
remuneration: outside family 95; unremunerated, as distinct from unpaid work 88–90
reproduction 8, 59, 169–70, 184, 188, 193, 202; distinction of reproduction and production 74, 142–5; theories of reproduction 8, 169–70
respect, men's need for, as cause of women's oppression 184–91
revaluation, of women's bodies 194–7
revolution: need for feminist 75; origins of revolutionary impetus 150
revolutionary feminists 143
Rich, A. 116
Righini, M. 208
Roberts, H. 28
Roberts, L. ap 57
Rubin, G. 25
rural crisis/dis accord 54, 61, 63; families, use as examples 10–11, 45; sociology 10; women 9–11

Sahlins, M. 203
St Augustine 191
St Paul 191
Sartre, J.-P. 190
science 150–3, 213–14; feminist science 159, 212; marxism as Science 155–7
second marriage, economic pressures towards 98; *see also* divorce
self-consumption, production for 63–7, 80–90; evaluation of self-consumption 63, 80
self-hatred, struggle against 9, 112–13, 118–19, 132; and Black struggle 111–12; and left-feminism 132
serfdom 59, 101–2, 105, 158, 186
servants 42–3, 121, 125, 158, 186
sex, relationship to gender 144; *see also* gender

Further Pamphlets published by the
Women's Research and Resources Centre.

Some Processes in Sexist Education
by Ann Marie Wolpe   £1.00

**Inspiration and Drudgery: Notes on Literature
and Domestic Labour in the 19th Century**
by Sarah Elbert and Marion Glastonbury   £0.70

**Girls Will Be Girls: Sexism and Juvenile
Justice in a London Borough**
by Maggie Casburn   £0.60

**"Black Friday": Violence Against Women in the
Suffragette Movement**
by Caroline Morrell   £1.95

Obtainable from your local bookshop or direct by post from
1a Gladys Road, London NW6 2PU